Television Plays

BY

Paddy Chayefsky

A TOUCHSTONE BOOK
PUBLISHED BY
SIMON AND SCHUSTER

Holiday Song was suggested by an article, "It Happened on the Brooklyn Subway," by Paul Deutschman, which appeared in the *Reader's Digest*.

FIRST TOUCHSTONE PRINTING

SBN 671-21133-1 TOUCHSTONE PAPERBACK EDITION
LIBRARY OF CONGRESS CATALOG CARD NUMBER: 54-9800
MANUFACTURED IN THE UNITED STATES OF AMERICA

To Susie

Contents

Foreword

There are a number of illusions in the theatrical mediums that are unnecessary and artificial and sometimes in the way. One of these is the idea that the writer has a paternalistic attitude toward his scripts. People in the theater like to describe a writer's play as his "baby," and they refer to his creative struggles as his "birth pains." Most writers I know are not so involved with their scripts, especially in television, where the constant urgency of time does not allow for the self-indulgent mannerisms usually associated with the creative spirit. If the writer has to cut five minutes, he simply cuts it, or someone else will cut it for him.

In television, the writer is treated with a peculiar mixture of mock deference and outright contempt. He is rarely consulted about casting, his scripts are frequently mangled without his knowing about it, and he is certainly the most poorly paid person in the production. Some programs don't allow the writer to attend rehearsals of his own show. At the same time, he is granted the proud title of playwright, and, in every respect but his work, he is treated with a dignity inherited from the stage.

When a television writer has an idea for a script, he has first to submit it in the form of an outline. This is read by the producer, the director, and/or the script editor of the program. The writer is then called in for a conference with one or another of the production staff, and revisions are suggested to him. My own experience has been that these conferences are a waste of time. For one thing, the writer has only a nebulous concept of his proposed script no matter how meticulously he prepared his outline. No writer I know knows literally what he is going to write until the first stumbling scenes of the first act have been written and his characters have begun to assume a physical reality to him. I have never written an outline that retained its rigid structure all the way into a final draft. Scenes that

I reckoned to be eight pages in length turn out to be six lines of dialogue, and scenes I never conceived suddenly demand to be written. Most writers count on the impetus of their dialogue to disgorge new lines of dramatic movement, new insights into their characters, and even a new tone or flavor to the over-all script. Outlines do serve a vital function for the writer in that they keep him from plunging into the actual writing before he has thought out a general line for his story, but no outline should ever be used as a basis for judgment. Nevertheless, outlines are almost always required by every program. The producers and the advertising agencies representing the sponsors do not know the work of their writers well enough to trust them and with some justification want an indication of what they are paying for. In any event, the outline is submitted and the writer either makes a living or not on the basis of it.

When the writer has revised his outline, he submits it again. If approved by the producer and director, it is forwarded on to the advertising agency. I have no idea what happens to it here, but it usually stays here for about a week or ten days or longer and is studied, not for its theatrical merit, but for its palatability. The advertising agencies are not villains whose sole purpose is to destroy the artistic integrity of a dramatic script. But, by definition, they are concerned with selling their clients' products, and the twenty-two or fifty-three minutes of drama that go between the commercials are considered as essentially part of the sales talk. The agency is most concerned with neither offending nor disturbing possible customers, a policy that stringently limits the scope of television drama. (The taboos of television, though much is made out of them, are really no worse than those governing the movies or the slick-magazine short story. Only on the Broadway stage or in the novel form is there any freedom of topic, and even the stage has produced little in the last ten years that could not have been done on television.)

At any rate, the outline is either accepted or rejected by the advertising agency, or it is returned with more revisions suggested. Eventually, the writer is faced with the problem of transforming his outline into a script. At least two weeks, and probably a good deal more, have passed since he handed in his original outline.

Whatever artificial enthusiasm he had for his story has long since evaporated, but he sits down to his typewriter and begins to regenerate his energy. Like every other member of the theatrical mediums, the writer has to lift himself into a suspended attitude of work. He has no discipline but his own training and his need for money. Writing is a compulsive type of work. No writer I know wakes up in the morning with eager anticipation for the day's work. Each writer develops his own series of little morning habits which graduate into the business of sitting down to his typewriter. Actually, the work of writing a given script is the easiest part of the writer's life. It is on those dreary and empty mornings between scripts when he awakens to an amorphous world of aimless thinking, of poking about into the unformed recesses of the air about him for a new thought, a new character, an incident, a fragment of feeling, anything to start him off—it is on these mornings that the writer considers other trades. Right now, of course, the writer has this accepted outline to do, a concrete chore. He reads through the outline and he sets about conceiving his first scene.

My own experience in television has been confined almost exclusively to the hour-length drama and to one specific program at that, the Philco-Goodyear Playhouse. I enjoy writing television a good deal for personal reasons and because the Philco-Goodyear Playhouse allows me to write as well as I care to. Most of my friends are not so lucky. They write for shows that demean their talents or twist their good work when they do put effort into it. They feel very little pleasure when they set out on their first act. They work from under a hard coat of defensive unconcern, finding whatever reward they can in the mechanical excellence of their craft rather than in their artistry. They affect the attitude of the skilled artisan, and they go about their work with the diffident detachment of a carpenter. It is a laborious kind of writing with very few kicks in it. The patterns of creation are always the same. There are some writers who can block out a "Danger" or a "Suspense" idea for you in half an hour. Most writers take from two to five days to hack out a half-hour script. In the hour-length shows, the demands are somewhat greater, depending on the program. Philco-Goodyear expects a certain amount of artistic effort. I have spent two months in plotting out one or another of the scripts collected in this volume. Sometimes they come easier, sometimes harder; but no script has ever come without intensive work.

When the script is finished, the writer brings it in to the director and the producer. Again script conferences are called, revisions suggested. The mood of these conferences varies with the personalities involved. In my case, I have been almost childishly dependent upon the reactions of Fred Coe, the producer (at this writing) of the Playhouse, Gordon Duff and Bill Nichols, his associates, and Delbert Mann, who usually directs my shows. By the time I have finished my first draft, I have long since lost my perspective and will accept just about any suggestion they make. It must be made clear that these four men are inordinately talented at their jobs. I don't believe there is a better story mind in the business than Fred Coe's. Delbert Mann is an extremely gifted director who has a precise affinity for my kind of writing and a sharp understanding of his own needs in conveying the values of the script to the actors and cameramen.

Most dramatic programs are not so efficiently organized. Some shows present their suggestions for revisions as mandatory, and, if the writer cannot satisfy, the director or producer may peremptorily rewrite the script himself. Certainly, once the script goes into rehearsal, unless the writer is there to do the rewriting and cutting, the director and even the actors will butcher it for him. On those shows that keep the writer out of rehearsals, most of the scripts end up a bloody business indeed, and the writer who takes his work seriously will be sick to his stomach when he sees what comes out on the television screen.

A writer must attend rehearsals for his own self-respect and because so much can be done. If all directors were superior talents, if all actors were uncommonly gifted, and if all scripts were flawless, then the writer could sit comfortably at home and begin a new script. But despite the currently overevaluated concept of the director, he is a mundane man like the rest of us and as limited in his ability. And actors as a class are perhaps the least realistic people alive. And no script is ever flawless. The transformation of the written word into a full-bodied moment of reality is a vast one. Words that read well on paper are often dull gasps of literature in the actor's mouth. The actor may find his part incomprehensible or beyond his own sense of reality. The words have to be changed, the scenes reconceived. Rehearsals can be the best part of television, for this is where the real fascination of theater lies—in the quick, nervous, day-to-day maturation of a script, in the sometimes incredible blossoming of actors as they wrench their roles open and expose innumerable hidden subtleties. There is nothing in the professional world to compare to a bunch of responsive theater people engaged in a genuinely co-operative work. On the other hand, nothing is more miserable than those rehearsals in which everyone concerned has contempt for the script, himself, and the entire production.

Of course, I work with a director who likes me and will accept my meddling. If your director is defensive or belligerent, as is more frequently the case, there is little you can do. The point is to find a producer you respect and a director you can work with. The personalities in any theatrical medium are edgy and difficult, or they wouldn't be in the theater in the first place. Generally, however, it is possible to feel out productive workaday relationships, and rehearsals can be fun and the final show a reasonably proud piece of work.

Well, the show is done. Ten minutes after the last commercial, the actors have vanished and the studio is empty. Anywhere from a month to six months have gone by since the writer submitted his first outline. He has put perhaps three weeks to three months of concentrated work into the show. For his troubles he will have received as little as three hundred dollars for some half-hour shows and as much as the three thousand dollars reserved for the better-known hour dramatists. A successful hour dramatist may do four, five, or six shows a year with a thin hope—a very thin hope—of reselling one of his scripts to the movies, provided he has been careful enough to keep the rights to his work. He may make as much as twenty-five thousand dollars in a top year. For this he has written the equivalent of three full-act plays. He has no guarantee that his next year will be as fruitful; in fact, most writers live in a restrained terror of being unable to think up their next idea. Very few television writers can seriously hope to keep up a high-level output for more than five years. Television is an endless, almost monstrous drain. How many ideas does a writer have? How many insights can he make? How deep can he probe into himself, how much energy can he activate?

For my part, television has been a kind medium. I came out of the legitimate theater, and I want to go back again. When I do, I will not be able to calculate the debt I owe to television for the amount of sheer craft I have learned in these past two years. I have achieved a discipline and a preciseness of thinking and even a certain notoriety, upon which every writer feeds whether he admits it or not. I have never written a script in television of which I was not at least partially proud. I hope to continue writing for the medium as long as I can.

PADDY CHAYEFSKY

December, 1954

Holiday Song

DIRECTED BY: GORDON DUFF
PRODUCED BY: FRED COE

Cast

CANTOR	Joseph Buloff
ZUCKER	Herbert Berghof
NAOMI	Frances Chaney
MRS. DAVIS	Dora Weissman
GIRL	Irja Jensen
YOUNG MAN	Werner Klemperer
RABBI	David Kerman
GEORGE	David Opatoshu
WOMAN	Ann Dere
SHORT GUARD	Martin Greene
MAN	Fred Sadoff

ACT I

MONTAGE: Suburban town on outskirts of New York—quiet shaded streets, etc.

DISSOLVE TO: Simple square synagogue.

DISSOLVE TO: Announcement box, meticulous little white lettering:

HIGH HOLY DAY SERVICES
WED., THURS., SEPT. 9TH & 10TH.
EREV ROSH HASHANAH, WED. EVENING 7:16 P.M.
SERVICES WILL BE CONDUCTED BY
CANTOR LEON STERNBERGER.

The camera narrows down on name: "Cantor Leon Sternberger."

DISSOLVE TO: Photograph of Cantor Sternberger in full robes of his office. Camera moves back. We are in a plain living room. (Cantors don't make very much money.) The camera carefully pokes about the dimly lit room. It picks up the high black turreted cantor's hat resting on a chair beside a hat brush—then the long white robes on an ironing board. They are being carefully ironed by a woman in her middle thirties. This is Naomi, Cantor Sternberger's niece. For a moment we watch her, nearsighted and intense, ironing the Cantor's robes. The doorbell rings. She looks up, carefully sets the iron into a harmless position, and nervously hurries to answer the door. An elderly man of sixty, birdlike and at the moment apparently concerned over something, stands in the doorway. This is Zucker.

ZUCKER: *Well, what's the matter?*
NAOMI: [Agitated] *Sssssss . . . sssshhh . . .*
She closes the door behind Zucker.

ZUCKER: *Well, what's wrong? Is he sick? What's the matter?*

3

NAOMI: *He's been lying in his bed for two days, looking at the ceiling. Like I told you over the phone, I bring him in his meals. He doesn't touch a thing. I ask him—are you fasting? What holiday is it that you're fasting? He looks at me like a dying man. Then he looks back at the ceiling.*

ZUCKER: *Did you call a doctor?*

NAOMI: *I asked him, I said—Uncle Leon, are you sick? Shall I call a doctor? He lies there, Mister Zucker, I don't know what to do . . .*

ZUCKER: *All right, all right, all right. Let's siddown a minute, and you'll tell me what happened from the beginning. . . .*

They take seats at either end of the living room table.

NAOMI: *Like I told you over the phone . . .*

ZUCKER: *What happened? He came home from the synagogue!?*

NAOMI: *He came home from the synagogue . . .*

ZUCKER: *This was Sunday?*

NAOMI: *This was Sunday.*

ZUCKER: *All right, he came home. What happened?*

NAOMI: *I was in the kitchen, making a roast. It's Sunday you know. On Sunday I make roasts. So I hear the door open and close. I look up. There he is. He's as white as a sheet. I said, Uncle Leon! What's the matter? So he looks at me. . . . "God alone knows what's the matter!" he cries. And he goes in his room, and he closes the door.*

ZUCKER: *Well, you know what happened. They broke the window in the synagogue.*

NAOMI: *When was this?*

ZUCKER: *I'm telling you. This was Sunday. The two of us were standing there talking to the Rabbi, when whoever it was threw the stone in the window. All the glass came crashing down at our feet, well, listen, it was a dreadful experience. A sensitive man like your uncle, well I could see he was disturbed by the whole incident. And the Rabbi* said, "*Cantor, you don't look well. Go home and lie down . . .*"

NAOMI: *So he came home, and he lay down, and he hasn't come out in two days. And, listen, Mister Zucker, tomorrow night is Rosh Hashanah! The High Holiday!*

ZUCKER: *I know!*

NAOMI: *I said to him, Uncle Leon! Tomorrow night, you've got to go to synagogue—you've got to sing! And he looks at me like . . .*

ZUCKER: *All right, I'll talk to him . . .*

NAOMI: *I didn't know what to do, so I called you, Mister Zucker . . .*

ZUCKER: *I'll talk to him . . . I'll talk to him .*

He sits a moment, frowning in contemplation. Then, pursing his lips, he rises slowly from his chair.

What shall I do? Shall I knock, or shall I go right in?

NAOMI: [Rising too, crosses to door to the Cantor's room.] *Wait, I'll look, see if he's asleep.*

She carefully opens the door, peeks in . . . then calls softly and with gentleness.

Uncle Leon . . . Uncle Leon . . . Mister Zucker, the Sexton, is here. . . . He wants to talk to you . . . Uncle Leon . . .

She waits for an answer. There is none. She comes softly back to Zucker.

He's sitting in his chair now.

ZUCKER: [Nods nervously] *All right, I'll go in and talk to him. . . .*

Takes a deep breath, advances on the door, opens it, bends in.

Cantor? . . . Cantor? . . . This is Zucker here . . . I understand you don't feel well. I'd like to come in and talk to you a minute . . .

He stares anxiously across the simple, bare, unlit room to the chair. The camera follows his gaze across the floor, up the side of the chair, to the rigid form sitting thereon. This is Cantor Sternberger, a gentle little man in his fifties—a scholar, generally confused by the outside world. His lean, sensitive face is gaunt with inner pain. Deep, pained eyes regard Zucker in the doorway. The head nods involuntarily a few times, then slowly reverts to its previous position of staring fixedly at the floor.

Zucker darts one anxious glance back into the living room, where Naomi is nervously ironing away, then softly closes the door and pads to the Cantor.

ZUCKER: [With deep compassion] *Hello, Leon. How are you, my dear friend? What is it that troubles you, my friend? Your niece was so worried, she called me on the phone. She said, come over right away, my uncle won't eat anything. Is it the broken window in the synagogue that has affected you so much? . . .*

The anguished head remains motionless.

Don't worry about the window. It will surely be replaced before the services tomorrow night. . . .

The gentle, pained face turns to Zucker, and the eyes fill with tears. The Cantor stares at his old friend in mute abjection.

Would you like me to turn on a light for you? You don't want to sit here in the dark? . . . Would you like me to leave, Leon? Would you like to be alone? . . .

He leans forward, waiting for an answer. There is none. Zucker slowly shuffles to the door. He reaches for the knob . . .

CANTOR: *Zucker! . . . Zucker! Stay here with me.*

Zucker turns at the door.

ZUCKER: *Sure, Leon.*

He comes quickly back.

CANTOR: *I am sorely afflicted, Zucker.*

ZUCKER: *I tell you, Leon, for some time now, I have noticed that you seem to be moody and brooding.*

CANTOR: *I have fasted for two days.*

ZUCKER: *You used to be such a cheerful fellow. Everybody used to say—"Here comes Cantor Sternberger. Now we'll have a few jokes." But I don't see you laugh no more.*

CANTOR: *What's to laugh?*

He rises from his chair and pads to the bed. On the bed table lies a newspaper. He picks it up.

*Here, Zucker, read. Read! Read any page! Did something
nice happen in the world today? Murder! Graft! A pag-
eant of oppression. Famines and wars. I defy you to find
me one inch of pleasure in all those words.*

ZUCKER: *Well, listen, these are terrible times.*

CANTOR: *What's on the radio? Let's listen. A murder? A
death? A war?*

ZUCKER: *My friend, it is not up to us to discern the will
of God.*

CANTOR: *The will of God!* [With growing fervor] *Is God a
mortician, Zucker, that he desires all this tragedy?*

ZUCKER: *It says in Isaiah: "And ye shall be scattered over
the earth, and ye shall tremble before your enemies like an
aspen leaf."*

CANTOR: [Crying out] *Why?*

ZUCKER: *Because God in His infinite wisdom willed it so.*

CANTOR: [Trembling with emotion] *What kind of a God
wills so much misery?*

> Zucker, unnerved by the turn of the conversation, looks un-
> easily at the Cantor, then away. The Cantor moves shakily to
> his old friend, his eyes wide with some unknown fear.

ZUCKER: *My friend, I am not a scholar, but did I not read
in the Book of Job—What? Should we accept the good
alone from God, and the evil we should not accept?*

CANTOR: *Zucker, I . . . I . . . I believe I have lost my faith!*

ZUCKER: *What do you mean you have lost your faith?*

CANTOR: *I have lost my faith!*

ZUCKER: *Well . . . well—what do you mean you have lost
your faith?*

CANTOR: *I mean that I'm sitting here and I'm doubting the
existence of the Almighty One.*

> There. It is out. The two old friends stare at each other in
> shock and consternation.

CANTOR: *Zucker, you have known me from my earliest
days in the seminary. We were always as brothers to each*

other. If I could not tell this to you, to whom could I tell it?

ZUCKER: *My friend . . . my dear friend . . .*

CANTOR: *All my life, Zucker, you have known me as an up-right man. I have feared God, and I have eschewed evil.*

ZUCKER: *Sternberger, believe me, I . . .*

CANTOR: *I have never questioned or doubted. When my parents died an unnatural death, I did not sin with my lips or attribute any injustice to God. The Lord giveth and the Lord taketh; may the Name of the Lord be blessed. Then suddenly—it was like I went to bed one night, and I woke up the next morning—and I was thinking: What sadness in this world! I seem to hear nothing or see nothing but sad-ness. And at night, I would hear in my head like a drum—God-God-God. What sort of a God is it who would allow this? I would awake in the night and desperately try to pray. And in the darkness of the room I felt a moment of peace. But it would come again into my mind—like a drum —What kind of God is this? What kind of God is this . . . What kind of God is this?* [Crying out in anguish] *Zucker! I am sorely afflicted!*

ZUCKER: *Leon . . . Leon . . . if you don't mind, please, I would like a glass of tea . . .*

DISSOLVE TO: Living room. Close-up of teapot. Dolly back to see Naomi as she crosses the room and serves tea to Zucker and the Cantor, who are now sitting at the table.

ZUCKER: *Well, so what are we going to do?*

CANTOR: *I don't know. Tomorrow night is the Eve of the High Holidays. I am expected to lead the congregation in prayer.*

ZUCKER: *Yes, I know.*

CANTOR: *And it seems to me that if a man is going to lead the congregation in prayer he should at least have some faith in God.*

ZUCKER: *It seems that way to me too.*

CANTOR: *Well, then, how can I sing tomorrow night?*

ZUCKER: *Well, listen, this is a serious business. I wouldn't presume to advise you on such a delicate spiritual issue. My advice is to go to our Rabbi and get his advice.*

CANTOR: *I couldn't do that, Zucker.*

ZUCKER: *You couldn't? Why couldn't you?*

CANTOR: *He is such a young man, Zucker. And I couldn't admit to him my loss of faith. It took all my courage to admit it to you.*

ZUCKER: *He's a nice fellow . . . Naomi, please, if I could have a little jam.*

NAOMI: *Oh, didn't I put the jam on the table?*

ZUCKER: *Well, now, if you don't want to go to our Rabbi, do you know who you could go to?*

CANTOR: *Who?*

ZUCKER: *Rabbi Marcus of New York City. A sage on earth! Men in torment make pilgrimages from all over the world to this man.*

CANTOR: *Rabbi Marcus is a learned man. A sage among sages.*

ZUCKER: *May his name be blessed.*

CANTOR: *May his merits hover over all of us.*

ZUCKER: *The first thing tomorrow morning, you should go to the railroad station, get on the train, and go to New York to see Rabbi Marcus. I'll go with you.*

CANTOR: *Why should you go with me? Am I a child to be led across the street by the hand?*

ZUCKER: *Naomi, please, if I could have a little piece of lemon? . . . Well, listen, Leon, I think the best idea would be if I wrote you out instructions how to get there. It's a little complicated, and a simple soul like you could wind up the Almighty One alone knows where. You know, listen, it's been a good couple of years since I myself went to New York. All right, Leon . . .*

CANTOR: *What?*

ZUCKER: *Tomorrow morning, Leon, we'll take you down to the railroad station, and we'll put you on the train. All*

*right, when you get on the train, Leon . . . are you lis-
tening?*

CANTOR: *I'm listening, I'm listening . . .*

ZUCKER: *When you get on the train, find a kindly-looking
gentleman, and tell him to put you off at East New York
Station. Did you hear me, Leon?*

CANTOR: *I hear, I hear . . .*

ZUCKER: *I wrote it down for you . . . East New York Station . . .*

CANTOR: *You don't have to write it down. There are plenty
of people to ask.*

ZUCKER: *All right, when you get to East New York Station,
go to the Atlantic Avenue subway, look for a subway
guard. Go to the subway guard, and say—"Mister, I want
the Manhattan train." Now, Leon, there are two trains.
One goes to Manhattan, and the other goes to Brooklyn.
Tell the subway guard you want the train that goes to
Manhattan. You hear?*

CANTOR: *I hear, I hear . . .*

ZUCKER: *Not the Brooklyn train.*

CANTOR: *Not the Brooklyn train.*

ZUCKER: *Manhattan . . .*

CANTOR: *Manhattan! Manhattan!*

ZUCKER: *All right . . .*

DISSOLVE TO: Film—Long Island train pulling into station.

DISSOLVE TO: Subway platform, people passing by subway
guard.

CUT TO: Long shot—big, tall, magnificently impressive subway guard at far end of platform.

CUT TO: The Cantor makes his way down platform to the
big, tall subway guard.

CANTOR: [Tugging at guard's sleeve] *Excuse me . . .* [Guard
hardly knows he's there.] *Excuse me, please . . . Mister . . .
Hey, Mister . . .* [Guard turns slowly to him.] *Excuse me,*

*but I would appreciate if you would put me on the train
to Manhattan. I was told to stress to you, the Manhattan
train.* Not *the Brooklyn train. The Manhattan train . . .
please . . .*

> The guard nods a little impatiently. A subway train slides to a
> halt in front of them. The door opens. The guard rather for-
> cibly escorts the old Cantor through the door. The door closes.
> The camera moves up on the placards in the window of the
> train. They read: "New Lots Avenue—Brooklyn." The train
> begins to chug out.

> CUT TO: Close-up—the Cantor frowning a little nervously.
> He notices the Brooklyn placard in the window.

CANTOR: [Confused] *Excuse me, is this the Brooklyn train,
or the Manhattan train?*

> The question has been addressed to the air around him, but
> now he turns, a little confused, to find someone with whom
> he can verify his suspicion.

> CUT TO: Interior of subway car, looking down the aisle to-
> ward one end. It is absolutely empty. The Cantor takes a few
> tentative steps down the aisle.

CANTOR: [Calling lightly] *Excuse me, anybody here could
tell me, is this the Manhattan train, or is this the Brooklyn
train?* [Indicates the placards in the window] *. . . Seems to
me, this is the Brooklyn train . . .*

> He stares helplessly around the empty car. Then he perches on
> the edge of the seat, frowning and at a loss. He folds his hands
> nervously between his knees. For a moment he just sits there,
> and then, over the click-clack of the train, we hear faintly a
> woman sobbing. The old Cantor looks up. The woman sob-
> bing again. The Cantor rises slowly, moves slowly down the
> aisle, following the sobbing. He stops, stands motionless,
> looking. . . .

> A pretty young woman in her twenties is standing by the
> open door at the end of the car. She is sobbing. She leans for-
> ward. . . . Crescendo clacking train noise. . . . Suddenly she

starts to loosen the guard chains and prepares to jump. The Cantor grabs her.

CANTOR: *Madam, what are you doing? Please—please—Madam!*

She struggles for a moment, then stares at the Cantor and flings herself onto his breast sobbing.

DISSOLVE TO: Film—subway train hurtling along. Fade out film . . .

FADE IN: Hallway of a cheap, dark, dank boarding house. The Cantor and the girl enter, cross to end of hall, and go into the girl's room.

CANTOR: *Ten o'clock in the morning and look how dark it is in here. . . .* [Crosses to window, lifts blind] *What a depressing room. You should move away from here. Why don't you look for another room?* [The Cantor moves across to her.] *Ah? . . .*

GIRL: *Was denn?*

CANTOR: *I said, you should look for another room. You shouldn't stay in a room like this. It's very depressing . . .*

The girl nods vacuously, stares down at her hands, folded limply in her lap. The Cantor regards her for a moment, touched, concerned; then he takes a seat beside her.

So tell me, where in Holland are you from?

GIRL: [Tonelessly] *Utrecht . . .*

CANTOR: *Utrecht! I was born not far from Utrecht! How do you like that! A little village called Landau. Do you know of it?*

The girl, momentarily interested, looks up, nods.

Yes, yes, I was born in Landau. I have still, I believe, one or two distant cousins living there. I remember, once a month, my mother would take me to Utrecht to go to market. Even to this day I remember. It was a very lovely city . . .

GIRL: [Looking down at her hands] *Ja . . .*

CANTOR: *Have you been very long in this country?* [The

girl shakes her head.] *How long?* [The girl mutters. The Cantor doesn't hear. He bends forward.] *I'm sorry. I didn't hear you.*

GIRL: [Stumbling between her Dutch and English] *Drei . . . drei . . . drei week. . . .*

CANTOR: *Three weeks. And do you know anybody here? I mean, do you have friends or relatives or . . .* [The girl shakes her head bleakly.] *Well, now you know me, so that's one friend.*

> The girl tries to smile her appreciation of the old Cantor's sympathy, but her lips tremble, and she only succeeds in beginning to cry again. She quickly regains control of herself.

CANTOR: [Gently] *Were you married?*

GIRL: [Barely audible] *Ja . . .*

CANTOR: *Dead?*

GIRL: *Ja . . .*

CANTOR: *Children?*

GIRL: *Ja, zwei . . . Alle . . alle tot . . .*

CANTOR: *The Nazis? . . . Were you in a concentration camp?*

GIRL: *Auschwitz . . .*

CANTOR: *The same sadness. Everywhere I look, the same sadness.*

GIRL: [Mumbling] *God . . . God—*

> CLOSE UP tight on Cantor's face.

CANTOR: *God? . . . Dear, dear young lady—there is no God!*

> FADE OUT.

ACT II

FADE IN: Grandfather clock showing half past eleven. Camera pulls away. We are back in the Sternberger home. The rooms are bright with the morning sun. Off in the kitchen, we see Naomi baking cookies. Suddenly the phone rings. Naomi comes hurriedly out of the kitchen into the living room, picks up phone.

NAOMI: *Hello? Hello? Who? . . . Who? . . . Oh, Mister Zucker, he's not home yet . . . No, I didn't hear nothing . . . What? . . .* [The doorbell rings.] *Wait! Wait! The door just rang! Hold the wire a moment! . . .*

She puts the telephone down, hurries to door, opens it with air of expectancy. Standing in doorway is a round little woman of forty dressed in holiday fashion, especially a gaily plumed hat. This is Mrs. Davis.

MRS. DAVIS: [Beaming] *Happy Holiday.*

NAOMI: *A Happy Holiday, a happy year. Listen, Mrs. Davis, I'm on the telephone. Come in please. Sit down. I'm talking on the phone . . .*

Naomi hurries back to the phone. Mrs. Davis comes in, closes the door, finds a seat.

NAOMI: [On phone] *Hello? Hello? Mister Zucker? . . . No, it was Mrs. Davis . . . Mrs. Davis . . . All right, I'll call you as soon as he comes in . . . All right . . . Good-by.* [Hangs up—turns to Mrs. Davis] *Excuse me just one minute more, Mrs. Davis. I have cookies baking in the oven. Cinnamon cookies.*

MRS. DAVIS: *Go right ahead, Naomi. I just dropped in to tell you he's here.*

NAOMI: *Who's here?*

MRS. DAVIS: *Who's here? My brother is here. My brother from Cleveland. The one I told you about. The one with the jewelry store in Cleveland. Remember I told you, my*

14

brother from Cleveland with the jewelry store, I was inviting him here for the holidays. I wanted you to meet him.

NAOMI: [A little flustered] *Oh, your brother from Cleveland with the jewelry store.*

MRS. DAVIS: *Yes.*

NAOMI: *Well, sit down, Mrs. Davis.*

Mrs. Davis perches on the edge of the overstuffed chair and folds her hands in her lap. Naomi sits down opposite Mrs. Davis and straightens out her skirt.

MRS. DAVIS: *Naomi, I'm going to tell you something. George is a better match than I thought he was.*

NAOMI: *He is?*

MRS. DAVIS: *When I first mentioned him to you, Naomi, I told you he was not an especially good-looking fellow. But, after all, he is a successful man with his own jewelry store and he makes quite a good living, and, after all, Naomi, you're thirty-four years old yourself, Naomi . . .*

NAOMI: *Thirty-three . . .*

MRS. DAVIS: *Thirty-three? Well, anyway, I met him at the station, and, in the four-and-a-half years that I haven't seen my brother George from Cleveland, I'm going to tell you something, he has gray hair on the sides, and he looks extremely dignified. Well, needless to say, Naomi, I have told him everything about you. What a marvelous and well-respected young woman you are. And how pious you are. The niece, after all, of our Cantor. And, believe me, I told George, a good-looking young woman. To my eyes at least, you are a good-looking young woman.*

NAOMI: [Blushing a little] *Thank you, Mrs. Davis. Let me get you a cookie.*

Naomi is immediately off her chair and into the kitchen. Mrs. Davis calls after her.

MRS. DAVIS: *I also told him what a marvelous cook you are, and I can tell you, he is bursting to meet you . . .*

Naomi pops back in from the kitchen with a plate and some cookies.

NAOMI: *Well . . . well . . . I . . . do you think . . . I . . . Well, how . . . how . . .*

> She collects herself. She draws herself up a little, gathers a little composure, and advances on Mrs. Davis with her plate of cookies.

It so happened of course that the batter didn't come out so good this time. As a rule, I make a much tastier cookie . . . people tell me I have a talent for baking. I . . . I . . .

> She sits down again, looks down, a little embarrassed, at her nervous fingers.

I would like very much, Mrs. Davis, to meet your brother George from Cleveland with the jewelry store.

MRS. DAVIS: *Naomi, I know you are asking yourself this very minute—is this brother of Mrs. Davis a devout man.*

NAOMI: *Well, I . . .*

MRS. DAVIS: *I mean, after all, you're the Cantor's niece. It's perfectly legitimate that the Cantor's niece, when she considers a match, has to take into account the spiritual character of the man.*

NAOMI: *Listen, Mrs. Davis, I'm thirty-four years old . . .*

MRS. DAVIS: *You just told me thirty-three.*

NAOMI: *All right, you caught me. I'm really thirty-four. And at thirty-four, I am not going to insist that my husband be a Talmudic scholar.*

MRS. DAVIS: *Well, I can tell you, my brother George from Cleveland is a Talmudic scholar. My brother George is a devout man.*

NAOMI: *I would surely like to meet him.*

MRS. DAVIS: *And I mean devout. I mean, my brother George goes to synagogue every day for morning prayers, for afternoon prayers, and for evening prayers. And he even fasts on days when it's not such a sin to nibble a bit of food here and there. I'm going to tell you, Naomi—my brother George is a fit husband for the niece of such a scholarly man as your uncle.*

NAOMI: *You make him sound so attractive that I ... well, how could a meeting be arranged?*

MRS. DAVIS: *He's right outside.*

NAOMI: *What do you mean, he's right outside?*

MRS. DAVIS: *He's right outside, waiting in the car.*

NAOMI: *You left him waiting in the car?*

MRS. DAVIS: *Well, I didn't want to come barging in without giving you a little warning, a chance to put on a little lipstick ...*

NAOMI: [Up and all excited again] *Lipstick! Well, I mean, the poor fellow ... well, I mean, to leave him sitting outside in the ... Well, go call him in, Mrs. Davis ... Go call him in ... Look at me. Isn't this ridiculous?*

MRS. DAVIS: *Don't be so excited, Naomi ... I've already told him all about you. He's just as nervous as you are.*

NAOMI: [Herding Mrs. Davis to the door] *You better go call him in ...*

Mrs. Davis exits into the street. Naomi closes the door after her—then thinks better of it, opens the door a little. She takes a few steps back into the living room, frowns, tries to get a grip on herself. She notices the kitchen towel lying on the table, picks it up, stuffs it into her apron. Then she realizes the apron is no costume in which to greet Brother George from Cleveland, hurriedly takes it off, looks nervously around for some place to put it, finally throws it into the grandfather's clock.

At this point there is a knock, and the door opens. Mrs. Davis comes in, followed by a pleasant man of forty-odd, just a little bit ill at ease, but likewise keeping a good grip on himself.

Naomi turns to greet them.

NAOMI: *Please come in, please come in ...*

MRS. DAVIS: *Naomi, this is my brother George from Cleveland, with the jewelry store.*

NAOMI: *How do you do?*

GEORGE: *Happy Holiday ...*

NAOMI: *Happy Holiday, happy year . . .*

MRS. DAVIS: *George, sit down over there.*

NAOMI: *Yes, please sit down.*

They enter and find seats at the table.

GEORGE: *I'm sure that this is a big interruption to you, and an imposition on your time, but my sister insisted we drive over to see you.*

NAOMI: *Sure, and we left you sitting out there in the car, and . . .*

MRS. DAVIS: [Extending the cookie plate to George] *George, have one of these cookies. Naomi just made them right out of the oven.*

GEORGE: *Thank you . . .*

He takes a cookie. For some reason, a silence falls on the three as he takes a bite.

This is very, very, very good. I really mean it. This is an extremely tasty cookie.

NAOMI: *Thank you.*

For a moment they just sit. A hush falls over them.

MRS. DAVIS: *Well, look how we're sitting here. Like children. Listen, we all know why we're here.* [Rising] *Well, I'm going to leave you two. Talk a little. Make a date. Don't eat too many cookies, George, because we're having lunch in a couple of minutes. This time I'll go wait in the car.*

GEORGE: *All right, Sylvia, I'll be out shortly.*

Mrs. Davis goes to the door.

NAOMI: *Good-by, Mrs. Davis.*

George turns with a sweet smile to Naomi.

GEORGE: *Well, you have heard the case stated. I am forty-two years old. I am established in business. I would like to get married. My sister tells me what a wonderful girl you are.*

NAOMI: *Well, I wouldn't say a girl. I'm thirty-four years old. I would like to get married. I'm a good cook. At least, people tell me I have a talent for cooking. Perhaps you would like to come to dinner some evening this week?*

GEORGE: *I would like that very much.*

NAOMI: *Come on Monday. I would like you to meet my uncle.*

GEORGE: *I'll be here.*

NAOMI: *Let's see. What else can I tell you about myself?*

GEORGE: *My goodness, you don't have to tell me anything about yourself. I'm the one who should make myself attractive to you . . .*

NAOMI: *Is there . . . is there to be a question of dowry?*

GEORGE: *Dowry?*

NAOMI: *My uncle makes only a modest income. I . . .*

GEORGE: *Naomi! It is I should bring a dowry to you! For heaven's sakes! I consider it an honor and a privilege to be considered a suitor for your hand. You are a cantor's niece. To me, honestly, I tell you, it is the greatest honor to marry into a cantor's family. I don't know whether my sister told you, but I am a religious man, and to me, your uncle—I . . . I can hardly wait to hear him sing tonight. Let us talk no more of dowries! I have a comfortable business of my own. Let us talk no more of dowries. Dowries! Really! What a European thought!*

NAOMI: *To tell you the truth, I'm not a very modern person.*

GEORGE: *To tell you the truth, neither am I.*

NAOMI: *Occasionally I put on a little lipstick and even then I feel a little bit sinful, and that's how modern I am.*

GEORGE: *I think we are going to be very happy together, Naomi . . .*

NAOMI: *Of course it's hard to tell just the first time we meet, but it seems we have the same tastes.*

GEORGE: *It seems that way to me too. Listen, I'm going to be here for the rest of the holidays. We'll go to the movies. We'll go for rides. We'll discuss with each other. We'll see how compatible we are. I think . . . I think this is going to be a good thing.*

NAOMI: *I think so too, George.*

GEORGE: [Rises] *Well, I'll see you in synagogue tonight. I'd better go now because my sister is a nervous woman, and she's waiting there, and . . .*

NAOMI: *I'll look for you tonight.*

GEORGE: [At door] *Fine . . . Good-by, Naomi.*

NAOMI: *Good-by, good-by.*

George exits. Naomi stands at the door for a moment, strangely expressionless. Then she begins to smile. She doesn't know quite what to do with herself. She shuffles aimlessly back into the room. She is beginning to hum a Chassidic wedding dance. She sits at the table. The humming picks up. She begins to rock slightly back and forth in rhythm to her humming. Slowly the wedding dance swells within her, and in a moment she is on her feet, stamping and whirling, her skirts flaring about her as she executes several steps from a European wedding dance. As suddenly as she started, she stops. She sits down again, still smiling a vague, aimless smile.

The door behind her suddenly opens. The Cantor enters. She whirls to him.

NAOMI: *Uncle Leon! . . . Uncle Leon, how are you? Did you see the famous rabbi? What happened? Did it go all right?*

CANTOR: *I didn't even go . . . I got on the wrong train . . . the subway guard there put me on the wrong train.*

NAOMI: *Listen, Uncle Leon, you know Mrs. Davis who has the brother in Cleveland? They were just here five minutes ago! Maybe you saw them when you came in?*

CANTOR: *It was an omen! An omen! It was meant for me to meet that girl.*

NAOMI: *I invited him here Monday for dinner! What shall I make? Shall I make a roast? Or an old-fashioned chicken dinner with noodle soup.*

For the first time, the Cantor is aware that he and Naomi are shouting about different things. He stares at his niece.

CANTOR: *What are you talking about? What noodle soup?*

NAOMI: *They were just here five minutes ago ...*

CANTOR: *Who?*

NAOMI: *Mrs. Davis and her brother from Cleveland. His name is George.*

CANTOR: *What Cleveland ... What are you telling me of Cleveland? I'm telling you about a girl on the subway.*

He whirls away from her, furious, opens the door to his room, strides in.

Cleveland! What is she telling me of Cleveland? ...

Naomi follows him a step into his room.

NAOMI: *Uncle Leon—I think I've made a match ... a match! Mrs. Davis talked to me about him some time ago, and now he has come here, and we just met, and, if after the High Holy Days, we still like each other, then we will be married ... subject to your consent, of course, Uncle Leon. Oh, Uncle Leon, he seems so gentle. I am sure you will like him.*

The old man stares at his niece, the news slowly registering.

CANTOR: *Mrs. Davis' brother wants to marry you?*

NAOMI: *And a devout man! A man who fasts even when it is not required. He is so anxious to meet you. To tell you the truth I think he was more anxious to meet you than he was to meet me. He is so determined to be a cantor's nephew.*

The Cantor surveys his niece with swift compassion.

CANTOR: *A cantor's nephew. But I am no longer a cantor, my child. I must go to the Rabbi and tell him to find another cantor. You see, I was on the train there, on my way to New York. [Sits] It was the Brooklyn train actually. The subway guard put me in the wrong train. There was a young woman there, who was about to leap upon the tracks when I stopped her. She told me a story that made me tremble. I didn't even go to see Rabbi Marcus. What for? To what purpose? What could he say to me? What arguments could he have put up against that poor unfor-*

tunate girl? I don't believe in God, and that's all. I am no longer a cantor—I am an atheist. If Mrs. Davis' brother is so devout, I do not think he will be so determined to be my nephew.

NAOMI: *I . . . I don't understand exactly what you're talking about, Uncle Leon.*

CANTOR: *I am saying that Mrs. Davis' brother will not come to dinner on Monday. The soup will be as molten lead in his mouth, and he will revolt at the chicken. You are cursed with a disillusioned uncle, my child. Men of piety will turn away from you. If this young man is so devout, he will not marry you, Naomi. You must prepare yourself for his denial.*

NAOMI: *I don't understand how one day you can believe in God, and the next day you can't.*

CANTOR: *My dear child, do you think I understand?*

NAOMI: *Mrs. Davis' brother is only going to be here till the end of the holidays. Couldn't you reserve your decision on God just for two weeks, just till after the Day of Atonement?*

CANTOR: *Naomi, what do you want from me? Am I not in torment as it is?*

Naomi looks at him, rises, slowly crosses, and sits on bed. The Cantor watches her. He reaches halfheartedly for his prayer book, opens it at random, knits his brow, and tries to pray. Naomi watches anxiously.

CANTOR: *"Who is this that darkeneth counsel*
   By words without knowledge?
   Gird up thy loins like a man;
   For I will demand of thee, and declare thou unto me.
   Where wast thou when I laid the foundations of the earth?"

He snaps the book shut.

No! I cannot lead the prayers tonight. It would be profane. I must go and tell the Rabbi to find a substitute

He starts for door, turns back to Naomi—sympathetically.

Well, perhaps he's not so devout. Perhaps he will forgive you a disillusioned uncle.

NAOMI: *It's not so important, really. I just got a little excited there for a minute. Well, listen, I managed this long without a husband, I can manage longer.*

CANTOR: *If I believed in God, I should pray quite sharply to him about Mrs. Davis' brother.*

He turns, starts for door.

Happy Holiday, Naomi.

NAOMI: *Happy Holiday, happy year.*

The Cantor exits . . . Naomi remains sitting on the bed, expressionless.

CUT SHARPLY TO: Interior, the Rabbi's study. This is a small room with a flat desk, pictures of bearded patriarchs on the wall, and piles of books all around. The Rabbi himself is seated at the desk, poring over what should be a book of Talmudic lore. He is a young man in his thirties with the clergyman's air of premature wisdom. He wears a sober suit of Oxford gray. There is a knock on the door.

RABBI: *Yes?*

The door opens, and Zucker pokes his head in.

ZUCKER: *Rabbi . . .*

RABBI: *Yes, Zucker, what?*

Zucker slips into the room, closes the door behind him.

ZUCKER: *Cantor Sternberger is here. He would like to see you a minute.*

RABBI: *Is it important?*

ZUCKER: *I think you should see him right away.*

RABBI: *Is something wrong?*

ZUCKER: [Shrugs] *He says he's lost his faith in God.*

The Rabbi regards Zucker with a mildly startled eye.

RABBI: *He's lost his faith in God?*

ZUCKER: *He doesn't believe in God any more.*

RABBI: *Cantor Sternberger?*

ZUCKER: *His niece called me up last night, she says: "My uncle is sick." So I went over. I said: "Leon, what's the matter?" So he says: "Zucker, I have lost my faith in God." Well, what can you say when somebody says something like that to you?*

RABBI: *Well, what did you say?*

ZUCKER: *I disputed with him. In the end, we decided he should go see Rabbi Marcus of New York. Well, I don't know what happened. But he did not see Rabbi Marcus. And he is sitting in the synagogue now, and he tells me we'll have to get another cantor.*

RABBI: *Cantor Sternberger? . . .*

ZUCKER: *Thirty minutes past twelve before the Eve of the High Holidays, he tells me we'll have to get another cantor! The services start at sixteen minutes past seven! Who can we get on such short notice?*

RABBI: *Zucker—please, really.*

ZUCKER: *Well, then, who shall sing? Schulman, the butcher, perhaps, who likens himself unto an opera singer? He has a voice like a frog. Well, really, we shall be without a cantor tonight, I assure you. What is Rosh Hashanah without a cantor? A wedding without a bride!*

The Rabbi goes out into the corridor and across into the synagogue proper. He is followed by Zucker. They both slowly approach the Cantor, who is now sitting—abject and bowed—on one of the rear benches.

RABBI: *Peace be with you, Cantor.* [The Rabbi seats himself beside the old man.] *What is it, Leon? Why are you troubled?*

CANTOR: *Rabbi, I can't sing tonight. I feel empty. I feel naked and hollow. God was my life. Now, nothing. What was my day but the simple rituals of my religion? I would awaken in the morning and hurry through the streets to the synagogue to don my long white praying shawl and my phylacteries . . . and it seemed to me, Rabbi . . . It seemed to me that God was shaking my hand and wishing me a good morning . . . Was it sacrilegious, Rabbi, to have felt so friendly with God?*

RABBI: [Gently, with deep compassion] *No, of course not, Leon.*

CANTOR: *I don't feel Him around me any more. I wouldn't recognize Him if He passed me on the street.*

RABBI: *Was it not Micah who stated: "And ye shall meet Him in the strangest places."*

CANTOR: *No, Rabbi, excuse me. The quotation is actually attributed to Zechariah, and its states: "And ye shall know Him in the strangest costumes and in the strangest places."*

RABBI: *Well, Zechariah then, so be it.*

CANTOR: *So, Rabbi, I have come to tell you that you shall have to get another cantor. I would suggest Mr. Schulman the butcher who was helpful on those occasions when I was ill.*

Zucker, who has been impatiently listening to the disputation between the Cantor and the Rabbi, now bursts out.

ZUCKER: *Schulman, the butcher! He will drive the congregation from the temple! Really, on Rosh Hashanah, we should have a cantor! One holiday out of the year, there should be singing. Rabbi, I am not a scholar, but I would like to raise a question of rabbinical law.*

RABBI: *Yes, Zucker, what is it?*

ZUCKER: *Rabbi, what in essence is the cantor? Is he a religious functionary who must have faith to perform his duties, or is he merely a hired employee of the congregation. For is it not written in the Commentaries, Rabbi, that employees of the congregation need not be devout? This is the issue I would pose to you for clarification.*

RABBI: *It's a casuistic issue, Zucker. It is clearly stated by Rabbi Gamaliel that the cantor is as a teacher to the congregation, even as a rabbi. But on the other hand . . .*

ZUCKER: *Yes, Rabbi?*

RABBI: *Does not the cantor of a congregation have a social obligation like a mayor or a policeman to fulfill his duties even though he is ill or taken with disease? Indeed, is not the loss of faith to a cantor even so much as the death of a loved one to a civil functionary? This is a very interesting point. I would have to study the Commentaries for a precedent.*

ZUCKER: *It's half past twelve, Rabbi. We don't have time to study the Commentaries.*

RABBI: *It's an issue I am not adequate to judge. I would suggest that Cantor Sternberger go to New York and present the issue to Rabbi Marcus.*

ZUCKER: *A sage on earth!*

CANTOR: *Actually, Rabbi, I was on my way down to see——*

RABBI: [Nodding] *Yes, that is the best solution. Well, then, Leon, you will go to Rabbi Marcus, and you will pose him the following problem: Which deserves first consideration —the social obligations of the cantor's position or the religious requirements? Do you understand, Leon?*

CANTOR: *I understand all right. It's just that I . . .*

RABBI: [To Zucker] *Zucker, take the Cantor down to the station, because I really don't think there is too much time . . . Does he know how to get to New York?*

ZUCKER: *Rabbi, I'll give him instructions, don't worry.*

CANTOR: *What's the matter with you? How many times are you going to give me these instructions?*

ZUCKER: *Leon, I'm going to put you on the train. Ask somebody to put you off at East New York Station. Do you want me to write it down for you?*

CANTOR: *You don't have to write it down.*

ZUCKER: *All right, when you get to Atlantic Avenue, look for a subway guard . . . Say to the guard—I want to stress this point—say to him: "Please put me on the Manhattan train."*

CANTOR: *Manhattan . . . Manhattan . . .*

ZUCKER: *Not the Brooklyn train . . .*

CANTOR: *Not the Brooklyn train, but——*

BOTH: *The Manhattan train!*

DISSOLVE TO: Film clip—Long Island train pulling into station.

DISSOLVE TO: The subway platform. The Cantor walks down the platform looking for the subway guard. The big, tall guard is at the end of the platform. The Cantor comes up to him.

CANTOR: [Tugging at guard's sleeve] *Excuse me, Mister . . . Hey, Mister . . . You remember me? I came over to you this morning . . . I asked you to put me on the Manhattan train, remember? And you made a mistake. You put me on the Brooklyn train . . . Well, listen, even if you don't remember, please, this time don't make a mistake. I want you to put me on the Manhattan train. Not the Brooklyn train. The Manhattan train. Now, don't make a mistake, please . . .*

The guard nods. A subway train comes roaring into the station. The doors open. The subway guard pushes the old Cantor onto the train . . .

CUT TO: Interior subway train. The old Cantor looks quickly at the placards in the car window. They read: "New Lots Avenue—Brooklyn."

CLOSE-UP: The Cantor, furious. He runs for the door. The door closes in his face. Sound of train picking up steam. Train starts into motion.

CLOSE-UP: The old Cantor's face covered with futility, pressed against subway car window as train slowly moves out of focus . . .

FADE OUT.

ACT III

FADE IN: Interior subway car. The old Cantor just snorting with exasperation. He looks down length of subway car, again strangely empty except for a young man who sits quietly reading a newspaper. The Cantor perches on seat opposite the young man, but he cannot remain seated long. He sighs angrily once or twice, folds and unfolds his hands, suddenly stands, goes to the door, stops, stares at the young man. He is bursting to tell his exasperation to somebody. Finally, he can no longer resist. He goes to the young man, sits down beside him, and speaks.

CANTOR: *Excuse me, Mister. Hey, listen, you want to hear something?* [The young man looks up from his paper.] *I mean, this is something should be complained about. I mean, this is something crazy. Let me tell you what happened* ... [The young man regards the Cantor with polite interest.] *This morning I got on the train to go to New York. So I came over to the subway guard and I said to him, "Please put me on the Manhattan train." Well, he put me on the train* ... *I look up* ... *I see it's the Brooklyn train.* ... *Obviously he made a mistake. Well, what can you do about it? We are all human. We can all make mistakes. But just now, I came over to the same subway guard —a big tall husky fellow—looks like a general. Perhaps you saw him standing there* ... *No?* ...

YOUNG MAN: *Ah* ... *ah* ... *I'm not speak English too—uh good* ...

CANTOR: *No?*

YOUNG MAN: [Shaking his head] *No. I am in this country* ... *ah* ... *small time* ...

CANTOR: *Ah, so. Are you Dutch?*

YOUNG MAN: *Ja.*

CANTOR: *I thought so. I recognized the accent. I am of*

28

Dutch birth myself. I came to this country at the age of sixteen.

YOUNG MAN: *Oh, yes?*

CANTOR: *Yes.*

YOUNG MAN: *I am from the city of Utrecht.*

CANTOR: *Utrecht! Isn't that strange? I come from a small village about ten kilometers from Utrecht. My mother used to take me to Utrecht on market days as a child. And just this morning, I met a young woman—also Dutch, recently arrived in this country—It's remarkable how many times I have heard the name Utrecht today. Utrecht— what a lovely city.*

YOUNG MAN: *I remember only sad things in Utrecht . . . My wife . . . my children all dead . . . My wife in Auschwitz . . . I myself in labor camp four year . . . I come back, all dead . . .*

The old Cantor has been frowning during this stumbling recital.

CANTOR: *Auschwitz? . . . Did you say your wife was in Auschwitz?*

YOUNG MAN: *Ja . . .*

CANTOR: *Of course, this is foolish, but could you tell me, was your wife's name Marya?*

YOUNG MAN: [Suddenly alert] *Yes . . . Marya . . . Do you know of her?*

CANTOR: *Well, this is a very remarkable thing perhaps. I don't know. Did you have two children and did you live with your mother-in-law? . . .*

YOUNG MAN: [Excited] *Yes . . . Yes . . .*

CANTOR: *Is your wife a tall, handsome woman . . .*

YOUNG MAN: [Half standing, shouting] *Yes! Do you know of her?*

CANTOR: *I . . . I . . .*

YOUNG MAN: *For heaven's sakes, my friend, who are you?*

CANTOR: [His eyes blinking with confusion] *My friend, we*

are coming to a station. Would you come with me to a telephone?

CLOSE-UP: The frantic young man, staring wide-eyed at the Cantor.

CUT SHARPLY TO: A wall telephone ringing in the hallway outside Marya's room. Camera moves down hallway into Marya's room. Ringing continues off. Camera moves slowly across the room to bed . . . Marya lies on bed, her arms rigidly at her sides. Only sign of life is her open eyes, and they stare fixedly at the ceiling.

CUT SHARPLY TO: Subway phone booth. White tiles. The Cantor is pressed to the phone. The young man hovers over him.

CANTOR: *Of course, this is a little fantastic, and you mustn't put too much hope in this. I just met the girl for a few moments this morning, and . . . Hello, Hello . . . there doesn't seem to be any answer . . .*

YOUNG MAN: *Please—let us wait a little longer . . .*

CANTOR: *The phone is in the hallway, and she may not hear it.*

CUT SHARPLY TO: Hallway outside Marya's room. The phone is still ringing. A woman of fifty or so, wearing an old woolen bathrobe with towel around her neck and hair in curlers, comes to the phone and picks it up.

WOMAN: *Hello. Hello. What do you want? . . . What? . . . Marya who? . . . There's nobody named Marya here . . .*

CUT SHARPLY TO: Cantor in subway booth.

CANTOR: *Madam, if you would only knock on her door, just down the hall, just see if she's in . . .*

CUT SHARPLY TO: The woman.

WOMAN: *Oh, that one. Oh, she went out this morning. I saw her go myself . . . All right, just a minute . . .*

Woman shuffles down hall to Marya's door. Knocks. No answer. Turns and goes back to phone; picks up receiver.

Well, she's not in. I told you she wasn't in . . . Good-by . . .
> She is about to hang the receiver up.

> Cut to: Marya's door open. Marya stands there.

MARYA: *Did you knock, please, Missus?*

WOMAN: *There's a phone for you . . .*
> Lets the receiver drop from her hand to dangle by its wire.
> Turns and walks away.

> Cut Sharply to: Cantor and the young man in the phone
> booth.

CANTOR: [About to hang up] *She doesn't seem to be home.*

GIRL'S VOICE: [On filter through receiver] *Hallo! . . .
Hallo! . . .*
> The Cantor looks down at the receiver in his hand, picks it up
> again, puts it to his ear.

CANTOR: *Hello. Could I please speak to a girl named
Marya . . . Oh. This is Cantor Sternberger, do you remember? . . . This morning . . . Yes . . . Yes . . . Listen, my dear,
a strange thing has happened to me, and I was wondering
if you could answer . . . if you could tell me . . . My dear.
was your married name Rakin? . . . What? . . .*
> He turns slowly to look at the young man in the booth with
> him, the receiver pressed against his ear.

*Was his first name Leopold? . . . Please don't be excited,
madam . . . If you will hold the wire for a moment, madam,
please . . .*
> He puts a hand on the young man's arm.

*My friend, do not be excited. But a miraculous thing is go-
ing to happen to you . . .*
> Extends the phone receiver to the young man.

Here . . . You are going to talk to your wife . . .
> The young man takes the receiver tentatively, swallows,
> squeezes to the phone.

YOUNG MAN: *Hello? . . .* [Then in Dutch] *. . . This is Leopold Rakin. Am I talking to my wife, Marya? . . .*

Suddenly the tense restraint leaves the young man, and he screams in Dutch into the phone.

Marya! ... Marya! ... This is Leopold! This is Leopold! ... How are you, my darling! How are you! Where are you! How ... Marya! I am ... Where! ...

His eyes are glistening, and he can hardly restrain his emotion. [Beginning to cry] *Marya, Marya ...*

CUT TO: The Cantor, a beaming spectator. Then slowly, the expression of delight passes to one of troubled introspection. He cocks his head in concentration.

CUT TO: Film—subway train, hurtling through the dark tunnels.

DISSOLVE TO: Interior of subway car, this time with usual crowd—men and women hanging from straps, swaying to motion of car, others reading newspapers. Camera pushes its way through field of bodies to the Cantor, who sits still rapt in thought. A man reading a newspaper sits next to him. He touches the arm of the man; the man scowls at him.

CANTOR: *Excuse me ...*

MAN: *What? What? Waddaya want?*

CANTOR: [Thinking aloud] *The most extraordinary thing happened to me today. On two separate occasions ...*

MAN: [Impatiently] *What? Waddaya want ... ?*

CANTOR: *On two separate occasions, I was pushed into the wrong train, and now that I come to think of it, it seems to me that on both times, the car was strangely empty ...*

MAN: *Look, Mac, you don't like it here, why don't you take a taxi? Waddaya bothering me for? Who am I, Impellitteri?*

He angrily returns to glowering at his newspaper.

CANTOR: [Still thinking aloud, obsessed with his thoughts.] *And isn't it the most remarkable coincidence ... absolutely fantastic ... that on the first time on the wrong train, I should meet a wife who has lost her husband. And then on the second time, I should meet the husband who has lost his wife . . . What a remarkable thing!*

GUARD'S VOICE: [Off] *Atlantic Avenue! . . . Change here for Long Island trains! . . .*

The conductor's voice jerks the old Cantor back to reality. There is a sweeping motion through the subway car, and, as the door slides open, the old Cantor is carried out onto the platform on the wave of outgoing passengers. . . . Here, on the platform, he looks about for the tall subway guard. People pass around him, whizzing in every direction. At last the old Cantor sees a subway guard. This one, however, is a much shorter chap. Nevertheless, the old Cantor wends his way over to him.

SHORT GUARD: [Calling out] *Atlantic Avenue. Change here for Long Island trains.*

CANTOR: *Excuse me, my friend . . .*

SHORT GUARD: *Step along—Atlantic Avenue. Change for Long Island* [Ad lib., etc.] [Turns] *Yeah, what is it?*

CANTOR: *My friend, I am looking for that big, tall subway guard that was here the earlier part of the day.*

SHORT GUARD: [Ad-libs to crowd, then turns to cantor] *Wadyou say?*

CANTOR: *I said, could you tell me where I could find that big, tall subway guard . . . the very big fellow . . . the one that looked like a general.*

SHORT GUARD: *Not on this platform. I'm the only guard on this platform. I been here all day.*

CANTOR: *My friend, I tell you, I had occasion to talk to the man twice, I . . . This is the Atlantic Avenue Station, isn't it?*

SHORT GUARD: *Yeah, this is the Atlantic Avenue Station.*

CANTOR: *Then there must be a tall subway guard . . .*

SHORT GUARD: *Mister, I been on this platform since eight this morning, and there ain't been no other guard here.*

CANTOR: *You mean, there was no other guard?*

SHORT GUARD: *No other guard.* [Ad lib.—exits]

CANTOR: [Standing alone, frowning] *The big, tall fellow*
...He had the ...

> The guard has turned away and is moving down the platform
> ... The Cantor stares after him, his eyes widening.

CLOSE-UP: The Cantor.

CANTOR: *And ye shall know Him in the strangest costumes*
and in the strangest places.

> He looks up in the direction of the sky—then quickly down
> again. He hunches his shoulders and starts quickly down the
> platform. Fade out ...

FADE IN: Candles. The Synagogue. The Cantor stands facing the pulpit. He raises his voice in the age-old intonations of
the service. He wears his white robes. As the music swells, cut
to George in his prayer shawl, listening; then cut to Naomi
and some of the ladies, listening; then to Zucker in his prayer
shawl and some of the other men, listening. Cut back to the
Cantor. He turns slowly to face the congregation. His eyes are
glistening. The choral voices crescendo up into a roar.

FADE OUT.

THE END

Holiday Song

Holiday Song was ostensibly an adaptation. That is to say, I was given the basic story and asked to adapt it to an hour script. I am not good at adaptation, and my final draft was only vaguely related to the original property.

In television, the writer is paid considerably less for an adaptation than he is for an original script on the premise that the idea for the story, its characters, and incidents are already provided him. Actually, the material to be adapted is rarely of any use to the adapter. It is usually in the shape of a novel or a short story, two literary forms that do not lend themselves comfortably to dramatic exploitation. The convenient introspection of the prose style is difficult to capture in dialogue and action, and the adapter usually winds up picking a kernel of story from his material and improvising his own characters and insights.

Occasionally, the writer is asked to create a drama based upon some magazine article or newspaper item. This was the case in *Holiday Song*. The material provided me was a short article in *Reader's Digest* entitled "It Happened on the Brooklyn Subway." It dealt with a photographer, a man of confirmed habit, who always took the same train into New York every morning. One day, on a sudden impulse, he decided to visit a friend in Brooklyn and switched to the Brooklyn train. This train was packed; but, by chance, the passenger seated in front of him left the car, and the photographer took his place. Seated next to him was a young man reading a Hungarian newspaper. Being Hungarian himself, the photographer struck up a conversation. The young fellow told a harrowing tale of having been in Nazi concentration camps. There was something familiar in the story to the photographer. A few months before, he had met a Hungarian girl who had told him of very much the same sort of experience. On a hunch, the photographer called

35

the girl, who turned out to be the young fellow's long-lost wife. The author of the article drew the conclusion that God had been riding the Brooklyn subway that day.

The incident is not a good one for dramatic purposes. Despite the fact that it involves bringing together a husband and wife who believed each other dead, there is little emotion involved. There is a certain element of suspense, but suspense is a poor substitute for drama. It would be possible to use this incident as the opening scene of a story and then follow the course of events resulting from the meeting of a long-separated husband and wife. But this isn't what the subway incident is about. The incident has only one dramatic meaning, and that is: there is a God. The incident is what I call a third-act incident: it proves something. If in the beginning of the play there was a character who didn't believe in God, then this incident could prove to him that there is a God. Of course, the character would have to be someone who would accept such a symbolic interpretation of the incident; and as a writer, it is your job to create such a character. Now the wheels begin to turn. What sort of man would construe this chance meeting on a subway as a machination of God? Certainly he would have to be a man of pronounced religious conviction almost to the point of naïveté. Your photographer, then, has to be a deeply religious man. But the line of your story dictates that he begin the story as a man who doesn't believe in God so that he can mature to some new conviction by the end of the story. So then he must be a deeply religious man who has lost his faith. Now you are beginning to poke around in genuine dramatic areas. A religious man who has lost his faith in God is a good character to explore. So you have the first and last scenes of your show. You open your script showing a religious photographer who has lost his faith in God, and you end your script with this subway incident which restores his faith to him. What is missing is the story or what I call the urgency. Why is it so urgent that the photographer regain his faith in God? What terrible consequence will occur if he doesn't? As a writer, you sit down and painfully invent a series of circumstances that will be resolved by this incident on the subway

I do not mean to make this an exercise in story construction. Actually, the construction of *Holiday Song* is not a good one for television. It is much too complex and mechanically active and is better suited for a movie. All that I want to bring out is how far afield an adaptation wanders. Except in only occasional cases, the creative processes of adaptation follow the same tortured, stumbling steps required in the creation of an original story. Frequently, the material to be adapted, as in the article assigned to me, provides no characters at all; or if there have been delineated characters, they are usually impossible to accept. Writing is a highly personalized business. Each writer feels differently about a situation, and certainly no other writer would have adapted the subway incident quite as I did. I happen to be Jewish, and my understanding of the religious emotion is limited to the Jewish ritual, so my leading character automatically became Jewish. At the time I sat down to this adaptation, I was governed by an almost compulsive interest in Jewish folklore and humor. I had been wanting to write a show about synagogue life for years. I think that it was beyond my conscious control to keep from imposing this long-repressed synagogue story onto this adaptation. In the end, I had written what amounts to a completely, or almost completely, original work. Certainly, the work that went into the writing was no less intense than if I had started out cold on an original idea.

Holiday Song was the first hour television show I wrote, and it shows a lack of awareness of the television medium. I approached the script as I would have approached a movie. I actually patterned the story after a French film called *The Baker's Wife*. I wanted to tell a charming folk tale about a small Jewish community struck by the catastrophe of its cantor refusing to sing for the High Holidays. In the final version, it is apparent that the concept of the community disappeared and the story was sliced down to the less involved story of an old man who lost his faith in God. I meant the show to be a comedy after the fashion of Sholom Aleichem, but it came out a rather ponderous spiritual message. The celebrated actor Joseph Buloff played the leading role and was an incredible success. To my mind, Mr. Buloff was not quite accurate in the role. I meant the Cantor to be a simple old man who knew how to get from his home to the synagogue and back again and nothing more, so that to make a thirty-mile subway trip to New York was much like the pilgrimages made by devout Jews of the last century to the High Rabbi of Wilno. I saw the old man as a wan little scholar, confused when outside the sheltered confines of his synagogue. Mr. Buloff, who has great charm as an actor, was nevertheless too strong for the role. He came out an imposing intellectual, and the net result was to give the play a weight that should never have been there. This is, of course, my own opinion and I have yet to find five people who will agree with me. *Holiday Song* was a fantastic success, measured by television standards. Mr. Buloff received more than four thousand letters, and Ben Gross, the television editor of the New York *Daily News*, suggested that the show be done annually at High Holiday time—and I am afraid it may well be.

In the production of *Holiday Song*, the thing to guard against is extravagance. It is only natural for actors to play their lines for all they are worth, and I have met only a few directors who have the taste and delicacy to keep the actors within the bounds of realism. Directors, indeed, usually have a passion for the theatrical themselves—searching into the scripts for explosive moments and intense close-ups. *Holiday Song* can easily degenerate into a mawkish piece of sogginess. The main element of comedy has to be stressed to avoid plunging into the cheap tragedy. The fact that the Cantor has lost his faith in God is not a heavy thought. Among Jews especially, religion has a highly intellectual quality. The second-act scene, for example, where the Rabbi and Zucker engage in a Talmudic discussion was intended to be rank comedy. Perhaps a better clue to the basic level of the show lies in the first scene of the play when the Cantor first confesses his loss of faith to Zucker. The actor playing Zucker will inevitably stare aghast at the Cantor, blanch, perhaps turn aside in terror at this awful confession. Actually, Zucker doesn't know quite what the Cantor is talking about. It would be as if the Cantor had announced to Zucker that he had just jumped off the Brooklyn Bridge and broken every bone in his body. Zucker's reaction would obviously be: "What are you talking about? I don't see any broken bones." Anyway, just what does it mean—to lose your faith in God? Faith being a nebulous thing, how do you lose it? Zucker should be played in this scene much like the man in the talking-horse stories. He is aware that something extraordinary is going on, but he isn't quite sure what it is.

The quality of *Holiday Song* is that of the folk tale, European and never more than poignant. It is a gimmicky kind of show; that is, its plot is more important than its characterizations. Another thing to be guarded against is the tendency of serious actors to make more out of their parts than is called for. Actors, like everyone else, like to think of themselves as creative artists; and if they want to, they can develop the most complicated characterizations. The characters in *Holiday Song* are no more than the words indicate them to be. Some of the scenes are little more than burlesque sketches, especially the little routines between the Cantor and Zucker in which the latter gives subway instructions to the former. You need real professional actors for this kind of improvisation, men who have played vaudeville and a lot of comedy. In this kind of thing, nobody in the world is much better than Mr. Buloff.

Generally speaking, *Holiday Song* is a comedy. Seen in the smallness of a living room, it may play with no more than a smile; but in front of a house audience it should get continual laughter. Under any circumstances, this should be the basic approach to it.

Printer's Measure

DIRECTED BY: DELBERT MANN
PRODUCED BY: FRED COE

Cast

MR. HEALY	Pat O'Malley
BOY	Martin Newman
MOTHER	Peg Hillias
NEIGHBOR	Ann Dere
BOSS	Joseph Boland
LINOTYPE OPERATOR	Joseph Mantell
LUNDY	Wyrley Birch
UNION OFFICIAL	Irving Winters
FAULKNER	Frank Tweddell
SON	Peter Gray
WIFE	Virginia Robinson
SISTER	Melinda Markey
MRS. HEALY	Ann Sullivan
NARRATOR	Douglas Taylor
STREET PASSERSBY	S. K. Hershewe George McCoy Norton Bloom Shirley Wood
GRANDDAUGHTER	Pidgie Jamieson
STREET URCHINS	Bobby Galli Michael Mann

ACT I

Fade in: A wooden sign swaying ever so little in a May morning breeze. . . . The sign is old and battered, and the words "Emperor Press" are barely discernible.

The camera moves slowly down across a store window so dirty you can hardly see through it. Again dimly visible, "Emperor Press." The window display is a number of samples of the printer's work—all printed at least ten years ago, the edges curling up, and covered with dust.

NARRATOR: *In 1939 when I was seventeen years old, I went to work in a print shop on West Twenty-sixth Street in New York . . .*

The camera moves toward the door, which is one step down from the sidewalk, opens the door, moves in. We are faced with a railing that separates the customers from the shop proper. We push through the swinging door of the railing and face the shop. It is a crowded, dark, dank little place. The only illumination is provided by work bulbs over the stone and over each press. The floors are black from years of spilled ink and littered with balls of crumpled paper. The air is dense with the smell of kerosene. Along the right wall of the shop are rows of type cabinets about waist high. Over them, space cabinets and furniture cabinets. Along the left wall, a row of three presses, a large hand press, an Automatic Kluege, which is clacking away at the moment—its automatic arm plunging and backing with mechanical preciseness—and a small job press. Between the type cabinets on one wall and the presses on the other, there is a tortuous passage. The camera slowly moves down the shop, ducking the moving arm of the Kluege press.

NARRATOR: *My job was to clean the press, fill the fountains with ink, a little distributing, a little compositing . . .*

At this point the apprentice, who had been bending down between two presses, suddenly pops into view, sweeping the floor industriously.

and other duties . . .

The camera continues its slow movement to a second railing, which separates the machines from what is known as the office. This consists of a small cleared area, in which squats an old roll-top desk. The rest of the area is used to store cartons and cases of paper. There are a small paper-cutting machine and a Ludlow machine. Seated at the desk is a heavy-set man in his fifties. He is wearing a soiled printer's apron. . . . At the moment he is scowling at some bills.

NARRATOR: *My Boss . . .*

The camera clambers past the stacks of cartoned paper so that all that is left to see in the shop is the rear wall. There is a door which obviously leads to the bathroom. On the door hang several coats. There is also an incredibly filthy washbasin. In the bowl of the basin are three cans of Trusolvent.

The door to the bathroom opens, and a round-shouldered, bandy-legged, crusty-looking little man in his sixties comes out, tying his blackened printer's apron behind him. Under his apron he wears an old-fashioned undershirt with elbow-length sleeves and a collar that buttons to the throat. A somewhat bizarre effect is created by the fact that he always wears an old, worn, gray fedora hat.

NARRATOR: *The only other worker in the shop was the compositor . . . Mister Healy. I shall never forget Mister Healy as long as I live.*

Mr. Healy moves down the length of the shop to the type cabinets, opens one of the drawers, fetches a compositor's stick from the wall behind him, props up his copy on the space cabinets before him, and begins setting up a composition.

CLOSE-UP: Mr. Healy's hands working so fast they form a blur. The deft fingers flick in and out of the cabinet, plucking the letters from their compartments and plunking them into place on his stick.

DISSOLVE TO: Close-up of Mr. Healy's hands blocking in the composition into a frame, snapping the wooden furniture into place, tightening the quoynes, etc.—all done with a sure touch that indicates the finished craftsman.

DISSOLVE TO: Close-up of Mr. Healy's hands clamping the frame into place in the press, setting the tympan, the quads, and then running off one impression.

CUT TO: Mr. Healy holding the proof up to the light over the stone, peering at it, squinting, frowning.

CUT TO: Close-up of Mr. Healy's hands as he feeds a job press. The press is clacking away for all it's worth. Mr. Healy's hands flicker in and out, as methodical as the press.

The camera dollies slowly back to see Mr. Healy finishing the last of his feeding. He leans over, pulls one of a profusion of wires coming out of the wall, and the press slowly rolls to a halt. Mr. Healy turns to the pile of newly printed letterheads piled on the shelf at his right elbow and begins expertly to straighten them. He darts a quick glance at the boy, who is still sweeping the floor down at the front of the shop.

MR. HEALY: *Hey! Come here! . . .*

The boy looks up and comes scurrying down the shop, dodging the poking arm of the Kluege press, and comes to Mr. Healy. Mr. Healy pulls out a letterhead, points to a line of print.

MR. HEALY: *What kind of type is that?*

BOY: *Twelve-point Clearface.*

MR. HEALY: *How do you know?*

BOY: *It's lighter than Goudy, and the lower-case "e" goes up.*

MR. HEALY: *Clearface is a delicate type. It's clean, it's clear. It's got line and grace. Remember that. Beat it.*

The boy hurries back to the front of the shop to finish his cleaning. Mr. Healy now stands, regarding the unsuspecting figure of the boss, bent over his desk, still scowling at bills.

MR. HEALY: *Hey!*

The boss looks up.

BOSS: *What?*

MR. HEALY: [Flourishing the letterhead] *Why do you keep buying this twenty-pound stock? It's wrapping paper. How many times I told you not to buy this twenty-pound stock?*

BOSS: *Watsa matter with you now?*

MR. HEALY: *If you're going to buy twenty-pound, buy watermarked, will you? Stop buying this wrapping paper. What are you, a grocery store or a printer? Aren't you ashamed to hand your customers letterheads like this?*

He lifts his head imperiously, calls to the boy.

Hey, boy, come here . . .

The boy, dragging his broom, scurries down the length of the shop, dodging past the Kluege. Mr. Healy thrusts the paper at him again.

MR. HEALY: *Feel that. It offends your fingers, don't it? That's twenty-pound stock, no rag content. It has no texture, no taste. When I get some time, I'll show you how to feel paper. Wrap these up neat. It goes out this afternoon.*

He turns abruptly, shuffles bandy-legged down to the front of the shop, muttering to himself. He is a mutterer.

Twenty-pound . . . twenty-pound . . . It demeans the craft . . .

He raises his voice for the benefit of the boss.

This place is turning into a real Sixth Avenue shop, a real dump . . .

He plucks a sheet of printed matter from the pocket of the Kluege press and examines it with a querulous scowl . . . muttering steadily and inaudibly to himself. He pulls another of the thousand wires coming out of the wall, and the Kluege comes to a halt. He takes a pica stick from a pocket, lays it quickly on one of the finished printed papers, flicks it quickly across the page, and measures the margin a second time. Then he casts a quick scornful glance at the boss, bends over the tympan, and resets one of the quads the tiniest fraction of an inch.

The boy stands behind him, watching, open-eyed with fascination. Mr. Healy, conscious of the boy, looks up at him, winks suddenly, then as abruptly goes back to resetting the quad. Finished with this, he straightens up, slaps the magazine back into place, pulls another wire, and the Kluege is off again.

The old man shuffles down to the stone, muttering inaudibly away. He plucks a copy from a clipboard containing the day's work, automatically fetches a compositor's stick from the wall behind him, pulls open a drawer of type.

MR. HEALY: *Hey, boy! Come here!*

The boy, still at the Kluege, comes over slowly and waits for the little round-shouldered man to say something. The old man clips the stick to its right length, reaches up to the space cabinet for a slug, plunks it into the stick, and then stands a moment, scowling down at the open type drawer before him, obviously preparing a philosophical speculation.

MR. HEALY: *Boy, if you was my kid, I wouldn't even let you near a print shop. It'll take you twenty years before you're even a half-good printer. By the time you're a printer, you could be ten doctors. I got a boy, thirty-eight years old. When he was fifteen, he said to me, he wanted to quit school and work down the shop with me. I whacked him one across the head, he's still talking about it.*

Mr. Healy pauses here. For a moment, it seems he has finished his dissertation. The boy waits, then decides it's over, starts back to his chores.

MR. HEALY: *Stay here, boy!*

The boy dutifully returns to the old man's side.

When I say printer, I mean printer. I don't mean these kids, come out of some school, come walking in, tell you they're compositors.

He indicates the copy propped up on the space cabinet in front of him.

Whoever set this up is a real Sixth Avenue printer. . . . Look at this "W." The face is breaking in half—I don't like Bodoni. It looks like a vaudeville poster. There's no design here. There's no flow in the lines. There's no grace—The compositor who set this up, he figures it's just a lousy consignment book. He just threw a handful of type together, and flopped it into the press.

He waves a foreboding finger at the boy.

A good compositor takes a lousy consignment book like this and sets it up like he was Michelangelo painting the Sistine Chapel. [The boy starts to go.] *Hey, boy!* [The boy turns.]

BOY: *Yes, Mister Healy.*

MR. HEALY: *Do you like this trade?*

BOY: *Yes, Mister Healy, I like it very much.*

MR. HEALY: *You'll never get that ink out from under your nails. You're going to have dirty fingernails the rest of your life.*

BOY: *I like printing very much, Mister Healy.*

The old man suddenly reaches out and awkwardly pats the boy, two quick pats on the side of the head—then abruptly turns back to studying the copy paper in his other hand. He mutters.

MR. HEALY: *If you was my kid, boy, I wouldn't even let you near a print shop.*

CLOSE-UP: The boy's face—quite touched. The boy then goes back to his pile of papers, picks up his broom. . . .

DISSOLVE: SLOWLY OUT.

FADE IN: Interior of shop, looking out to the street.

NARRATOR: *I remember one morning Mister Healy came in, clutching a brown package . . .*

The door to the shop opens and Mr. Healy comes in. He has on his perpetual hat and his topcoat, and he is holding close to his chest a thin brown-wrapped parcel about the size of a book. He shuffles down the length of the shop to the rear, nodding

quickly to the boy's good morning. At the rear wall, he carefully sets the book down on the stacks of paper. The boy, who
is opening a can of ink, watches him. The old man takes off his
coat, his jacket, hangs them up. Every now and then he darts
a quick, suspicious look at the boy, who smiles and nods back.
The old man unbuttons his vest, frowning and scowling. He
takes off his shirt, reaches for his printer's apron, pauses in the
action, darts another quick look at the boy.

MR. HEALY: *Hey, boy, come here.*

The boy obligingly sidles down to the old man, who reaches
for the package and carefully unwraps it. Then he extracts a
thin, brown book and he slowly extends it to the boy. The boy
reaches for it.

MR. HEALY: *Don't touch it, boy. Just look at it.*

The old man is peering at the boy with suppressed excitement. The boy looks down at the book. It is a beautifully
leather-bound book. The old man slowly opens it. The paper is
thick and soft, the printing exquisite. The boy is impressed.

BOY: *It's beautiful, Mister Healy.*

In the dim light of the rear of the shop, the old man's face
glows with an almost forgotten sense of craftsmanship.

MR. HEALY: [In a whisper] *I set that book myself, every
bit of it. In 1922 I printed it and bound it, and I bought
the leather for the cover. You don't see books like that
around. I etched that cover. I etched it myself. With a
red-hot needle. With my hands I did it, boy, with my
hands. There wasn't a machine in the whole process. Isn't
it clear? Look how level the impressions are. Look how
the letters seem to cling to the paper. Oh, it's a beauty!
A beauty! A rare piece of work! A rare piece!*

He stares up at the boy, his eyes wide and his mouth slightly
ajar with his immense pride. The boy regards the book with
genuine respect.

BOY: *It's beautiful, Mister Healy.*

MR. HEALY: *Do you really mean it?*

BOY: *I really mean it, Mister Healy.*

The old man's head bobs. Then he turns and begins quickly to rewrap the book.

MR. HEALY: [Without looking up] *I'll buy you a beer to-night before you go home . . .*

> DISSOLVE:

> FADE IN: The old wall clock on the wall by the front window. It reads nine o'clock. The camera looks down at the door, which now opens to admit the boy, in street clothes, coming in for work.

NARRATOR: *This is the story about Mister Healy and the linotype machine . . .*

The boy shuts the door behind him, pushes through the swinging door of the railing. Mr. Healy is already at work, standing in front of the cabinet, his inevitable composing stick in hand. He is in a bad humor.

BOY: *Good morning, Mister Healy . . .*

The old man says nothing, just deepens his scowl. The boy moves past him and makes his way to the rear of the shop. He just about gets to the Kluege, which is halfway, when his progress is arrested by a mighty roar from behind him. He turns to see Mr. Healy flourishing his composing stick in the air like a machete.

MR. HEALY: [Roaring] *I quit! That's all! I'll finish this off, and then I quit!*

The boy looks quickly at the long-suffering boss, who is in the rear of the shop by the Ludlow machine. The boss casts a glance of appeal to the ceiling and goes back to his Ludlow. The boy, a little unnerved, continues quietly to the rear of the shop, offering a quick hello to the boss as he goes. The boss acknowledges the greeting with a nod. The boy takes his coat off, hangs it over the coats already hung on the back of the bathroom door. He takes off his jacket, hangs it up . . . starts on his tie. He is again given pause by a roar from Mr. Healy at the front of the shop.

MR. HEALY: [At the top of his lungs] *I won't work in no shop that got a linotype machine!*

BOSS: *Ah, come on, John, act your age.*

An exchange now follows between the two old friends, each at opposing ends of the shop, neither pausing in their work as they bellow at each other.

MR. HEALY: *You heard me!*

BOSS: *Act your age.*

MR. HEALY: *Better call the union, get another comp.*

BOSS: *If you had your way, printers would still be carving letters out of wood.*

MR. HEALY: *I ain't working in no shop that got a linotype machine. I'm a printer; I ain't a stenographer. A linotype machine is nothing but a big typewriter. You'll be hiring girls to do all your printing for you.*

BOSS: *Yeah, sure.*

MR. HEALY: *Better send the boy to the bank, pick up my close-out pay. I ain't working here no more.*

BOSS: *You'll be working here when we're all dead.*

MR. HEALY: *Yeah?*

BOSS: *Why should I send out eight thousand bucks worth of linotype to Schmidt every year? It's just Vogue and Garamond. I can set that stuff up right here.*

MR. HEALY: *I don't want no linotype machine in this shop.*

BOSS: *John, we been friends for twenty-seven years, so I'm taking the privilege of telling you you're an old lunatic. Every time I bring a new machine into this shop, you raise the roof. When I brought in the automatic Kluege, you threw a can of ink right through the window. All right, I'm telling you, I need a linotype machine in this shop. You can't set everything up by hand . . . Those days is gone forever.*

MR. HEALY: *Yeah?*

BOSS: *Yeah. You're still living in the Middle Ages. We do printing with machines now. I'm going to haul this old job*

press out. Tomorrow morning, there's going to be a lino-
type machine which cost me twenty-eight hundred dollars
sitting right over there where that old job press is now.
You just get used to the idea.

DISSOLVE TO: Interior Seventh Avenue dairy cafeteria—
Mr. Healy and the boy, carrying trays of food, wending their
way through a few people. The boy wears his apron. Mr. Healy
has his jacket on. Mr. Healy is muttering dark imprecations to
himself. They make their way to a table at which sits another
old-timer cut from the same mold as Mr. Healy. His name is
Lundy. Mr. Healy and the boy set their trays down and sit.

MR. HEALY: *They're putting in a linotype machine in my*
shop.

Mr. Lundy is immediately all sympathy.

MR. LUNDY: *Is that right, John? Well, that's a bad bit, isn't*
it?

MR. HEALY: *Oh, it is. I don't know what the trade is coming*
to. There's nothing but machines. He's got so many ma-
chines now in that shop I don't know whether it's a print
shop, or he's manufacturing Chevrolets. He says to me this
morning—and the boy here will bear witness—the days of
the handcraftsman is gone forever.

MR. LUNDY: *That's not what I had in mind, John. I was*
thinking that you might be out of a job soon.

MR. HEALY: *Oh, don't be daft. I been in that shop for*
twenty-seven years. It would crumble to dust without me.

MR. LUNDY: *Oh, I've heard those gallant words before.*
Didn't I say them myself? For isn't it just what happened
to me? The boss installed a row of linotypes, and within
the week, I was out on the street, poking my head into
shops, looking for a job. I haven't had an apron on in seven
weeks, John.

This is a thought that had never occurred to Mr. Healy.

MR. HEALY: [Frowning] *I'm not worried about my job.*
Why, the boss don't blow his nose, he doesn't let me meas-

*ure it off with a pica stick for him first. Ask the boy here.
I can walk into any shop in New York and command a
hundred dollars a week, and they'd wrench their bones
loose jumping for me.* [Mr. Lundy nods sadly.] *Seven
weeks is it now, Lundy, that you haven't worked?*

MR. LUNDY: *Seven weeks and I expect a lot more. Work is
rare. It's not like the old days when you could just march
into a shop, pick up an apron, and go to work.*

DISSOLVE TO: Bar.

DISSOLVE TO: Close-up—Another old-timer's face. We are
in interior of bar, typical Eighth Avenue beer joint. Mr. Healy
in coat and hat and the second friend—named Faulkner—likewise in coat and hat, over their after-work beers. Bartender
behind bar moving in and out of camera view.

MR. FAULKNER: . . . *Well, I give you six weeks before he
cans you.*

MR. HEALY: *Well, you're Mister Cheerful today, aren't you,
George?*

MR. FAULKNER: *Give the facts a good look in the face, John.
When your boss brings in a linotype machine, what's he
need a compositor for? For a couple of hundred bucks, he
buys himself a couple of magazines of type, and he'll be
rattling off printed matter like shelling peas.*

MR. HEALY: *The boss is an old friend. He's been up to my
house a hundred times—and drunk my whisky. He's an old
friend, and he isn't going to can me just like that.*

MR. FAULKNER: *Aye, and wasn't my last boss an old friend
who had been to the house for dinner more often than he
ate at his own home. And he drank my whisky. Oh, how
that man swilled my whisky. We had to hide an off bottle
when he was up to keep a swallow for ourselves. Well,
four months ago, he calls me into the office, and he says:
"George, I'm thinking of expanding a bit, magazines, and
pamphlets and that sort of thing. I'm bringing in a pair of
linotype machines, and I just want you to know you've*

*nothing to worry about." Well, two weeks had barely
sneaked by, when he called me into the office, and he says:
"George, we're closing out the hand-press department.
You're fired." Well, he's no friend of mine no more . . .*
[To the bartender] *Fill that up again, will you, Mister? . . .*
[Back to Mr. Healy] *Oh, things are black. There isn't work
around for no one. My old boss, fourteen years ago, Old
Man Kleinberg, flung himself off the roof of the Stowe
Building yesterday. There was a bit in the papers about
it, did you see it, John? I'm sorry to hear about that lino-
type, John. But if you like, we can go job-hunting together.*
MR. HEALY: *Well, I'm surely glad I bumped into you,
George. You've brightened my day immeasurably.*
MR. FAULKNER: *It's my disposition to be cheerful.* [Drinks]
Cheers, John. [To bartender] *Oh, it's a bad year for printers. The bosses are flinging themselves off the roofs like
pigeons. I been looking for work for three months now
and seen nothing but gloomy faces . . .* [Drinks] *Well,
cheers.*

> DISSOLVE TO: Living room of Healy home. Family is eating
> dinner. Pan from Mr. Healy's wife to his son (thirty-eight),
> his daughter-in-law (thirty-five), his granddaughter (four-
> teen) and at last to Mr. Healy, who sits staring down at his
> plate of food without eating. The rest of the family is eating,
> but in silence—oppressed by the old man's gloom.

MR. HEALY: *. . . So I thought I'd try it out, see if things was
as bad as all that. So I went up to Sixth Avenue and opened
the door and leaned into the shop, and I said "Need a
good comp?" And the boss there just looked up and shook
his head. And then I tried another shop. "Need a good
comp?" And it was the same. And I must have poked my
head into half a dozen shops, and, oh, my blessed Saint,
it was like 1931 when the whole town was gray and locked
up. That dreadful feeling that there isn't a dollar in the*

*whole city, and the men lined up for blocks to buy a bowl
of rice for a penny.*

SON: *Oh, now, Dad, it isn't as black as that.*

WIFE: *Well, it's a shame now, isn't it? A shame and a scan-
dal, that a man devotes his whole life to a trade, to be cast
off at the age of sixty-six for a machine.*

SON: *Now, he hasn't been canned yet, Ma. We're all being
a bit premature. The boss is an old friend. He's been up
to this house a hundred times and drunk our whisky . . .*

Mr. Healy deepens his scowl at this.

MR. HEALY: *We'll keep the bottle hidden if he comes again.*

SON: *And if he cans you, then what? You're sixty-six years
old, Dad, with a good bit in the bank. You've worked a full
life, and perhaps it's time, Dad, to enjoy the autumn of
your years.*

Mr. Healy picks his head up imperiously at this.

MR. HEALY: *The autumn of my years?*

SON: *You'll sleep till ten and no more elbowing about in
the subways.*

DAUGHTER-IN-LAW: *I sometimes wish I was sixty-six so I
could sit in the park and contrive ways to spend my pen-
sion.*

MR. HEALY: [Jerking his attention to the daughter-in-law]
Oh, do you?

SON: *Perhaps you'll buy a little car and go bucketing down
to Florida with Ma, and play checkers with the old chaps
down there. Take it easy and loll in the sun, the rewards
of a fruitful life.*

DAUGHTER-IN-LAW: [To granddaughter] *Eat your soup.
The rest of us are on the meat already.*

SON. *You'll be out of that musty shop, Dad. What a place
to work!*

The old man suddenly stands and stares at his son aghast.

MR. HEALY: *That's my trade, man! That's my trade! I'd
crumble into my coffin without my trade!*

He takes a step from the table as if to leave the room. Stops. *I love that work! I'd rather be a printer than Ambassador to Ireland!*

He stares at his son, and then at the others, and then turns and goes off into his room. The others pause in their meal, then begin again.

SON: *Well, he hasn't been canned yet, and there's no sense being premature. We'll just have to wait and see what happens . . .*

CUT TO: Doorway of the print shop. Two sweating, cussing freight men, the boss, and the boy are trying to dolly a huge linotype machine down a ramp into the shop. The linotype machine is on casters. This spectacular operation has attracted quite a group of sidewalk spectators, who can be seen lined up, outside the front window, pressing their noses against the glass. A couple of unkempt neighborhood kids have actually contrived to watch the unloading from inside the shop. They are having the time of their lives. The two freight men, the boss, and the boy are struggling and sweating the machine through the doorway.

AD LIBS: "Watch your fingers, you nut!" . . . "Watch out, the wheels is coming off on this side." . . . "Get your end over, will you?" . . . "Hey, get those kids outta there." . . . "Beat it, you kids." . . . "Hey, boss, get that thing sticking out there." . . .

At last the machine is through the doorway. The freight men and the boss carefully wheel it down the ramp into the front of the store.

AD LIBS: "Will you kids get outta here!" . . . "How we gonna get this in the back with that thing over there jumping in and out?" . . . "All right, wait a minute while I turn the press off." . . . The boy hurries down to the Kluege and shuts it off.

FROM THE DOORWAY, SPECTATORS OFFER ADVICE: "Hey, boss, did you get a permit from the housing department to put a machine like that in here?" . . . "Hey, you guys'll never get that thing down the back." . . .

The freight men and the boss slowly wheel the linotype machine on its rollers through the swinging door of the railing.

Ad Libs: "Hey, boss, push in that drawer." . . . "Wait a minute, lemme get on the other side." . . . "Push in that drawer." . . . "Watch out for my hand, you jerk!" . . . "All right, push." . . . "You push, who are you, the foreman?" . . . "Hey, watch your head." . . .

Slowly the linotype machine is moved down the length of the shop, preceded by the neighborhood kids—who are being crowded farther into the shop. A couple of sidewalk spectators step into the shop. "Hey, boss, what kinda machine is that?" . . . "That's a press." . . . "That's no press. That's a paper cutter!" . . . "You wouldn't know a paper cutter from a can opener." . . .

The machine, with its thick wooden platform, is now wheeled into the empty area left by the removed job press. "How far in you want it, boss?" . . . "That's fine right where it is." . . . "You want this hose sticking out the back here?" . . . "That's fine. Just get the casters out." "Boy, I'm sweating like a dog." . . . "This must weigh twenty-five tons." . . .

The freight men now carefully remove the dollies under the platform. "All right, everybody get out of the way. Louie, hold that end there. Get that beam in here." . . . One of the freight men has got a thick beam under the press, while the other yanks the flat dolly out. Slowly the heavy machine is levered to the ground. The first freight man now pulls his beam out.

Suddenly, now that the machine is in place, a silence falls upon the shop. A magnificent engineering feat has just been accomplished, and the freight men, the boss, the boy, the kids, and the spectators are all impressed and hushed.

The boss stands, his chest heaving from his exertion, looking down on the linotype machine with understandable pride.

The camera slowly examines the machine. It is a large greenish-gray thing with a keyboard not unlike a typewriter's. The camera now slowly moves away from the machine toward the rear of the shop. It passes over the boss and the freight men and the boy to the railing that separates the office from the shop. Standing by the railing in the shadows of the rear is Mr. Healy.

The camera moves up for a close-up of Mr. Healy. He is re-regarding the linotype machine with patent hatred and gloom. His grumpy old face is scowling and muttering. Then he leans a bit to the boy, who stands on the other side of the railing with his back to the old man.

MR. HEALY: *That machine'll be the death of me, boy.*

He turns abruptly and heads off for the washroom in the rear of the shop.

FADE OUT.

ACT II

FADE IN: Close-up—Linotype machine as seen from the rear. It is in action. We stay on the machine for the manufacture of one whole slug of type, then slowly move around the machine and see the linotypist at work. His fingers flick rapidly over the keyboard.

NARRATOR: *And so the linotype machine was brought into the shop, and a linotypist was hired—and Mr. Healy declared war on both of them. First he challenged the machine to a race . . .*

The camera dollies back so that we can see the whole shop. In the middle stands the boy, his hand raised like the timer at a foot race. At the linotype machine, the linotypist sits poised, read to start. At the other end of the shop, Mr. Healy, composing stick in hand, waiting for the signal. The boy looks at him. He nods. The boy turns and looks at the linotypist. He nods. . . . The boy's arm comes down, and the race is on.

CUT TO: Close-up of linotype machine flicking away like mad.

CUT TO: Close-up of Mr. Healy's hands moving in a blur.

CUT TO: Close-up of linotypist—his fingers flicking over the keys. Then, with a broad smile, he lifts his head. He's done.

CUT TO: Mr. Healy bleakly examining the half-finished line of composition in his stick. Muttering.

SLOW DISSOLVE.

NARRATOR: *Then he took the tack that the linotype machine had a personal grudge against him . . .*

FADE IN: Mr. Healy sidling into the small area separating the Kluege press from the linotype machine. He bends down to pick up a proof that has fallen to the floor there. When he straightens up, he bangs his head against a projecting gimmick

59

of the linotype machine. Mr. Healy starts back, ready to do battle. He eyes the machine, daring the machine to try that again. Muttering, he sidles back into the aisle and starts for the back of the shop. He pauses in his tracks—looks quickly here and there to see if anyone is watching him. Then surreptitiously he gives the machine a quick kick on its base. Muttering, he moves on. SLOW DISSOLVE.

NARRATOR: *Or else he would suddenly be seized with a paroxysm of coughing* . . . [Mr. Healy in rear of the shop suddenly being seized by paroxysm of coughing] . . . *which he claimed was due to lead fumes that were filling the shop* . . . [Mr. Healy hacking away] . . . *and he would look around at the rest of us, amazed that we were immune to it all* . . .

Mr. Healy, controlling his cough, darts quick nervous looks from under his glowering eyebrows at the others in the shop . . . then mutters . . . shuffles out of view.

DISSOLVE TO: Interior, the boy's home, living room with hallway leading to front door. Lower-class apartment, the furnishings drab. The shades have been drawn on the one window, and the only light in the quite dark room is provided by two small lamps. The boy's mother sits stiffly in an old chair, her hands folded limply in her lap. Her face is drawn. In the next chair, bent forward in a position of consolation, sits another woman, a neighbor. She is mumbling solicitous words to the mother. Standing beside the mother is the boy's sister, a girl of about twenty, likewise solemn of aspect. The boy is standing by the darkened window. All three of the family wear black mourning bands.

NARRATOR: *In June 1939, my father died. . . .*

The consoling neighbor leans a little closer to the mother.

NEIGHBOR: *Oh, he was a man of cheer. Wherever he went, he brought a spark of laughter. I've been weeping myself dry these last four days. Look at my eyes, swollen and red. When I told my husband the news, he stood up from his*

*chair, so shocked he was, and said: "I'm going out for a
pot of beer." Oh, what a blazing drunk my husband put
on, so distressed he was at the news . . .*

    The doorbell rings.

MOTHER: *Tom, go see the door.*

    The boy leaves his post by the window and starts down the
    hallway to the door. Behind him, we hear the fading words of
    the neighbor's consolation.

NEIGHBOR: *It seems that all the good folks are dropping
off these days. Now, if there are so many heart attacks,
why couldn't one be visited upon our landlord, who didn't
give us a pound of steam this whole last winter and hasn't
painted our flat since we moved in . . .*

    The boy has reached the door, opens it. Standing in the door-
    way is Mr. Healy, head cocked to one side, peering quizzically
    up at the boy.

MR. HEALY: *Hello, boy . . .*

BOY: [Shocked at this visit] *Hello, Mister Healy.*

MR. HEALY: *I hope you don't mind, but I brought a basket
of fruit which I think is customary on these occasions.*

    He proffers a small basket of fruit.

BOY: *That's very nice of you, Mister Healy. Really, that's
very nice of you.* [The boy is obviously touched.] *I mean,
that's nice of you to come over and pay your respects.
Would you like to come in the house, meet my mother and
sister?*

    The old man comes into the hallway. The boy closes the door.
    He leads the old man up the hallway to the room.

BOY: *Ma, this is Mister Healy, who is the compositor down
at the shop. He's brought a basket of fruit.*

    Mr. Healy crosses and offers his hand to the mother.

MOTHER: *Thank you very much, Mister Healy.*

BOY: *That's my sister.*

SISTER: *How do you do, Mister Healy.*

    The old man nods.

NEIGHBOR: [Now standing] *He was a man of cheer, Mister Healy.*

MR. HEALY: *I'm sure he was.*

NEIGHBOR: *Wherever he went, he brought a spark of laughter. He was struck down in the prime, and what will his family do? He left behind him only a pittance of insurance, which has gone into the rental of the hearse and a plot of grave.*

MOTHER: *Missus Gallagher . . .*

NEIGHBOR: *And the girl two years away from graduation.*

MOTHER: *Missus Gallagher, Mister Healy has come to pay his respects, not to take away the furniture.*

NEIGHBOR: *He was a man of cheer.*

MR. HEALY: *I'm sure he was.* [A short, uncomfortable silence falls over the group.] *Well, I'll say good-by then. I just came by to let you know you have a friend whom you might not have known about.*

MOTHER: *Thank you, Mister Healy.*

The old man turns abruptly and starts back down the hallway. The boy follows him. When they reach the door, the old man pauses.

MR. HEALY: [In a low voice] *Do you need some money, boy?*

BOY: [Also in a low voice] *I don't think so, Mister Healy.*

MR. HEALY: *When will you be back at the shop?*

BOY: *In a couple of days, I guess.*

MR. HEALY: *Are you sad?*

BOY: *I haven't had time to be sad, Mister Healy. Ten minutes after my old man collapsed on the floor, my Uncle Frank had me in the kitchen telling me I had to start making a better living. Because my mother doesn't know a trade, you know. She can't even type. And my sister is two years in college, and my mother won't hear of her quitting, and somebody's got to pay the rent. We can't stay here. It's forty-seven dollars a month here, gloomy as*

*it is. I was thinking of hitting up the boss for a raise. Do
you think he'll give it to me?*

MR. HEALY: *Sure he will. You're the best boy we ever had
in the shop.*

BOY: *I was thinking of asking seventy-five cents an hour.
That's only thirty dollars a week . . .*

The strain of the week is beginning to tell on the boy. He
begins to cry quietly even as he talks.

*He was a tough guy, my old man. He gave me a lot of
hard times, but we used to get along good . . .*

He is crying openly now, trying to control it, biting his lip.

The old man examines the crying boy with a sudden
sweetness.

MR. HEALY: *Oh, it's a lot of responsibility you have for a
seventeen-year-old. But you'll make out. I'll talk to the
boss first thing in the morning, and when you'll come back,
you'll be seventy-five cents an hour. And I'll teach you to
composite. In the evening after work we'll stick an hour
a day, and I'll teach you the finesse. You've got the feel
for it, boy. You'll make a good printer some day.*

The gentle words of sympathy only unleash a new flood of
tears. The old man smiles fondly at the boy. . . . Then he puts
an arm around his shoulders, and the boy rests his head on
the old man's chest and cries.

CLOSE-UP: Mr. Healy, his own eyes a little wet.

MR. HEALY: *We'll make a good printer out of you, boy . . .*

DISSOLVE TO: The boy's mother, lying on the sofa. She is
wearing an old house robe . . . underneath that, an old-fashioned nightgown. It is some hours later, and she is ready for
bed. She lies on the sofa, unmoving, her eyes open, looking at
the ceiling. The room is darker now, one of the lamps being
turned off. Her face slowly turns to the second lamp, on the
other side of the room, which is still on.

MOTHER: *Tom, go to bed.*

The camera moves across the room to where the boy is sitting
in a chair underneath the lamp.

BOY: *Are you going to sleep out here again tonight, Ma?*

MOTHER: *Yes.*

BOY: *Listen, Ma, I've been thinking. I know how determined you are that Polly finishes college, but I think it's pretty silly.*

The mother makes a soft "shush," indicating a closed door
with an almost imperceptible motion of her head.

BOY: [Lowering his voice] *Look, the best I can make right now is thirty dollars a week, and . . .*

MOTHER: *You better come over here, Tom.*

The boy rises a little sulkily, pads across the room to his
mother, stands over her.

BOY: *Ma, the best I could hope to make for the next six months at least is thirty bucks a week, and, after that, I might get a small raise, maybe another couple of bucks a week, and, I mean, now, let's be sensible.*

MOTHER: *Tom . . .*

BOY: *So what if she goes to college? I don't see what's so important.*

MOTHER: *All right, don't talk so loud.*

BOY: [Lowering his voice almost to a whisper] *I think she ought to go out and get a job, contribute to the house. She can get some kind of a job, and if she can make another thirty dollars a week, then we'd be all right. But this way she don't earn nothing, and she has to buy all those books every term. She must spend a hundred bucks every term just on books. We can't afford that, Ma. You know that.*

MOTHER: *We can manage.*

BOY: *We can't manage.*

MOTHER: *It gives me pleasure that she goes to college. She has a fine mind, and it would be criminal to take her from her classes.*

BOY: *What does a girl have to go to college for? She's just going to get married. She'll have a raft of babies, and in*

ten years she won't remember one chemical from another.
Physics! I mean, what is she studying physics for? What
is she going to do with her physics?
MOTHER: *All right, Tom, sit down.*
BOY: *She's a good-looking girl. Why don't she get mar-*
ried? Who does she think she is, Madame Curie?
MOTHER: *Tom, sit down, and don't talk so loud. She'll hear*
every word you say. [The boy sullenly sits in the chair be-
side the sofa.] *I know you feel bitter against your sister.*
BOY: *I don't feel bitter.*
MOTHER: *You do. I can see every thought in your mind.*
You're going to have to scrape and scrimp to put a sister
through college. And you're only seventeen years old.
You'd like to be out kissing girls instead of worrying under
the burden of a grown man. Well, it'll only be two years.
She'll crowd in as much as is humanly possible and finish
it off quick. Now, don't twist in your seat. She's very good
at this physics, and someday she may poke out some ra-
dium like Madame Curie, and they'll make a moving pic-
ture out of her. You're as fogy as your father, and all that
you see in women is a drudge to cook your stew. Well,
times have changed, and it's something marvelous that a
sister of yours has a turn of mind to explore atoms. I can't
tell you the pleasure it gives me to see her bent over her
books, and when she's not home, sometimes I open up her
notes and see these fantastic diagrams and pictures, and
I never get over the shock of it. If she was just a pallid
student, I'd have said to her long since, you've got to go
to work. But she's strong at this physics, Tom. She'll make
something out of it. They may not do a movie about her,
but somewheres in some fine thing for mankind, she'll
have a finger. I'm not going to argue from day to night
about this with you, Tom, as I did with your father. It's
got to be clear between us.
BOY: *All right, all right.*
MOTHER: *Not all right, all right. When I was a girl, your*

father came to my father's house and knocked at the door, and announced: "I'm after a bride." And he and my father went into the other room and talked it out, and I sat in the kitchen with my hands in my lap and waited to hear. I thought nothing of it, because it was done that way when I was a girl. But the world is changing, and, if a woman's got a spark, it's her right and privilege to make a thing of herself. It's like this old friend of yours in the shop. The machine is there, but he won't accept it. I'm not saying that it's good or bad that a machine does a man out of his work, but the machine is here. It's part of our world, and the thing to do is to make our lives better with the machine, not worse. If we cannot hold on to old things, we must make peace with the new. Your sister has a talent. You had best make peace with that, Tom.

BOY: *It's the truth, Ma. She's a clever girl, and you know that I'm very proud of her underneath, you know what I mean, Ma?*

MOTHER: *I know what you mean, Tom. You're a solid boy, and I think very wise for your years. Else I couldn't talk to you as I do.*

BOY: *It was only natural that I should feel a little bitter.*
MOTHER: *It was only natural, Tom.*

BOY: *But it's going to be hard, Ma. Thirty bucks a week. Maybe, I could pick up a side job somewheres. It's going to be hard, boy.*

MOTHER: *Oh, don't I know that.*

The boy stands, smiles at his mother.

BOY: *You're a decent woman, Ma, and just to show you how much I like you, I'll go get you a blanket out of your bedroom.*

MOTHER: *No, Tom, the talk has done me a lot of good. I don't think I'll mind sleeping in the old room again.*

BOY: *I'm going to bed.* [Starts for the door to a room off . . . shaking his head and muttering] *It's going to be hard . . .*

He exits through the door. . . . Camera goes back to his

mother, who is still lying on the sofa, her eyes open, staring at the ceiling. Suddenly her eyes close and a trace of a smile appears on her gaunt face.

CUT TO: Linotype machine clacking away—linotypist sitting casually in front of machine, fingers flicking. Every now and then he sneaks a glance at his copy, fetches a cigarette from his shirt pocket with one hand, all the while typing away with the other. Beside the linotype machine there is a small stove for melting down lead, and along the wall are about a dozen "pigs," small oblong chunks of lead. The boy is watching the linotypist with quiet fascination.

LINOTYPIST: *Put another pig in.*

The boy nods, picks a pig from the wall, goes to rear of machine, drops it carefully into the pot.

BOY: *How much you make a week, Joe?*

LINOTYPIST: *A hundred.*

BOY: *No kidding.*

LINOTYPIST: *Yeah.*

BOY: *That's a lot of money. Mister Healy only makes eighty-five and he's sixty-six years old.*

LINOTYPIST: *I made as high as a hundred fifty. I once worked for a couple of guys on Broadway and Twenty-fifth. They had four linotypes and a proof press. They were racking in easy two, three hundred bucks apiece every week. You know, little shops like this one here, they don't usually have a linotype machine. They usually send their linotype work out. Sixteen cents a line . . .*

His hands flick over the keys, and a line of lino flips out onto the plate.

Sixteen cents . . .

BOY: *It must be tough to get to be a linotyper.*

LINOTYPIST: *Aaah, you go to school for a year. That's all I went. Then I went out to Paterson, New Jersey, for a joint called The Monarch Publications, Inc. Used to print comic books. That wasn't bad. At least, it was interesting*

*work. Then, I got a job in Buffalo, New York. Used to print
fire-insurance laws. That's all I ever printed there, fire-
insurance laws. Used to drive me crazy. Sorry I ever left
those comic books. Of course, that was nonunion work,
only paid sixty bucks. But I always remembered those
comic books. That was the only interesting material I ever
worked on. You ever read a comic book called* Jungle
Judy?

BOY: *No.*

LINOTYPIST: *Boy, that was good. Hey, kid, put in another
pig.*

The boy puts in another pig.

BOY: *All you went was one year in linotyping school?*

LINOTYPIST: *Yeah.*

The boy ponders this for a moment. Then he looks down the
shop to where Mr. Healy is bent over the stone.

MR. HEALY: *Hey, boy, you've got four trays of distribution
waiting for you.*

BOY: *Okay, Mister Healy. What's the name of that school,
Joe?*

LINOTYPIST: *American Linotyping School.*

MR. HEALY: *Hey, boy, did you hear me?*

BOY: *Yeah, okay, Mister Healy.*

LINOTYPIST: *Before you go, kid, put in another pig.*

BOY: *It's pretty full now, Joe. It may spurt.*

LINOTYPIST: *Put it in. It won't spurt.*

The boy picks up a pig. Mr. Healy stands regarding the linotypist and his machine with ineffable scorn.

MR. HEALY: *Oh, this is a very clever machine you have
here. Oh, look at the little things flipping around like bugs.
But it broke down yesterday, didn't it? It took two and a
half hours and thirty dollars for a mechanic before you
was able to clack away again.*

LINOTYPIST: *What do you want from me now? Why you
always bothering me? Do I always bother you? . . .*

MR. HEALY: *Well, now . . .*

LINOTYPIST: *Do I always come down the front and stick my head over your shoulder, while you're puddling away with that crummy hand type . . .*

MR. HEALY: *Crummy hand type, is it?*

LINOTYPIST: *Leave me alone for a couple of minutes, will you?* [To the boy] *This old loony, he drives me crazy.*

BOSS: [Calling from the back of the shop] *Hey, John, leave the man alone, will you?*

MR. HEALY: *I was just commenting on the fact that it took two and a half hours and——*

BOSS: *All right, John . . .*

MR. HEALY: *. . . thirty dollars to set this machine . . .*

LINOTYPIST: *He's driving me nuts, this old character . . .*

MR. HEALY: *. . . back into operating condition yesterday.*

LINOTYPIST: *These old comps, they're all off their rockers. I come in here yesterday, I find him standing in the middle of the shop, cussing out the machine like it was human.* [To the boy] *Put that pig in, will you?*

The boy, who has been engrossed by this hot exchange, now drops the pig in.

BOY: *Watch it, it's spurting!*

With a screech, Mr. Healy darts back.

MR. HEALY: [Roaring to the world at large] *Did you see that! Did you see that! . . .*

BOSS: *What happened, John? . . .*

LINOTYPIST: *Aaah, it just spurted. It just stings a minute . . .*

MR. HEALY: [Holding out his hand like a trophy] *The unholy thing sprayed me! Did you see that now!*

LINOTYPIST: *I been sprayed a hundred times. . . .*

MR. HEALY: [Still holding his hand out as if it were lepered, stares aghast at the boss.] *Suppose it had gone into me eye? We'll all be blind before the year is out! The machine's a hazard to one and all!*

BOSS: *All right, John, what are you yelling about?*

MR. HEALY: [Still holding his hand out] *This unholy monster is a threat to life and limb, and I demand that it leave this shop! Either it goes, or I go! But I'll not take my life in my hands from this moment on!*

LINOTYPIST: *You just got a couple of lead drops on your arm. Just wipe them off.*

MR. HEALY: *Did you hear me, boss?*

BOSS: *All right, all right, take it easy, will you? Nothing happened. The pot spurted a little.*

Mr. Healy thrusts his arm out for the boss to see.

MR. HEALY: *Will you look at it? Mottled with lead!*

BOSS: [Roaring] *All right, John! Cut it out, will you! You'd think it was radioactive, for heaven's sakes! It's just lead! Wipe it off! And stay away from the linotyper, will you! You're driving him crazy!*

The old man stares up at the boss, shocked by his old friend's anger. Then he abruptly turns and starts back down to the front of the shop.

DISSOLVE TO: Exterior building . . . engraved lettering or sign or whatever it may be: "United Brotherhood of Printers, Linotypers, and Pressmen."

DISSOLVE TO: Mr. Healy sitting stiffly in front of a desk. Behind the desk, a slim, dark, sympathetic young man wearing glasses.

MR. HEALY: *My name is Healy. I been a member of this union since it was founded. I've never been remiss in my dues, and I want to register a complaint. I'm a compositor. I work in a small shop, the Emperor Press, at 283 West Twenty-sixth Street, a bit of a shop, two job presses and a small Kluege. I've worked there for twenty-seven years. Eight weeks ago, my boss installed a linotype machine, which is a safety hazard and a danger to the whole community . . .*

The union official gets the drift. He smiles patiently.

The shop is always filled with noxious lead fumes which is leading me to an early grave, and just this afternoon, the horrible machine burst into a geyser of molten lead,

*covering me from head to foot . . . You better make some
notes on this, boy . . .*

The union official nods, picks his pencil up, waits.

*Now, I'm sure this machine is a violation of some safety
rule or another, and I want to have it removed. . . .*

Mr. Healy now contrives a few coughs.

*It may very well be I have taken a case of tuberculosis as
a result of those noxious lead fumes.*

UNION OFFICIAL: *Does the boss have a hose running
through the wall to the street?*

Mr. Healy scowls a moment.

MR. HEALY: *Yes.*

UNION OFFICIAL: *Does he have a permit from the Department of Labor for that machine?*

Mr. Healy looks down at his gnarled hands.

MR. HEALY: [In a low voice] *Yes.*

The union official leans forward sympathetically.

UNION OFFICIAL: *Mr. Healy, the truth of it is that you just
don't like the machine, isn't that the truth of it?* [Mr. Healy
makes no answer.] *My old man was like you, Mr. Healy.
He hated machines. Printing was a hand trade to him. It
didn't make any difference if he was setting up a bill book
or a Bible. When he died, he wanted to be buried in his
apron.* [Smiles sympathetically] *If you want us to, Mr.
Healy, we'll send a man down to look it over.*

Mr. Healy rises slowly.

MR. HEALY: [Mutters] *No need.*

Turns and shuffles for the door. Turns again.

*When I die, I'll be buried in my apron too, if I'm not as-
phyxiated by those noxious lead fumes first.*

He opens the door and exits.

DISSOLVE TO: Interior print shop, looking out to the street
door. The door opens, and Mr. Healy comes in, dressed as in
previous scene, inevitable hat and worn topcoat. He comes
surlily into the shop, muttering to himself, moves past the boy,

who is standing by the type cabinets distributing. The boy
looks quickly up at him, but the old man mutters past. He
shuffles past the Kluege press and past the linotype machine,
where the linotypist is clacking away. He pushes past the railing into the office of the shop, where the boss is squaring off
some stock in the paper-cutting machine. The boss looks up at
him, but the old man pays no mind. He takes off his coat,
hangs it up, then his jacket, then his tie. He picks his apron
off the top of a carton of stock and begins to tie it on. The boss
comes over to him.

BOSS: *I'm sorry, John, I lost my temper, but you know you
can drive somebody crazy.* [The old man doesn't even
look at him.] *Come on, John, what do you say? I'll buy you
a pot of beer after work tonight. . . .*

The old man moves off back down the shop again—past the
linotyper, the Kluege—and joins the boy at the type cabinets.
He plucks a copy from the clipboard on the stone, looks at it
quickly, sets it up on the space cabinets, reaches behind him,
fetches his composing stick off the nail, opens a drawer, and
begins to set up a composition. The boy and the man now
stand shoulder to shoulder, each before his respective open
drawer of type. The old man is composing, the boy is return-
ing old type to the proper compartments. The old man is muttering. It takes a moment before the boy realizes he is muttering to him.

BOY: *Did you say something, Mister Healy?*
MR. HEALY: [Muttering a little louder] *I said, I want you
to stay an hour after work tonight. I'm going to give you
your first lesson in compositing. I'm going to make a
printer out of you. This is a great trade. It's not going to be
crushed under a bunch of machines.*

The boy is obviously disturbed. He continues his slow distribution for a moment.

BOY: *I can't make it tonight, Mister Healy.*
MR. HEALY: *What's the matter?*

BOY: *I got an appointment. I'm filling out an application for a school.*

MR. HEALY: *What school?*

BOY: *A linotyping school.*

MR. HEALY: *What are you talking about?*

BOY: *Mister Healy, I got a mother and a sister to support. My sister won't be out of college for two years. I spoke to the boss about it. He says he'll let me off an hour early every night, and I can go to this linotyping school in the evenings.*

The boy hasn't looked up once during this explanation. The old man stares at him.

MR. HEALY: *Hey, boy . . .*

The boy turns to look at the old man. Suddenly the old man's hand lashes out and strikes the boy flat across the face, sending the boy back a startled step. He regards the trembling old man for a moment, then turns back to his distribution. The old man slowly turns back to his own work. They work in silence. The camera slowly dollies away from them.

FADE OUT.

ACT III

FADE IN: Interior, Mr. Healy's home, that night. The wife and the son and the granddaughter are sitting listening to the radio. The daughter-in-law is off in the kitchen, but occasionally crosses camera view. In short, typical middle-class evening at home. Mr. Healy is nowhere to be seen.

The doorbell buzzes. The son rises, crosses to door, opens it. The boy is standing there.

SON: *Yes, sir?*

BOY: *I'd like to see Mister Healy if he's in. I'm the boy that works down his shop.*

SON: *What's that?*

BOY: *I said I'm the boy who works down his shop.*

SON: *Oh. Oh, well, come on in. Just a minute . . .*

He starts for the bedroom door.

WIFE: *Is anything wrong, George?*

SON: *It's a kid from the old man's shop.*

He knocks gently on the old man's door, opens it a bit. The camera follows his view. It is a small, two-by-four bedroom containing little more than a bed, a dresser, a lamp, and a straight-back chair. There is no light in the room, just what streams in when the son opens the door and a trace of moonlight that outlines the furniture. The old man is sitting stiffly in his chair, his hands folded in his lap, deep in a black reverie. At his son's entrance, he looks up—a little startled.

MR. HEALY: *What is it, George?*

SON: *There's a boy from your shop to see you.*

MR. HEALY: *Who?*

SON: *A boy from your shop.*

MR. HEALY: *From my shop? Oh. Well, send him in.*

SON: *In here?*

The old man has turned away, a little nervous. The son turns and beckons to the boy, who comes up to the doorway, then

74

enters a tentative step or two into the room. The old man
turns to him.

MR. HEALY: *Hello, boy, is something wrong?*

BOY: *No, I just come by because of the fight we had, and
I felt so lousy about it, you know what I mean? So I asked
the boss for your address, and I just come up, that's all, to
apologize if I said anything to hurt you.*

The old man looks across at his son, still standing in the
doorway.

MR. HEALY: *Close the door, George.*

The son nods, backs out of the room, and closes the door,
leaving the two alone in the suddenly darkened room.

MR. HEALY: [Indicating the bed] *Well, sit down, boy.*

The boy shuffles across the room to the bed, sits down with a
reluctant creak from the mattress spring.

BOY: *I'm sorry if I said anything to get you mad, Mister
Healy.*

MR. HEALY: *Well, I surely had no call to smack you one
like that. I'm not your father.*

BOY: *I know how you feel about linotyping and things like
that.*

MR. HEALY: *Well, that's how I feel. I surely can't expect all
the world to shake my hand.*

BOY: *I don't run across many people who I really like, Mister Healy, and I sure don't want to have any bad feelings
between us.*

MR. HEALY: *Thank you, boy.* [A pause falls between the
two.] *Did you go to that school?*

BOY: *Yes.*

MR. HEALY: *Did you get accepted?*

BOY: *Well, I filled out the papers. It costs quite a chunk of
money. I'll have to talk further with my Ma, and probably
my Uncle Charlie, who will have to loan me the tuition.
But the school guarantees to get you a job as soon as you
graduate. Out in the sticks somewheres, but I think it's
worth the investment.*

MR. HEALY: *Well, you've got a lot of responsibilities, and you've got to think of those.*

BOY: *Yes.* [Again, the pause] *Mister Healy, look at it this way. If I just stick around, I guess I could get to be a two-thirder in a couple of years. Then, I'd kick around from shop to shop, learning the trade, and, maybe when I'm about forty, I could say I was a compositor and get a pretty good wage. And then what? If I work steady and save some dough maybe when I'm fifty, I could get a mortgage on some little shop somewheres. Out in the sticks somewheres, printing up wedding invitations, five bucks for a hundred. Maybe I can make a hundred, a hundred and a quarter a week. I take in some stationery supplies and sell Christmas cards, and where do I go from there? This way, bang! One year out of school, I'll make fifty, sixty bucks out in New Jersey. I know I sound like all I'm interested in is money, but you got to take a realistic view of these things.*

MR. HEALY: *Sure, boy.*

BOY: *I like printing. I get a real kick out of it. I mean sometimes when I'm feeding the press, I forget that's nothing but an old broken-down machine. I think to myself, that's a black monster who's going to snap off my fingers if I don't keep him tame. You know what I mean?*

MR. HEALY: *I often have the same image myself.*

BOY: *When I go out on deliveries, I always wear my apron because I want everybody in the street to know I'm a printer.*

MR. HEALY: *Boy, I never met a linotyper who liked his job.*

BOY: *They like their job on payday, I bet you.*

MR. HEALY: *They sit all day, plunking keys. There's no craft to it. There's no pride.*

BOY: *Nowadays, I don't know you have to be so proud. Mister Healy, I just figure there ain't much future in being a compositor. I mean, what's wrong with linotyping? If they didn't have linotype machines, how would they print all the books in thousands and thousands of copies?*

MR. HEALY: *Are there so many good books around? Are the authors any more clever?*

BOY: *How are you going to set up daily newspapers? You can't supply the public demand for printed matter by hand setting.*

MR. HEALY: *Are the people any wiser than they were a hundred years ago? Are they happier? This is the great American disease, boy! This passion for machines. Everybody is always inventing labor-saving devices. What's wrong with labor? A man's work is the sweetest thing he owns. It would do us a lot better to invent some labor-making devices. We've gone mad, boy, with this mad chase for comfort, and it's sure we're losing the very juice of living. It's a sad business, boy, when they sit a row of printers down in a line, and the machine clacks, and the mats flip, and when it comes out, the printer has about as much joy of creation as the delivery boy. There's no joy in this kind of life, boy—no joy. It's a very hard hundred dollars a week, I'll tell you that!*

The boy stares down at his feet.

BOY: *Well, I don't agree with you, Mister Healy.*

MR. HEALY: *Aye, it's very hard to want to be poor when you're seventeen.*

BOY: *The world changes, Mister Healy. The old things go, and each of us must make peace with the new. That's how I feel. It's an honest difference of opinion.*

MR. HEALY: *Aye.*

BOY: *I just want you to know that we're still friends.*

MR. HEALY: *You're a good kid.*

The boy stands. The mattress spring creaks again.

BOY: *I better get home because I don't like to leave my mother alone these days.*

MR. HEALY: *I wish you luck.*

BOY: *I'll see you tomorrow in the shop.*

MR. HEALY: *I'll see you tomorrow.*

The boy crosses to the door, opens it, pauses in the shaft of light that pours into the black room.

BOY: *I'll buy you a pot of beer after work tomorrow.* [A sob almost escapes the old man. He masters it quickly, turns away.] *I'll see you.*

Goes out, closes the door. The old man remains sitting in the dark room, slack, his body suddenly limp and tired. He sits unmoving, his eyes closed. The camera moves slowly up to a close-up. Suddenly the old man gets off the chair, crosses to the closet in his room, opens the door, fetches out his coat and hat, begins to put them on.

DISSOLVE TO: Interior, the shop, an hour later, around ten o'clock at night. The shop is pitch-black. The light from a street lamp trickles onto the front window, just enough to show the front door being unlatched and opened. Mr. Healy comes in, wearing hat and topcoat. He pushes surely through the railing to the stone and switches on the overhead work bulb. Instantly a cone of light shoots down, and the old man squints to adjust to this. The rest of the shop is shrouded in progressive blackness.

The machines sit idle and grotesque in the darkness. The old man is muttering. He shuffles down the length of the shop past the Kluege, past the linotype machine, through the second railing, and almost disappears into the pitch black of the rear of the shop. We can barely make out his movements. He seems to be bending down in the far corner by the washbowl. There is a quiet clank of some metal. He straightens and comes back now, just dimly visible. He stands in front of the linotype machine. He raises his hands over his head like a wood chopper. Then he brings his hands down. There is a flash of metal and then a horrible crunching, crashing sound as the sledge hammer Mr. Healy is holding crashes into the linotype machine. Mr. Healy is smashing the machine. Again and again he raises his hammer and brings it down on the machine. The whole action takes place in deep shadow, but it is manifest what he is doing. At last, he has exhausted himself. Breathing long, deep, rasping breaths, he shuffles back to the stone, holding onto the wall for support.

Back at the stone, he leans spent and gasping for air. The overhead work bulb shines mercilessly down on his sweating face. In his hand, we now see clearly the sledge hammer dangling. His chest rises and heaves from his exertion. Suddenly he begins to cry, at first quietly and then with loud, half-caught sobs.

The sledge hammer falls from his limp fingers and clatters to the floor. He just stands now, one elbow on the stone, hunched and heaving, sobbing unashamedly.

DISSOLVE TO: Looking down on smashed remains of the linotype machine. The next morning. A linotype mechanic is bent over the machine, examining the damage to the machine. The camera dollies back to show the boss, expressionless, watching the mechanic.

MECHANIC: [Exclaiming] *Boy . . .*

BOSS: *How much?*

MECHANIC: *It's gonna be at least four hundred bucks. Probably take a week to get this thing fixed.*

BOSS: *They going to have to take it out?* [Mechanic nods] *Okay, call them up and tell them to take it out as soon as they can, and fix it right away, and get it back.* [The boss turns and looks to rear of the shop, where Mr. Healy stands.] *Well, what are we going to do, John?*

MR. HEALY: *Send me the bill.*

BOSS: *Have you got four hundred dollars?*

MR. HEALY: *Send me the bill. I'll make you a check.* [To Linotypist] *I'm sorry, mister. It was a foolish thing to do. I must admit this machine makes a good even line of print and I'm sorry I smashed it up with the sledge hammer.*

LINOTYPIST: *Well, it's all right—as long as it was the machine and not me . . .*

MR. HEALY: [To boss] *Well, I'll be going then. I got a good bit in the bank. I thought I might take my old lady down to Florida—loll in the sun. More or less enjoy the autumn of my years. See if I can get this ink out from under my nails. Just send me the bill and I'll mail you a check.*

BOSS: *Where you going?*

MR.HEALY: *I'm retiring from the trade. . . .*

BOSS: *Yeah, sure, come on, go to work.*

He throws the apron to Mr. Healy.

MR. HEALY: *Now look here, mister, don't you be so grand or I'll put the sledge hammer to you. I'm sixty-six years old and if I feel like retiring, I will. I'll finish out the day's work just to help out. But the truth of it is the trade is beginning to pall on me. I'm weary of this dank little shop and the smell of kerosene is enough to choke a man. Why don't you clean up the shop once in a while—it's getting to be a real Sixth Avenue dump.*

Mr. Healy crosses back to stone and begins to work. The boy stands beside him, smiling and working. The camera backs out of the shop and comes to a halt on the sidewalk, looking at the front window with its barely legible "Emperor Press."

The camera looks slowly up the window to the battered old wooden sign "Emperor Press" as we . . . fade out.

THE END

Printer's Measure

A CONSTRUCTION

Printer's Measure is a good, sound piece of theater and is probably the best-constructed script in the book. It has neither the honesty of *Marty* nor half the characterizations that went into *The Bachelor Party* and *The Mother*, but it has a solid architecture and I like it.

When a writer tries to convey the sort of thinking that goes into the construction of a story, he runs into trouble. Dramatic writing is really nothing more than telling a story, and nobody ever tells a story quite like anyone else. In fact, no two writers will literally agree on what constitutes a story. There are some arbitrary rules of construction, but even these can occasionally be violated without losing your audience. I have only one rule that I consider absolute and arbitrary, and that is: a drama can have only one story. It can have only one leading character. All other stories and all other characters are used in the script only as they facilitate the main story. In *Printer's Measure*, the main character is manifestly the old compositor. Every other character in the story was constructed to move the main story along. The boy's story was created in order to make the second-act crisis in the old compositor's life. The crisis occurs because the boy, whom the old compositor has grown to love, deserts him and his trade. The boy had to be motivated for deserting the old man. Thus, the circumstances of the boy's father dying and the burden of making a better living were contrived. But even the boy's story, separate as it is from the old man's story, had to be tied together in theme, which accounts for the boy's sister and his relationship to her.

Dramatic construction, as far as I am concerned, is essentially a search for reasons. That is to say, given the second-act-curtain incident, construction consists of finding the reasons why the characters involved in the incident act as they do. Each reason must be dramatized by at least one scene, and the scenes must be laid out so that they inevitably grow into the crisis. Of course, this is about as elementary as you can get. The construction of a drama, like every other aspect of writing, never follows any precise line of logic. The writer frequently starts off on a drama with no idea of the crisis; he may have a character he wants to write about or a setting that has impressed him. Then he has to sit down and slowly work out the dramatic significance of his character or setting. Then he has to invent a basic situation that will best dramatize this significance. Eventually, however, he has to conceive his moment of crisis; and from this point he works back, motivating his characters so that they fit honestly into this moment of crisis. Sometimes, in fact usually, the moment of crisis is lurched at rather than sensibly worked to, and much of the difficult laying-out of scenes that went before its discovery must be thrown out and a new order of scenes invented. The point is that no matter how the writer approaches the construction of his script, it always comes down to justifying his moment of crisis, and this is what I call the search for reasons.

Perhaps the best way I can indicate the fumbling logic of construction is actually to reconstruct the first act of *Printer's Measure* as if I were approaching it for the first time. Needless to say, this will be a highly distilled picture of what my thinking was. An accurate version of a writer's thoughts in the course of construction would be far too jumbled to put down in words. I only intend to suggest the few half-steps of architecture that went into the relatively simple outline.

Printer's Measure was based on a short story I wrote in college. It was about a boy who comes to work in a print shop. He is befriended by a rancorous old compositor. The old compositor has an immense pride in his craft, but he knocks it down continually in the eyes of the boy. When the boy leaves for a better-paying if less rewarding job in a furrier's shop, the old compositor suddenly slaps the boy, revealing how deeply he is hurt by the boy's defection.

Well, it's not a bad story, really, even if it was written in college. It has a good character, a good emotional relationship, and even a

good crisis in that relationship. That's all you need for a good drama.
It even has a social significance, for the old compositor stands for
the dying handicraftsman in this world of machinery. The character
of the crusty old printer has charm and color, and the set is an interesting one: a little, dank print shop, stained black from years of
spilled ink, musty, dense with the smell of kerosene, overcrowded,
littered with piles of ems and ens—in short, my uncle's print shop.
Well, what have we got to start with? We've got the crisis, the slapping incident. It is always good to start a dramatization with a crisis
if you can get one. For one thing, it promptly tells you what your
basic story is and keeps you from getting confused with other story
elements. The crisis is where the old man slaps the boy and the
strange, rather tender friendship is ruptured. So the basic story line
is the friendship between the old man and the boy. The basic story
is always the emotional line of the script. Don't ever make the basic
line the social comment of the script. Drama is concerned only with
emotion. If your characters also carry a social value, that's fine. It
gives your play added dimension, but that's all it is, a dimension.
So we've got the basic story line, and we've got the crisis. The problem now is to justify the depth of friendship between the old man
and the boy. The old man must really love the boy if the boy's defection is going to pain him enough to merit a second-act curtain.
Why does he love the boy? Because the boy shares his love for printing. The boy is, of course, a nice kid—well mannered in a tradition
that the old man understands, respectful. But the old man represents the old handicraftsman, and the basic attraction between the
two must be on that level. Well, what have we got so far? A
crotchety old printer and a nice kid who are attracted to each other
by a common love for the handicraft of printing. That gives the kid
a pleasant quality—a sensitivity for other people and for his trade.
He's about seventeen, out of a lower bourgeois or working-class
family. He goes to a manual-training high school—is probably in his
last semester—and he got into printing because it was one of the
courses at high school that interested him. This is the case with most
printers' apprentices. (I happen to know this because I worked a
number of years in a print shop. If you don't know anything about

the printing business, you shouldn't be writing this story.) At any rate, the kid is pleasant, seventeen, sensitive to the old man. He recognizes the warmth beneath the crusty exterior. A deep fondness grows between them. What breaks them up? What leads to the incident of the face slapping? This is really a love story; we need the third angle of the triangle. The basic communication between these two is a common love for the craft of printing. The interloper would have to be someone who represents mechanized printing or the inexorable advance of the mechanized world. We need a symbol of the mechanization of printing. The mechanization of the compositor's function is the linotype machine. A linotype machine is installed in this shop. That gives us our basic situation. A linotype machine is installed, and the old man declares a personal war on it. That's a charming concept—a crotchety old man's personal war against a machine. He vies with the machine for the boy's love. This is the basic line. But if the boy loves the handicraft aspect of printing, why would the linotype machine have any attraction for him? Linotypists get more money, have a better future. But money is a shallow motivation; it makes the boy callous and unsympathetic. We must contrive a situation in which he needs money immediately and for sympathetic reasons. His father dies, and he has to support his family. We'll worry about that later. Let's stick with the old man and the linotype machine. The old man declares war on the machine. He despises what the machine represents in our way of life. The machine is taking the boy away from him. There is not enough urgency. There is nothing immediate about these motivations to make the story move along quickly. The linotype machine is a threat to his job. This means he is working in this shop at a job and is not his own boss. That makes sense because if he were his own boss, he wouldn't install the machine in the first place. That means we have to have another character—the boss. All right, we have three characters in this shop now—the old compositor, the boy apprentice, and the boss. The boss decides to install a linotype machine. Why? Well, why not? It's not too usual for a small shop like this to have a linotype machine, but there must be a certain level of production where it would be advantageous to the boss to have one. Check with

some printers to find out at what level a linotype machine is profit-
able. All right, the boss decides to install a machine. We must already have planted the love story between the old man and the boy,
and also the fact that they share a common love for printing. So
we need two scenes showing (1) the old man's almost medieval love
for his craft and (2) the growing affection between the old man and
the boy. Then the linotype machine enters their lives. But the actual
installation of the machine sounds like a first-act curtain, so we
need to plant the coming of the linotype machine before. And we
also have to establish that the linotype machine is a threat to the old
man's job. Let's block it out and see what we've got:

(1) Old man and the boy—establish the old man's skill and
love for his craft. Establish sweet friendship between old man
and the boy.

(2) The boss, the old man, and the boy—the boss decides
to install a machine. Show old man's violent distaste for machine and what it stands for.

(3) Need to establish threat to the old man's job. The boss
can't threaten the old man with firing him, or we don't have a
story. Our concept now is to keep the old man through two acts
of a personal war against the machine, so the boss can't fire
him. How to establish threat to old man's job? Well, another
old compositor who was fired when a linotype machine was installed in his shop would drive point home to the old man.
Make a sweet scene. Two old compositors bleakly regarding the
inexorable advance of mechanized civilization. We've had the
first two scenes in the shop. Set this scene in neighborhood cafeteria; gives us a change of scenery. Keep the boy in this scene.
We don't want to lose our basic emotional line.

(4) The actual installation of the linotype machine. We
have established what the machine means to the old man's
story. Cut to old man's grim face and fade out. Curtain.

This is all you need for an outline. Actually, when you sit down
to write these scenes, you will find that one scene with one old col-

league of the compositor is not enough to give the proper weight to the first-act curtain. The threat to the old man's job is vital, and somehow one such scene is thin and far outweighed by the preceding scenes. So you will invent a second old colleague, who will aggravate the old compositor's fears, and even a home scene for the old compositor, which will give you a proper graduation of urgency. Then, when you show the linotype machine being installed and cut to a close-up of the old compositor's bleak face, the full dramatic meaning of the moment is clear and balanced.

This is more or less the way I hacked out the first act of *Printer's Measure*. The logic of the thinking, such as it was, implies a few sub-rules which I think are rudimentary. The first of these is: there shouldn't be a character in the script who doesn't have to be there to answer the demands of the main character's story. The boss is there because somebody has to install the machine and because the old man's job must be threatened. The old compositor's friends are there to establish the threat to the old man's job. No matter how delightfully a character is written, he is a bore if he serves no definite plot purpose. George Bernard Shaw will drag in any number of peripheral characters just to indulge a dissertation, but he is guilty of this only in his inferior plays; and then, how many of us can entertain an audience simply by our wit and charm?

There is a second implication, which is that the character traits that go into the various characterizations are likewise contrived solely to satisfy the demands of the main character's story. It is a common illusion that dramatists sit down and preconceive a detailed biography and character study of each character in the script. To a professional writer, this would be a palpable waste of time. A writer usually starts off his thinking with a rough feel of the character absorbed from some experience in his own life. It is inevitable that the preconception of the character will change a thousand times during the course of construction in order to satisfy the demands of the story line. Drama unfortunately will not allow for the complex, contradictory impulses that constitute real-life people. The best you can hope to achieve in dramatic characterizations is an essence or basic truth of the character you had in mind when you started. Holding on to a preconception of a character is one of the worst stumbling blocks in the construction of the story. It keeps you from openly accepting or even looking for the correct incidents to tell your story because these incidents are not suited to the pre-conception of the character. In the end, you will have to change your preconception, but only after you have gone through hours of despair and excessive smoking. Generally, the characterizations are devolved from the incidents of the main story and not preconceived.

It is, of course, not as simple as all that. That is the difficulty with theorizing about such things as writing. Obviously, the characters are not deduced merely from the incidents—because the incidents are derived from the characters. Writing is such a confused business of backing and filling, of suddenly plunging into the third act while you are still pondering the first act. Writing is unfortunately an emotional as well as a mental trade, and the simplest steps in logic are obscured by the writer's own fears and anxieties, most of which he is unaware of. The writer's mind may flood with images or run raspingly dry so that he cannot pull himself out of a fruitless line of thought for hours, even days, sometimes never, and the script has to be abandoned in the middle. Nevertheless, the over-all logic of characterizing the people in the drama is one of devolution rather than preconception. *Printer's Measure* is not a good script for demonstrating this devolution, because the characters are simple and not particularly explored. The characters are symbols of social currents rather than psychological studies. My point would be a good deal clearer if I were discussing the characters of *The Mother*. Without getting too involved with that story, let me say that to justify honestly the daughter in that story—in her opposing her mother's going out to look for a job—I found myself involved in a study of subconscious guilts and resentments. I had to reconstruct meticulously the relationships between the mother and the daughter, between the daughter and her husband, between the mother and her other children and her own dead husband. None of these relationships was preconceived, at least not consciously, in my mind before

I came to the construction problem of justifying the daughter. I molded and remolded the characters until they were a far cry from the people I had in mind when I started.

All this dogmatic theorizing relates, of course, only to my own method of approach; and I really do not mean to be as dogmatic as I sound. If I had a sharp, clear-cut approach to construction, I would be delighted. But I have discovered that even when I do find a rule of construction, I promptly break it in my next script. For example, I usually like to start my subplot in the second act. In *Printer's Measure*, the subplot would be the boy's story. Having generally established the situation in Act I, I use my subplot in the beginning of Act II to let the audience know even more trouble is coming up. This rule is certainly not inviolable. In my next script, *Marty*, the construction followed no pattern I had ever used before—or have used since, for that matter. In *Marty*, the second act doesn't start with a new complication; it continues right off the head of the first act. *The Bachelor Party* has the most bizarre structure of all. It is literally a short story laid out scene by scene with almost no consideration for dramatic demands. It was an interesting experiment; but I must say that if it hadn't been for Delbert Mann's direction and Eddie Albert's acting, the audience might have turned their sets off in the middle. And in *The Mother*, the subplot suddenly turns up as the first major scene of Act I.

The point is that each story demands its own kind of construction, and each writer must construct his stories as best suits his ways. I wouldn't recommend that people just starting out as writers take this extravagant attitude, at least not at first. It is best to study the worn techniques of Ibsen or the wonderful preciseness of Lillian Hellman, after whom I carefully modeled my first dramas. *The Front Page* by Hecht and MacArthur is another fine piece of orthodox structure. And the television drama is really not too different in structure from the stage play. They differ in weight and approach and substance, but they are both in the three-act form and follow the lines imposed by that form. Eventually, the writer attains a security in his ability, and he breaks out here and there from the techniques of other writers and tells his own stories in his own way.

The Big Deal

DIRECTED BY: VINCENT J. DONEHUE
ASSOCIATE PRODUCER: GORDON DUFF
PRODUCED BY: FRED COE

Cast

JOE MANX	David Opatoshu
WIFE	Joanna Roos
DAUGHTER	Anne Jackson
HARRY GERBER	James Westerfield
DAUGHERTY	James Nolan
GEORGE	Joe Maross
COMPLAINER	Joseph Sweeney
WELL-DRESSED MAN	Nehemiah Persoff
SAM HARVARD	Louis Sorin
CONSTRUCTION MEN	Jerry Morris
	Bernard Kates

ACT I

FADE IN: Interior restaurant—not too posh, but the tables have linen tablecloths. Camera wends its way between two tables at which various chatting people are eating their luncheon. A waiter and a couple crowd their way past camera. General effect of crowded café.

We narrow our attention to a little man of fifty-odd years, seated at a table, studying a cup of coffee in front of him. He has on a blue pencil-stripe suit, single-breasted, and which somehow gives the feeling of the 1930's. His tie is tied into a narrow, elegant knot; but it is slightly askew. His shirt collar turns up at the edges. His fedora rests on the table at his elbow. This is Joe Manx. He looks up, and his face perks up a bit as he recognizes someone approaching his table. A moment later a pretty girl of twenty-six comes to his table . . . bends over him, gives him a quick kiss.

DAUGHTER: *Hello, Pa.*

JOE: *Sit down, Marilyn, sit down. You want something to eat? Eggs, a sandwich, anything like that?*

DAUGHTER: [Sitting] *No, Pa, I'm meeting George for lunch in about fifteen minutes.*

JOE: *Sure. Give him my regards when you see him. I won't hold you. I happen to need about ten, fifteen dollars if you happen to have it on you.*

DAUGHTER: [Promptly opening her purse] *Sure, Pa.*

JOE: *I ran across a very interesting proposition today, and I'd like to take the man out for a couple of drinks. I have an appointment with him at four o'clock.*

DAUGHTER: [Extracting some bills from her purse] *Are you sure fifteen bucks will be enough?*

JOE: *Oh, plenty, plenty. I'm just going to take him for a couple of drinks.* [Takes the bills] *I might be able to pay you this back on Thursday, because I'm playing a little pinochle over at Harry Gerber's tomorrow night, and I usually come out a couple of bucks ahead. Listen, Marilyn, don't let me hold you. I know you're anxious to get to see George.*

DAUGHTER: *All right, Pa. I'll see you later.*

JOE: *Just let me say that this is a very interesting proposition that I ran across today. I don't want to sound premature, but I have a feeling that this might be the deal I've been looking for. I won't bore you with the details. I only want to say this proposition involves Louie Miles, if the name is at all familiar to you. He happens to be one of the biggest contractors in the business. Eighteen years ago, he was a lousy little plasterer. I gave him his first work. Well, I was down the Municipal Building today. It happened that I . . . Well, look, I don't want to hold you. I can see you're anxious to see your boy friend. Go ahead, go ahead. Give him my regards. Don't tell your mother you gave me some money.*

DAUGHTER: [Who has been smiling fondly at her father throughout his speech] *Okay, Pa, I'll see you.*

JOE: *I'll see you. I'll see you. Have a good lunch.*

> The daughter exits off. Joe sits a moment, fingering the two bills his daughter has just given him. Then he suddenly lifts a hand imperiously and calls sharply out.

Waiter! Check!

> DISSOLVE TO: A section of one of those little restaurants you always find around hospitals. We see two booths. . . . Camera dollies past first booth, which contains two young doctors, one middle-aged doctor, and a young nurse—all in traditional white hospital uniforms.
>
> We move in on second booth, which contains the daughter and a young resident doctor named George. He is wearing the conventional white-jacketed uniform, with innumerable pencils and pens clipped into his outer breast pocket. They have their pie and coffee in front of them—also the dishes of

the meal they have just eaten, which have not been taken away yet. The daughter is eating her pie, but George is just fiddling with his fork. They are both obviously caught in deep discussion.

DAUGHTER: *I know these aren't ideal circumstances to get married in, but who gets married in ideal circumstances? Do you know what I mean?*

GEORGE: *I know, I know.*

DAUGHTER: *I mean, everybody has problems when they get married. They got parents to support, and finding a place to live, and they don't have enough money. These are just things everybody has to face when they get married. Look at Alex and Ann Macy. Neither of them had a job when they got married. We're lucky compared to them, for heaven's sakes.*

GEORGE: *Well, what do you want to do? You want to get married then?*

DAUGHTER: *Yeah.*

GEORGE: *Well, let's get married then. Let's get it over with.*

DAUGHTER: *Let's get it over with. You make it sound like I was going to electrocute you.*

GEORGE: *Look, Marilyn, marriage is a responsible business. I've got two more years of residency. You're going to have to support me for two years. That's the trouble with being a doctor. The first half of his life he has to be supported by somebody. It's a terrible thing to feel that somebody is sacrificing for you all the time. My mother and father, they went through torture to make me a doctor. Every time my old man sends me a check, I get a little sick in my stomach. And they don't understand, you know what I mean. They don't understand why I just don't rent myself an office on Halsey Street and open up a practice. I finished my year of interning. I'm an M.D. They don't understand why I'm taking all these years of residency at a salary of twenty-two dollars a month. . . . Well, I want to be an internist, that's why. I like internal medicine. I don't want to be a G.P. There's a thousand G.P.'s on Halsey Street now. Every ground-floor window you walk by, there's another G.P. . . .*

DAUGHTER: *George . . .*

GEORGE: *Well, the point is, Marilyn, I've got two more years of residency ahead of me, and you're going to have to support me for two years.*

DAUGHTER: *I'm making a good salary, George.*

GEORGE: *You're already supporting your mother and father.*

DAUGHTER: *I've got the five thousand dollars my Aunt Eva left me.*

GEORGE: *Look, Marilyn, you want to get married, it's all right with me. Let's get married.* [The daughter frowns down at her plate.] *I mean it. I'm not on call tomorrow. We'll go down to City Hall and get married. What do we need, blood tests? All right, I'll take you up the blood lab right now—finish your coffee—we'll go up the blood lab and we'll get our specimens taken. What do we have to wait, three days? What's today, Tuesday? All right, we'll get married on Friday.* [They both look down at their plates. A moment of uncomfortable silence.] *My mother is dead set against this marriage, you know that, don't you? Even my old man, who likes you a lot, says I can't afford to take on a wife at this moment.*

DAUGHTER: *Take on a wife! What am I, some kind of a bundle you're going to carry on your back?*

GEORGE: *I didn't mean it that way.*

DAUGHTER: *You're a boy, you know that? You're a seventeen-year-old boy. What do you think marriage is? Death in a gas chamber? Marriage is making somebody happy. You get better from marriage, not worse. Maybe you might find the next two years a little easier if you had somebody near you who wants you to be happy with all her heart and soul.* [The daughter's eyes are wet with tears now.] *I want you to be an internist! I want you to*

*finish your residency! I don't care if I have to support half
of Toledo, Ohio! It's no sacrifice to me if it makes you
happy! And I expect the same from you!*

She hides her eyes in her hand and tries to master herself.
George sits in the sudden vacuum left by the daughter's out-
burst, looking down at his hands folded in his lap. Then he
looks up and across at his girl friend and smiles gently.

GEORGE: [Rises—crosses around table—sits beside her]
*Marilyn, honestly, I don't know why I'm making such a
crisis out of this. I'm a little scared, that's all. You just forget how much you love the girl. I would like to officially
set our wedding for this coming Friday, if you'll have me,
and I promise to make you happy. So what do you say?*
DAUGHTER: *I finally collared you, eh?*
GEORGE: [Beaming] *Yeah.*

DISSOLVE TO: The front hallway of a four-and-a-half room
apartment. We are looking at the front door, which now
opens and admits Joe Manx. He closes the door behind him,
takes off his hat, puts it on the mail table. Then, carrying himself with a sort of bantam erectness, he passes into the living
room. The camera ambles along after him.

The living room is furnished with what had been good,
solid, expensive middle-class furniture two decades ago. The
dominating piece in the living room is a large dark mahogany
table with thick intricately carved legs. At the head of the
table is a massive chair with thick armrests, obviously the chair
of the master of the house. It is to this chair that Joe marches.
He takes off his jacket, drapes it around the back of the chair,
rolls up his shirt sleeves two turns, loosens his tie, unbuttons
his collar, and then sits down in the chair, placing his arms on
the armrests. For a moment he just sits there, enjoying a small
feeling of majesty. Then he lifts his head and calls out.

JOE: *I'm home!*

The wife appears in the kitchen doorway. She is a strong
woman of about fifty. She is dressed in a house dress and is

carrying a dish towel. On her face there is the anticipatory smile of someone who is about to impart a secret. Her secret becomes immediately apparent when the daughter appears behind her in the kitchen doorway.

WIFE: [Surveying her husband with that smile] *Joe, I got something in the nature of a pleasant shock to tell you, so get a good hold on your chair. I don't want you to fall off and hit your head on the floor.*

She comes into the living room, takes a chair at the far end of the table.

JOE: *I ran across a very interesting proposition today.*

DAUGHTER: [Also sidling into the room, wearing a smile] *Hello, Pa.*

JOE: *I was down the Municipal Building. I was with Martin Kingsley. Martin was having a little permit trouble, so he says to me: "Joe, come on down with me to the Housing Department." After all, Commissioner Gerber is a very good friend of mine. He figured I might put in a couple of good words for him.*

WIFE: *Did you talk to Harry Gerber about that other matter?*

JOE: *Doris, I'm telling a story, don't interrupt. Well, all right, I went down to the Municipal Building. I'm standing in the hallway by the water fountain. I went over to get a drink . . . so . . .*

WIFE: *Joe . . .*

JOE: *A man comes over to me. A big fat bald-headed man. He looks at me, he says: "Aren't you Joe Manx?" So I look at him, I say: "You'll have to excuse me. Your face is familiar, but I can't quite place you." So he looks at me, he says: "I'm Louie Miles!" Doris, you remember Louie Miles? Seventeen, eighteen years ago. He was a plasterer.*

WIFE: *Joe . . .*

JOE: *It seems he's a big construction man now in Cleveland. Well, that's neither here nor there. So anyway, we got to talking about this and that and it seems that he's bought himself a piece of land, about fifteen acres, out near Willaston, with the intention of putting up sixty or eighty houses, small ranch houses, fifteen thousand, maybe sixteen-fifty tops. Well, he starts to dig a little, and Boom! He runs into water. I said to him: "Louie, for heaven's sakes, if you would have asked me, I would have told you. The whole Willaston area is nothing but marshland." Well, the upshot of it is, he wants to sell the land. We made a date for four o'clock at the Statler Hotel. [Rises, crosses to his daughter] Sweetheart, I wonder if you would do me a very big favor.*

DAUGHTER: *Sure, Pa.*

JOE: *I wonder if you could get me a small glass of cold water. I'm very thirsty.*

DAUGHTER: *Sure.*

She promptly exits into the kitchen.

JOE: *Well, I began to do a little quick thinking. If I had one hundred and fifty acres of that land, that's six million square feet . . . with a fifty-foot frontage, I could put up a thousand houses. With a thousand houses, it's worth the trouble and expense of draining. Now, my dear lady, we are talking in terms of a million dollar proposition. One thousand small houses, nothing big, low-income houses, like that Levittown in New York. . . . Have you any idea how much money that man Levitt made? Countless millions! Countless!*

The daughter returns with the glass of water, which she sets at her father's place.

Thank you, sweetheart, thank you.

WIFE: *Joe, Marilyn also ran across a very interesting proposition today.*

JOE: *The upshot of it all was, at four o'clock, I went to the Statler. . . . I said: "Louie, what do you think of this idea? Louie," I said, "why don't we buy up another hundred and fifty, hundred and sixty more acres, and instead of setting up a lousy sixty houses, we'll set up a thousand!"*

*Well, I'll tell you something. If you ever saw a man get
shocked, you should have seen Louie Miles's face when
I said that. He looked at me like I was crazy.*

WIFE: *He was right, too.*

JOE: *That's very funny. When I built those houses on
Chestnut Street and Halsey Street and King Boulevard,
everybody also looked at me like I was crazy.*

WIFE: *That was in 1934.*

JOE: *That whole Chestnut Street district was nothing but
swamps. Snakes and frogs. The grass was so high you
could get lost in it.*

WIFE: *All right, Joe, what was the upshot of it all with
Louie Miles?*

JOE: *The upshot of it all was that he couldn't see it. He
wants to sell that fifteen acres. He wants to get out of the
whole deal. So I said to him: "Louie, what do you want
for that fifteen acres?" So he says: "Four thousand dollars." So I said: "Louie, I may take that land right off your
hands." And that's the way it stands at this moment.*

WIFE: *As long as you were down the Housing Department
today, did you go in and see Harry Gerber?*

Joe suddenly scowls.

JOE: *Doris, I want to get one thing straight right now. I
don't want to hear anything more about Harry Gerber. I
don't need your advice and counsel. It seems to be your
pleasure to make fun of me. . . .*

WIFE: *I don't make fun of you, Joe.*

JOE: *As far as you're concerned, I'm a big talker without a
nickel to his name, who thinks he's a big shot. All right,
I'm broke. I'm strapped. But I was once the biggest
builder in this city, and I'm still a respected name in the
trade. Go to Frank Daugherty and Sons. Mention the
name of Joe Manx, see what he says. Deputy Housing
Commissioner Harry Gerber still calls me up once or twice
a week for a little advice. State Senator Howard Schram*

*came halfway across a restaurant to ask my opinion about
a bill he's pushing through up in Columbus. So when I
tell you this is a million-dollar proposition don't be so
clever. Don't be so smart. When I die, there will be a million dollars in my will, don't worry.*

> Returns to his master chair, sits down, disgruntled and scowl-
> ing. An uncomfortable silence falls over the family. At last,
> daughter leans to her father.

DAUGHTER: [Smiling] *Pa, I'm getting married Friday.*

> Joe turns his head slowly and regards the daughter with open-
> mouthed shock.

JOE: *When did this happen?*

DAUGHTER: *Just at lunch, just after I saw you.*

WIFE: *I told you we had a shock for you.*

JOE: *Well, for heaven's sakes! Which one is this, the doctor? George?* [The daughter nods her head happily.]
*Well, where is he, for heaven's sakes? This calls for some
kind of a celebration. Seems to me we should have some
wine, a little festivity. For heaven's sakes! A man comes
walking home, and his daughter casually remarks, she's
getting married! Listen, call him up on the phone, tell him
to come over tonight ...*

DAUGHTER: [Smiling] *He's on duty tonight, Pa.*

JOE: *I'm taking the whole bunch of us out for a real celebration.*

DAUGHTER: *He's coming over tomorrow night, Pa.*

> Joe is staring at his wife, who is beaming.

JOE: *What are you sitting there in a house dress for? Your
daughter's getting married. Go put some lipstick on, for
heaven's sakes!*

WIFE: *I just found out myself fifteen minutes ago.*

DAUGHTER: *Pa ...*

JOE: *What's the fanciest restaurant in town?*

WIFE: *I got chicken in the stove now.*

JOE: *We'll eat it cold tomorrow.* [He is herding his wife

out of her chair.] *Come on. Into the bedroom. Put on a dress with feathers on it. Joe Manx's daughter gets married, this town is going to hear about it.*

DAUGHTER: [Laughing . . . to the wife, who is being crowded to the door] *All right, Ma. I feel like celebrating myself.*

WIFE: [Over her husband's shoulder to her daughter] *Marilyn, do me a favor. Go in the kitchen, turn off all the fires.*

DAUGHTER: *Sure, Ma.*

> The wife exits. The daughter goes into the kitchen. Joe stands by the kitchen doorway.

JOE: [More or less to Marilyn in the kitchen] *Well, this is certainly an occasion. A nice young fellow. He's going to make a success out of himself. In a couple of years, mark my words, he'll be making twenty, thirty thousand bucks a year . . .*

> Crosses to the kitchen doorway and stands on the threshold watching his daughter.

Under a little different circumstances, I would have given you two kids a wedding, the whole city of Toledo would talk about it for weeks. I'd have a thousand dollars' worth of cold cuts alone. You'd have some big shots at your wedding, believe me! State Senator Howard Schram would be there, I can tell you that. They'd pour the whisky out of barrels. The ballroom would be littered with drunks. Very important drunks. Men worth in the millions.

> The daughter joins him at the kitchen doorway and stands listening to him with a smile of deep fondness and understanding. For a moment Joe returns her gaze, obviously very fond of his daughter. Then his eyes drop.

JOE: [His voice lowered] *Marilyn, I'll need a couple of bucks to cover the evening. It might come as much as twenty, twenty-five dollars.*

DAUGHTER: [Smiling] *Sure, Pa.*

> She reaches out with her hand and lightly touches his face.

Then she turns and moves to the dining room table, where her purse lies. Camera stays on Joe for close-up. His eyes are closed. He has to control himself, or else he would cry.

DISSOLVE TO: Joe and Doris Manx's bedroom late that night. Actually, we open up on the wife, dressed now in an old batiste nightgown. She is standing by the window applying lotion to her hands and looking down, watching the operation. Then she turns and looks over to her husband and then back again to her hands.

The camera pans slowly to Joe, who is unbuttoning his shirt—also wrapped in his thoughts. The push and aggressiveness have gone from Joe. He seems tired and a little slumped.

The wife now shuffles down the aisle between the twin beds and perches on hers. She rubs the lotion into her hands, but it is clear that she is fishing for the best way to open the conversation.

WIFE: [Still looking down as she creams her hands] *Joe, she's going to have to support her husband for a couple of years. She isn't going to be able to pay the rent on this house no more. Maybe, we're going to have to move. I don't know. But we're not taking another penny from that girl. Even with Eva's five thousand dollars, it's going to be hard enough on her as it is.*

Joe sits on the far end of his bed, his back to his wife, a little slumped.

Harry Gerber says he has a job for you with the city. Why don't you at least go down and talk to him about it?
JOE: [Mumbling] *I'll see Harry tomorrow. We're playing pinochle tomorrow night at his house.*
WIFE: [Who didn't quite hear him] *I'm sorry, Joe. I didn't hear what you said.*
JOE: [A little louder] *I said, I'll see Harry tomorrow night. We're playing pinochle at his house tomorrow night.*
WIFE: *All right, you'll see him tomorrow night.*
Having finished rubbing her hands, she brings her feet onto

the bed and picks up a newspaper from the bed table between
the beds and starts to read.

JOE: [Muttering] *If you want to know, I went to see Harry
Gerber last week.*

WIFE: [Reading] *What did you say, Joe?*
Joe rises.

JOE: *I said, I went to see Harry Gerber last week, if you
want to know the truth.*
The wife looks up from her paper.

WIFE: *When was this?*

JOE: *Last week some time. I don't know. Tuesday,
Wednesday. What do you think, I don't want a decent
job? You think I like being supported by my daughter?
You don't think it hurts?*

WIFE: *So what happened with Harry Gerber?*

JOE: *It was some job he had for me. A building inspector.
Thirty-six hundred dollars a year. Thirty-six hundred dollars. Newspaper money. I put Harry Gerber into business.
He was a seventy-five-dollar-a-week accountant. I took
him in and made him a partner. He offers me a thirty-six-
hundred-dollar-a-year job. Now, he's a big shot. Deputy
Housing Commissioner. I told him what he could do with
his job.*
The wife, unable to think of anything appropriate to say, looks
back at her newspaper.

JOE: [Crying out] *I'm not a thirty-six-hundred-dollar-a-
year man!*

WIFE: *All right, don't yell so loud. She'll hear you.*
She puts the newspaper down, sits up. Joe moves around to
the inside of his bed, sits down on his bed, faces his wife.

JOE: *Doris, I was a big operator at one time.*

WIFE: *That was fifteen years ago, Joe . . .*

JOE: *All right, the bottom fell out of the real-estate market.
I went broke. All right. I still got it up here . . .* [Indicates
his head] *I can't think in terms of thirty-six hundred dollars a year. I'm not a candy store owner, keeping an eye*

on the kids so they won't steal the pennies off the news-
stand. I'm a businessman . . .

WIFE: *Joe, how many businesses have you tried? You tried
the trucking business. You tried the . . .*

JOE: *I was out of my element. I'm a builder. This is my
racket.*

WIFE: *I won't let you take any more money off that girl.*

JOE: *What do you want me to do? You want me to take
this job as a lousy building inspector?*

WIFE: *Joe, don't talk so loud.*

JOE: *You want me to walk around with my hand out, waiting for a five-dollar pay-off? I won't do it. Some of the
biggest men in the business are my friends.*

WIFE: *All right, Joe, sit down. Don't be so excited.*

> Joe, who has risen from his bed, now sinks back, his breath
> coming heavily.

JOE: [Looking down at his knees] *Don't worry about me,
Doris. We're not going to take another penny off that girl.
If you don't think it sticks me in my heart to ask her for
ten dollars here, fifteen dollars there, so I can play a little
pinochle. Don't you think I have a little contempt for myself? I don't have to be reminded. I love that girl. What
have I ever given her? I couldn't even afford to send her
to a decent college. I haven't even got a life-insurance policy so that she could at least benefit from my death.*

WIFE: *Oh, for heaven's sakes, Joe, don't be so dramatic.
We had money once, we don't have it any more. You've
had a long time to get used to that fact.*

JOE: [Pounding the bed table] *I'm going to leave that girl
a million dollars in my will!*

WIFE: *Joe, what are you yelling about? Go wash yourself
and let's go to bed. You're in one of your moods, and I
don't want to argue with you.*

JOE: *Listen, Joe Manx may be broke. He may be strapped.
But he still got it up here.*

WIFE: *Thirty-six hundred dollars a year would suit us fine. What do we need more? We're getting on in years.*

JOE: *There's a million-dollar proposition in that Willaston land. A little manipulation, a little maneuvering, and a man who hasn't got a nickel rides around in a Cadillac. Right now all I need is four thousand dollars. I want to pick up Louie Miles's land. You gotta have a piece of land to start with. You can't build without land . . .*

> Joe has forgotten his wife as he gets involved in his manipulations. He begins to pace slow, measured strides up and down beside his bed, his hands behind his back.

JOE: *All right, four thousand dollars. That's not so hard. I'll walk into Frank Daugherty's office, I'll say: "I want four thousand dollars," and that's all there is to that. . . .*

> The wife, long familiar with these mutterings of her husband, turns her bed lamp off, turns over on her side, and tries to go to sleep. The only light in the room now is the bed lamp over Joe's bed.

JOE: *But now comes the manipulation. One hundred and fifty acres, draining and construction costs the way they are today, it's going to run at least two hundred, two hundred and fifty thousand dollars . . .*

> He lies back on the bed now, his hands folded over his paunch, his eyes wide and glowing.

I'll have to have the land and at least fifty thousand dollars before I can go to the banks. I'll call Sam Harvard first thing in the morning. This is something that might interest him . . .

> Camera begins to move up slowly onto his face as he lies there dreaming aloud.

I could possibly realize two hundred thousand dollars out of this. A very interesting proposition. A very interesting proposition . . .

> The camera moves right into his eyes.

> FADE OUT.

ACT II

FADE IN: Film—Construction work going on in a city. A high wooden fence has been erected around the large corner area of the construction. Towering above fence are the skeletal girders of the proposed building. Noise and sounds of construction.

The camera pans slowly across this view and up and onto a huge wooden sign on which is written:

A NEW 12-STORY OFFICE BUILDING

WILL BE ERECTED ON THIS SITE—

TO BE COMPLETED SEPTEMBER 1953

FRANK DAUGHERTY AND SONS,

GENERAL CONTRACTORS.

Close in on name of Daugherty.

CUT TO: Interior, construction shack, crudely furnished. A wooden table, piled with papers and blueprints, a portable typewriter. A telephone. Coveralls hang from wall nails. On the wall an artist's conception of the proposed office building with Daugherty's name in bold printed letters at the bottom.

Two men are in the shop, both in their forties. Both are roughhewn types. Both wear baggy suits and hats, despite the fact that it is a July day. They are leaning over a large blueprint spread out on the table, muttering indistinctly to each other. Suddenly one bursts out.

FIRST MAN: *So what are we gonna do with all those guys sittin' out there?*

SECOND MAN: *Nothin'. The reinforcement rods aren't here yet.*

The two men return to the blueprint. There is a knock at the door.

SECOND MAN: [Without looking up, barks out] *Come in!*

The door opens and Joe Manx comes in, dressed as he was in

Act I. He closes the door behind him. Neither man looks at him.

SECOND MAN: *I knew that Andy Constantino would never come up with those five-eighths rods. So he said he would. So I said, drop dead. Well, who's right now, you tell me.* [Turns to Joe] *Wadda you want, mister?*

JOE: *I'm waiting for Frank Daugherty.*

SECOND MAN: *Waddaya wanna see him about?*

JOE: *I have a personal matter I want to see him about.*

SECOND MAN: *You can't wait in here. Wait outside.*

FIRST MAN: [Looking out the little window] *Here comes Frank.*

SECOND MAN: *Oh, he's gonna blow the roof off about those rods, boy. I told him yesterday, they ain't gonna be here, and he said* . . . [The door opens and a tall, angular Irishman of about fifty comes in.] *Listen, Frank, the rods didn't come in yet. I gotta whole crew outside waiting to get started. You told me yesterday, get them ready for the morning* . . .

DAUGHERTY: *Where's Andy?*

SECOND MAN: *I don't know. He ain't here yet either.*

DAUGHERTY: [To the first man] *Get Andy on the phone for me.* [To Joe] *Hello, Manx. Wadda you want?*

JOE: *I like to have a couple of minutes alone with you.*

DAUGHERTY: *I ain't got time now, Manx.*

Joe looks at Daugherty, then at the scowling faces of the other two men.

JOE: *I need four thousand dollars, Daugherty. I got a very interesting proposition.*

DAUGHERTY: *What is it?*

JOE: *I can get ahold of a piece of land* . . .

DAUGHERTY: *What land?*

JOE: *Fifteen acres out in the Willaston area.*

DAUGHERTY: *Not interested.*

FIRST MAN: [On phone] *Is Andy Constantino there?* . . . *Well, where is he? Get ahold of him, tell him Frank*

Daugherty wants to talk to him right away— [To Daugherty, as he hangs up] *He ain't there, Frank.*

SECOND MAN: *He's probably out trying to round up some rods now.*

JOE: *Daugherty, I know it's marshland. But if you think in terms of a thousand houses . . .*

DAUGHERTY: *That land won't hold houses. Louie Miles was around here yesterday, trying to sell me that piece-a-land. I tell you what I told Louie. I tried to build in Willaston five years ago. I was knee-deep in water. I don't want no part of it. I'm not interested.* [He crosses to door.] *Are we gonna have to pay those men-a-yours while we're waiting for those rods?*

SECOND MAN: *Yeah.*

DAUGHERTY: *Call the union. . . . Manx, that land won't hold any kind of foundation. I told Louie Miles to try and sell it to the city. They're looking for some land to put up a community playground.*

SECOND MAN: [On phone] *Is Herbie Swanson there? Daugherty wants him.*

DAUGHERTY: *That land might hold some tennis courts. That's about all it's good for.*

JOE: *I think you're making a mistake, Daugherty.*

DAUGHERTY: *It won't be the first time.* [Takes the phone from the second man] *Have you got them yet?* [Into the receiver] *Hello? Hello? This is Frank Daugherty. Who'm I talking to?*

> The camera moves onto Joe Manx. His face shows a mixture of envy for the activity going on around him and embarrassment at his futility in front of the other men. Over him comes Daugherty's voice.

DAUGHERTY: *Listen, Herbie, I got a crew of lathers here, but I can't use them for at least a couple of hours. Do I have to pay them? . . . Ah, come on, Herbie, for Pete's sakes. I can't afford to throw seven hundred dollars down the sewer. I'm doing this job close to the skin as it is . . .*

[Joe turns and starts out of the shack.] *Well, maybe, you can help me out this way. You know where I can get ahold of fourteen hundred rods right away? . . . I already tried Constantino. He was supposed to have them here this morning . . .*

Joe exits, closing the door behind him.

DISSOLVE TO: The restaurant of Act I, Scene 1. Actually, we fade in on a short, stout little man of about fifty, named Sam Harvard. He is hunched over his coffee, which he sips slowly and methodically in between small pieces of Danish pastry. Once he looks quickly across the table to Joe and then back to the pastry in his hand. He chews.

HARVARD: [Without looking up] *Joe, why do you always hit me for these interesting propositions of yours? Why don't you hit someone else for a change?*

JOE: *I came to you, Sam, because . . .*

HARVARD: *You came to me four, five years ago with some lunatic proposition about going into the trucking line, and I gave you two thousand dollars then, which I knew was money out the window when I gave it to you. And wasn't there something once about a tool-and-die plant you wanted to invest in, another of your interesting propositions that cost me a thousand, I think. Joe, why don't you hit somebody else for a change?*

JOE: *Sam, I'm going to tell you the truth. I went to Daugherty. I went to Irving Stone. I went to J. C. Shirmer Incorporated. They're getting old. They only want sure-fire propositions. Office buildings. Government jobs. I didn't want to come to you, Sam. I'm very conscious of the money that I owe you.*

HARVARD: *Don't be so conscious. You don't have to pay me. I don't need the money. But Joe, don't ask me for another four thousand dollars for such a lunatic proposition as this thousand ranch houses in Willaston.*

JOE: *I just want to remind you, I built houses before. I'm not a baby in this game. Go walk in the Chestnut Street area. Before I poured a footing there, the whole area was snakes and frogs. The grass was so high you could get lost ...*

Harvard breaks off another piece of Danish, looks up from under his heavy brows.

HARVARD: *Joe, the answer is no.*

He sips his coffee and chews slowly and methodically. We fade out.

DISSOLVE TO: A clock sitting on the buffet chest in the Manx's dining alcove. A telephone is ringing. The wife comes out of the kitchen to answer it. She wears what might be her best dress, but her sleeves are rolled up.

WIFE: *Hello? ... Hello, Joe, how are you? Where have you been all day? ... Oh, plenty of things have been happening here. You missed all the fun. The groom's father called up about four-thirty and invited us over to their house this afternoon. ... Yeah, we just came back about ten minutes ago. Quite a pair of in-laws we've inherited. ... The father is all right, but the mother is a real cold potato ...*

The daughter enters the room. The wife interrupts her phone conversation to speak to the daughter.

Marilyn, do me a favor. I started some water boiling for the vegetables. Put some salt in it. Then take the chicken out of the refrigerator ...

The daughter nods and passes on into the kitchen.

Well, Joe, when are you coming home? ... Why not? ... Don't talk so fast. I can't understand you ... Joe, did something happen today to upset you? You sound very depressed. Are you depressed? ... How do you feel, Joe? You don't sound good to me. Maybe you better give up the card game tonight and come on home and get some rest. . . . All right, don't get angry . . . all right, Joe, give me a call when you get to Harry Gerber's . . . good-by, Joe. . . .

Hangs up. She turns from the phone, frowning. The daughter comes out of the kitchen and sets a bowl of salad on the table.

WIFE: *He's not coming home for dinner . . . so let's just have the chicken from yesterday, and the vegetables, is that all right with you?*

DAUGHTER: *That's fine with me.*

The daughter goes back into the kitchen. The wife, still frowning, goes to the buffet chest, opens a drawer, and extracts some silverware. She starts setting two places, but her thoughts are elsewhere. She sits, brows knit in thought. The daughter comes back from the kitchen with a large plate on which sits a cold roast chicken, two other large plates, and some paper napkins, sets up places for her mother and herself.

WIFE: *I'm worried about him. I'm worried about him because he's beginning to talk like a fool. Four, five years ago, you listen to his big propositions, and you say: "Well, maybe. Maybe, some of his old friends will help him out." But now, it seems to me, he's beginning to sound like a comic character. What do you think, Marilyn?*

DAUGHTER: *Oh, he'll be all right, Ma.*

WIFE: *Do you think so? I don't think so. I think something terrible is going to happen to him. He doesn't talk like a completely sensible person any more. I look at him sometimes; it seems to me he's in another world, dreaming.*

The daughter sits across from her mother, studies the dish before her.

DAUGHTER: *He was a big shot once. He had a taste of what it was like. It's hard for a man of his age to adjust to new situations.*

WIFE: *It's not a new situation. It's fifteen years old. He's got to understand that it's not important to be the Governor's best friend. He was like that as long as I've known him, even as a boy. He was always the big spender. Be-*

fore we were married, he used to take me to the Hippodrome in New York City. At that time, the Hippodrome
was the big date of all dates. They used to have big spec-
tacles there, like circuses. It used to cost a dollar. In those
days, a dollar was a dollar. He used to take me every
week. I never knew where he got the money. He never
had a job in his life. He was always in this business or that
business. He was always what we used to call a sport. He
was the first one in our whole crowd to have a car. I'll
never forget. He came driving down the street, wobbling
from one sidewalk to the other. He was a kind, generous
man, your father. He had an open hand to everybody. You
were too young then. You don't remember. The parties we
used to give when we lived in the big house on Rogers
Boulevard! Every Sunday, I tell you that house used to be
filled till two, three o'clock in the morning. Well, we don't
give big parties any more. He'll have to change. Eat some
cold chicken!

DAUGHTER: *He's not going to change, Ma. Not at his age.*

WIFE: *He's got to go out and earn a living, Marilyn.*

DAUGHTER: *Ma, why talk foolish? He isn't going to go out
and get a job. In the first place where's he going to get a
job? Who's going to give it to him?*

WIFE: *Harry Gerber offered him a job.*

DAUGHTER: [Surprised] *Oh, yeah? When was this?*

WIFE: *A couple of weeks ago. It's a small job, a building
inspector. It would be fine for us. He don't want to take it.*

DAUGHTER: *Ma, don't push him. It isn't in him. He likes big
things. It would kill him to be a little man. I know that
you're probably nagging him to take this job. You're thinking what a burden you and Pop are on me, especially now
I'm getting married. It's no burden. Believe me. I don't
resent it.*

MOTHER: *Marilyn, you're not going to support Joe and me
any more.*

DAUGHTER: *Ma, I talked this all out with George long ago.*

I'm going to take a couple of thousand out of Aunt Eva's money, and we're going to put it down on a little house somewheres, probably out in Kingston, and you and Pop are going to live with us. George says it's perfectly okay with him. . . .

MOTHER: *You're twenty-six years old. It's time to have babies.*

DAUGHTER: *Sure, it's time to have babies. When a baby comes, we'll worry about it. Listen, Ma, you don't think George and I haven't discussed this a thousand times between us? But life doesn't dovetail so nicely. . . . Don't worry about us. We'll have plenty of babies.* [The doorbell rings.] *How much you want to bet that's George?*

She plucks a piece of chicken loose, rises, and goes to the door munching away.

The wife suddenly starts from her seat.

WIFE: *Oh, for heaven's sakes, I forgot the vegetables. The water's probably all boiled out already.*

She hurries into the kitchen.

The daughter opens the door of the apartment. It is, indeed, George standing there.

DAUGHTER: *I knew it was you.*

GEORGE: *I haven't seen you in an hour. I missed you. Well, what are you going to do?*

DAUGHTER: *Come on in. You want some cold chicken?*

George comes in. The daughter closes the door behind him.

GEORGE: *Tell you the truth, I figured we might go to a restaurant tonight, have a celebration. Because you know what?*

DAUGHTER: *What?*

GEORGE: *My mother likes your mother.*

DAUGHTER: *Hallelujah. Come on in, sit down for a minute.*

She leads him back to the dining table, where they take seats.

The daughter calls to her mother in the kitchen.

It's him again, Ma.

GEORGE: [Calling] *Hello, Mrs. Manx.*

WIFE: [Off in kitchen] *Hello, George. Give him some chicken, Marilyn.*

DAUGHTER: [Calling to the wife] *We're going to go out and eat, Ma, if you'll excuse us.*

WIFE: [In kitchen] *Sure. Go ahead, go ahead.* [She appears in the kitchen doorway, holding a saucepan.] *I burned the vegetables anyway. Go on out. Have a good time.*

    Disappears back into the kitchen.

    The daughter and George sit for a minute.

DAUGHTER: *My father was offered a job.*

    George looks up vaguely.

GEORGE: *Yeah?*

DAUGHTER: *Yeah. It would be nice, eh?*

GEORGE: *Sure. Is he going to take it?*

    The daughter thinks awhile, then shakes her head.

DAUGHTER: *I don't think so, George. But it would be nice. I could even quit my job after a year.*

GEORGE: [Smiles] *Yeah. Well, what do you say? You want to go?*

DAUGHTER: *Is this dress okay?*

GEORGE: *Sure.*

    They both stand. The daughter moves slowly to George, and for a moment they stand, hazily warm and comfortable in their communication. She looks softly at him.

DAUGHTER: *But it would be so nice.*

    George smiles at her.

GEORGE: *Sure.*

    The daughter turns her head to call good-by to her mother, is shocked to see her standing in the kitchen doorway, holding the saucepan, watching them with troubled eyes.

DAUGHTER: *Good-by, Ma.*

WIFE: *Good-by, Marilyn. Good-by, George. Have a nice time.*

GEORGE: *Good-by, Mrs. Manx.*

    The young couple move into the foyer, open the door, and

pass out into the outside hallway—closing the door after them.
The wife stands unmoving, watching them, even for a long
moment after the door has closed behind them. Then she
moves slowly to the telephone table, sets the saucepan down,
dials a number, and waits expressionlessly for an answer.

WIFE: *Harry? Is this Harry Gerber? . . . Harry, this is Doris
Manx. Listen, did I take you away from your dinner? . . .
Harry, I'll tell you why I called. Joe says he's coming over
to your house for cards tonight. . . . Yeah, well I'm a little
worried about him, Harry. He called up from downtown,
he sounded very depressed . . . Harry, make him take the
job. . . . I know, Harry, but please make him take the job . . .*

DISSOLVE TO: Joe Manx leaning forward over a table, reaching for some cards in front of another player. The camera
dollies back to show the pinochle game taking place in Harry
Gerber's living room. Four men sit around the table. On Joe's
right sits the Complainer, and directly across the table from
Joe sits the Well-Dressed Man, so named for reasons that will
soon be obvious. On Joe's left sits Harry Gerber, a heavy-set
sympathetic man of fifty. The living room is comfortably furnished: in particular, an easy chair. Joe has apparently just
won the last hand and is to deal the next.

COMPLAINER: [Leaning across to Gerber] *Why did you
play the king? You knew he was sitting there with a single-
ton ace? If you led the ace, I woulda put the king on . . .*
WELL-DRESSED MAN: *All right, all right, how much did this
hand cost me?*
GERBER: *Half a dollar.*

Gerber and the Well-Dressed Man send half a dollar to Joe's
little pile of money. Joe is riffling the cards. The Complainer
is still complaining to Gerber.

COMPLAINER: *If you run the government, Harry, like you
play pinochle, no wonder we're in the condition we're in.*
[To Joe] *How much do I owe you, Joe?*
JOE: *Half a dollar.*

COMPLAINER: [Pushing two quarters over to Joe] *I haven't won a hand all night, you know that? I get nothing but nines and jacks.*

WELL-DRESSED MAN: *So I was telling you, Harry, I went into this store, and I told the salesman: "Look, money is no object. I want a suit that will hold its shape in hot weather." So he takes out this bolt of cloth . . .*

Camera moves in on Joe as he riffles the cards. His eyes are down. He is obviously thinking of other things than the card game. Over close-up, we hear the others' voices.

COMPLAINER: *Right now, all I want out of life is to see one flush, preferably in spades.*

WELL-DRESSED MAN: *Harry, feel this cloth, will you? Have you any idea how much this suit cost me? A hundred and eighty-nine dollars. . . .*

Joe begins to deal out the cards, three at a time first round, then four at a time until the deck runs out.

COMPLAINER: *Joe, are we or are we not old friends?*
JOE: *Sure.*
COMPLAINER: *Then, deal me a decent hand, will you?*

WELL-DRESSED MAN: *Joe, take a guess. How much do you think I paid for this suit? A hundred and eighty-nine dollars. It's a special cloth, imported from Egypt. They wear this kind of material on the desert.*

COMPLAINER: [Picking up his cards as they come in] *Joe, what are you dealing me here? What are you trying to do, bankrupt me?*

WELL-DRESSED MAN: *This material is as light as paper, but it wears like iron . . .*

COMPLAINER: [Leaning over and showing his cards to Joe, who, as dealer, does not play in the hand] *Look what you gave me, will you? Do you see fifty points meld in this whole hand?* [To the others] *All right, all right, who bids?*

WELL-DRESSED MAN: *So, Joe, let me tell you about this suit . . .*

COMPLAINER: *Harry, what do you say?*

GERBER: *Three hundred. . . .*

WELL-DRESSED MAN: *So, Joe, this suit, rain or shine, it holds its crease. It doesn't wrinkle. I could jump in the river and swim in it, it won't wrinkle. The only trouble is, it makes me sweat so much. I'll be honest with you. I don't know how they manage in Egypt with it.*

COMPLAINER: *Hey, Lewisohn, what do you say?*

WELL-DRESSED MAN: *What?*

COMPLAINER: *Pick up your cards, will you? Gerber says three hundred. It's up to you.*

WELL-DRESSED MAN: [Painfully picking up one card at a time] *I was telling Joe about the suit.*

COMPLAINER: *Lewisohn, do me a favor. The next time you come for a pinochle game, come naked, will you? . . .*

WELL-DRESSED MAN: [Screwing up his face as he examines each card and puts it into place in his hand] *Let's see, what have I got here?*

> Silence descends over the cardplayers as they wait for the Well-Dressed Man to figure out his hand. In the silence, Joe leans forward, folds his hands on the table before him, and speaks quietly.

JOE: *Listen. I need four thousand dollars. Can you give it to me, you fellows?*

COMPLAINER: [Turning to him] *What?*

JOE: [To the Complainer] *What do you say, Davis? We've been playing pinochle together twenty years almost. Will you lend me four thousand dollars?*

COMPLAINER: [A little nervously] *Lend it! Another couple of hands, and you'll win it from me.*

WELL-DRESSED MAN: [Laying his cards down and turning to Joe] *What do you need the money for, Joe? Are you in trouble?*

JOE: *I need it for a business proposition. I want to buy a piece of land.*

WELL-DRESSED MAN: [Picking up his cards again] *Oh, land. Land I don't know anything about. If you were in some kind of trouble—if you needed an operation or if you wanted to pay off a mortgage, something like that, I might be able to dig up a couple of thousand for you. But land I'm not interested in . . .* [Studies his cards again] *Let's see. What's the bid to me?*

COMPLAINER: [With nervous embarrassment] *Come on, come on. Let's play cards. Gerber said three hundred. What do you say, Lewisohn?*

WELL-DRESSED MAN: *Three hundred is good with me.*

COMPLAINER: *It's good with me too. You want it, Harry, or not?*

Gerber is regarding Joe Manx with concern.

GERBER: *Joe, what is this proposition you want the four thousand for?*

Joe, in a sudden burst of irascibility, slams the table with his hand.

JOE: [Almost snarling] *Come on! Come on, Harry! Let's play cards! It's three hundred up to you! Do you want it or not?*

GERBER: [Without even looking at his hand] *I don't want it.*

JOE: *All right, throw in the hand. Here, deal.* [He pushes the discards, as they are thrown down, toward Gerber.] *Look. Are we going to play cards, or are we going to talk! If we're going to play, let's play! If we're going to talk, let's talk!* [He suddenly stands, growing more frenzied.] *My friends! My friends! My good friends! Four lousy thousand bucks! You can't lend me four lousy thousand bucks! What am I, some kind of a bum or something? I built plenty of houses in my time! Good double-brick houses, three coats of plaster!* [He seizes the few bills and silver in front of him and scatters the money on the table.] *Here! A couple more bucks for you!*

He turns and walks out. Gerber rises quickly from his seat.

GERBER: [Calling] *Joe!*

He moves quickly after his friend.

SLOW DISSOLVE TO: Joe Manx, sitting in the easy chair in Gerber's living room. Some time has passed—about an hour. The overhead lights of the previous scene have been turned off, and now the only illumination comes from the standing lamp behind the easy chair. There is enough light to see, however, as we pull back, that the cards still lie scattered on the table—except for a few that Harry Gerber is shuffling and reshuffling as he sits at the table. There is a cup of coffee in front of Harry Gerber, and Joe is holding his cup, sipping occasionally. He appears to have calmed down a great deal, even to the point of depression.

JOE: *I went to them all, Harry. I went to Daugherty, to Shirmer. I went to Sam Harvard, Marty Kingsley, Irving Stone. Some of these men used to mix cement for me. I couldn't raise four thousand dollars. I couldn't raise four thousand dollars! Daugherty brushed me off him like I was mud on his pants. I tell you, Harry, if somebody told me yesterday that Joe Manx couldn't raise four thousand dollars, I would have laughed in his face. What does it mean, will you tell me? What does it mean?*

GERBER: *Joe . . .*

JOE: *Tell me the truth, Harry, do they laugh at me when I'm not around?*

GERBER: *All right, I'll tell you the truth. You haven't got a name in this trade any more, Joe, and you're kidding yourself if you think you have. You can go on like this the rest of your life, or you can act like a* mensch *and face a couple of facts. I got a job for you. Come and take it. It's the best job I can get for you. I tried to get you a desk job where you could feel like an executive, but the flat truth is they wouldn't have you. I'm leveling with you, Joe. Take it or leave it. It's thirty-six hundred dollars a year. It'll pay your rent, and it'll give you a little self-respect.* [Turns his attention back to the few cards he is shuffling] *Joe, I'm your friend. Any time you need me, you know you can come to me. If I had four thousand dollars, I'd give it to you. But I want you to know I'd give it to you out of charity, and I'd never expect to see it again.*

JOE: [Studying his coffee] *Well, that's straight talk. I respect you for it. But I don't want your job.*

He sets the coffee down on an end table.

GERBER: *What is it, a question of pride? Are you ashamed to work for me?*

JOE: [Stands] *Harry, I've been a bankrupt for fifteen years. When you're a bankrupt as long as I am, thirty-six hundred dollars a year ain't gonna turn the trick. It isn't going to make up for all the failures.*

GERBER: *What failures?*

JOE: *You talk about facing facts! All right, let's face some facts! I failed as a man! I failed as a father! What did I ever give those two women?! What did I ever give them?! My wife wears the same cloth coat for four years, do you know that?!*

GERBER: *You haven't failed anybody, Joe.*

JOE: *From the age of ten I never bought my daughter even a birthday present! She's getting married Friday. What will my wedding gift be? A house for the newlyweds? A ten-thousand-dollar bond? Do you know how it haunts me that I can't buy that girl something? What contempt she must have for me!*

GERBER: *Joe, you're talking like a fool. You're a wonderful father. Your girl is crazy about you. Stop torturing yourself.*

JOE: *Look, Harry, don't worry about me. I'm having a little rough time right now, but I'll come out of it. I'm fifty-two years old. Maybe, I can't run around the block any more, but I'm still operating where it counts.*

GERBER: *Joe, sit down a minute.*

JOE: *Apparently, nobody has any faith in me, not even my best friend. Well, Harry, I'll dig up four thousand dollars somewheres, one way or another, and I'll buy fifteen lousy acres of swamp . . .* [His voice is beginning to rise.] *And*

I'll show you what Joe Manx can do with it! I'll put the Empire State Building on that swamp! I'm a man of respect! Bricklayers like Frank Daugherty will come on their knees to kiss my hand! [He suddenly smiles, but there is something almost wild about him.] *And, Harry, when I die, I'll leave thirty-six hundred dollars a year for you in my will.*

He nods his head once or twice—then turns and stumps out of the room.

FADE OUT.

ACT III

FADE IN: The bedroom of Joe and Doris Manx, later that
night. The room is dark. We fade in on the wife, lying on her
back on her bed, asleep. Suddenly her eyes open. Then her
head slowly turns in the direction of her husband's bed. The
camera slowly pans over to Joe's bed. It is empty. The blankets
have been pushed aside, and the sheets are mussed—indicating that Joe has recently been sleeping there.

The wife slowly sits up in bed, tense and apprehensive, but
outwardly expressionless. She moves quickly around the beds
to the door of the bedroom, opens it, passes into the dark hallway. She goes through the kitchen, opens that door, and steps
into the living room.

Joe Manx is seated in his large master chair, his arms resting
regally on the armrests. He wears his trousers and bedroom
slippers, but he has no shirt on. His hair is uncombed, and
there is a distraught quality about him. *Joe sits turned to look
out window.*

WIFE: *What's the matter, Joe? You can't sleep?*
Joe regards his wife with wide eyes.
JOE: *Doris, I'll tell you what I've been thinking. I think
I'm going to go away for a couple of days. I just called the
station. I can get a train to Saint Louis at four-forty-nine
A.M. Then I catch a flyer for Las Vegas.* [Stands, begins to
pace around, hands behind his back] . . . *the convention
last year in Atlantic City—a feller there from Las Vegas.
He told me, Las Vegas is just booming. He says, houses
are springing up overnight. A city jumping up out of the
desert. Like Florida in the 1920's. Well, I think I'll take a
look at this Las Vegas. Listen, a clever man can make himself a bundle.* [He's patting his pants pockets for cigarettes
now.] *Then too, I might have a look in California, see what
the situation on the Coast is. Listen, I've heard wonderful
things about the Coast. Los Angeles, San Diego. I've got*

121

some friends in San Diego. They told me: "Manx, any time you feel like switching your area of activity, there's plenty of room for you here."

WIFE: *Joe, come to bed.*

Joe comes to the table, leans intently across to his wife.

JOE: *Lady, I have a feeling Las Vegas is going to turn the trick. I was lying in bed thinking, and then, suddenly— like the burning bush—it came to me. It was like somebody spoke the thought aloud. "Go to Las Vegas." What am I pushing pennies in Toledo? Well, let's pack up a couple of things for me and a toothbrush.*

He starts briskly past his wife for the kitchen door, but his wife puts out a gentle hand on his forearm.

WIFE: *Joe . . .*

Her touch seems to crumble him. He turns to her suddenly gaunt and broken.

JOE: [Crying out in sheer anguish] *Doris! I gotta get outta this town!*

WIFE: *I know, Joe, I know . . .*

JOE: *They're squeezing me here! You understand?! They're squeezing me!*

WIFE: *I understand, Joe.*

JOE: *Look at me, for heaven's sakes. They all make a living but me. What's the matter with me?*

WIFE: *There's nothing the matter with you, Joe.*

He crosses to sofa, sits, slack and empty.

JOE: *I would just like to close my eyes and wake up with another name, because I'm sick in my heart of being Joe Manx.*

WIFE: *Joe, we don't want a million dollars from you. We love you, Joe, we love you if you build houses or if you don't build houses. We just want to have you around the house. We like to eat dinner with you. We like to see your face.*

Joe rises heavily from his seat and moves a few paces away. As he moves from the wife, he lets his hand rest lightly against her face in mute appreciation of her sympathy. The wife sits there, deeply weary herself.

JOE: [Muttering] *I don't know, maybe there's something in this Las Vegas.*

WIFE: [More sharply than she intended] *There's nothing in Las Vegas, Joe!*

She sits, trying to hold the edge of impatience inside of her, fishing desperately in her mind for something to say to her husband.

Joe, I'm tired myself. I'd like to have a little peace. I'd like to know we live in a certain place and that a certain amount of money is coming in every week, so at least we know where we stand. I don't want a lot of money. I just don't want to have to carry a sick feeling in my stomach all the time that you're going to come home depressed and miserable. I don't want to listen to you turning around in bed all night long. I want to be able to go to sleep peacefully, knowing that you're also having a good night's sleep. I don't have much strength left, Joe. This kind of living is eating us up.

Deeply exhausted, she rests her face in the palm of one hand. Joe stands silently. She has reached home with him. Finally he comes to her and gently takes her arm.

JOE: *It's all right, Doris, it's all right. Go to sleep.*

WIFE: [Still hiding her face in her hand] *You owe this to me, Joe.*

JOE: [Helps her from the chair] *Go to sleep. I want to do a little thinking.*

WIFE: *Joe, if I said anything that hurt you, it's because I'm all knocked out.*

JOE: [Helping her to the door] *You didn't hurt me.*

WIFE: *Let's go to bed. We'll get some sleep.*

JOE: *Go to sleep, Doris. You're all knocked out. I'm going to work out something, don't worry.*

They stand now in the kitchen threshold, looking wearily at each other.

JOE: *I don't deserve you, Doris.*

WIFE: *Come to bed, Joe.*

JOE: *In a couple of minutes.*

The wife turns and shuffles out of view. Joe watches her disappearing form for a few moments. Then he turns and begins again the slow, measured pacing up and down the dining room. We stay with him for four or five lengths of the room.

FADE OUT SLOWLY.

DISSOLVE TO: Close-up of daughter's face. She is sleeping. We are in her bedroom, which is just off the living room. It is dark. The daughter turns in her bed and then reverts back to her original position. Then—somehow aware that she is being looked at—she opens her eyes and awakens. She looks up. Joe is standing beside her bed, looking down at her. She is up on her elbow immediately.

DAUGHTER: *Is something wrong, Pa?*

JOE: [In a low voice] *I wonder if I could talk to you for a minute, Marilyn.*

DAUGHTER: *Sure.*

JOE: *Listen, Marilyn, I'm going to ask a terrific favor of you . . .*

DAUGHTER: *Sure, Pa . . .*

JOE: *First let me finish. I need your five thousand dollars. I want to buy Louie Miles's land. It's the only piece of land I can get my hands on, do you understand? It's a piece of swamp. It's marsh. But it's the best I can get. I have to have land before I can manipulate. I know what it means to you, Marilyn, the five thousand dollars. I know you need it for your marriage. But you have to have faith in me. I'll give it back to you a thousand times over. Marilyn, I wouldn't ask you this, but I need it.*

DAUGHTER: *Sure, Pa. I'll make you out a check now. You can cash it in the morning.*

She starts to sit up.

Joe stares at her, unbelieving. Then the accumulated tension breaks within him, and he begins to sob. He turns away from his daughter in shame and goes out into the living room, hiding his eyes in his hands, the sobs coming in hoarse, half-caught gasps. He walks aimlessly around the living room, hiding his eyes, crying uncontrollably. His daughter appears in the doorway of her room, watching him anxiously.

DAUGHTER: *Pa . . .*

He turns to her, still hiding his eyes.

JOE: [Brokenly] *What did I ever give you?*

He sinks down onto a chair, cupping his face in both hands now. The daughter moves slowly to him.

DAUGHTER: *Pa, look at me. Am I an unhappy girl? I'm happy. I love George. I love you. I love Mama. I got a responsible job. The boss is satisfied with me. That's what you gave me. I'll make you out the check.*

Joe has to shake his head a few times before he can answer.

JOE: *I don't want it.*

He rises weakly and starts for the kitchen door.

DAUGHTER: *Pa . . .* on, go on to bed

JOE: *Go to sleep, go to sleep . . .*

Wife enters, looks questioningly at Joe, says . . .

He goes into the kitchen, across it, and down the foyer to the door of his bedroom, opens it and goes in. His wife is lying on her bed and turns to watch his entrance. He doesn't look at her. He goes to his bed, sits down. He is over his tears now and is just breathing heavily. *Wife enters, stares worriedly at Joe*

JOE: [Mumbling] *All right, all right. I'll take the job with Harry Gerber.*

disbelievingly

WIFE: I didn't hear you, Joe. *Say that again Joe*

JOE: [Louder] *I said, I'll take the job with Harry Gerber. At least, they'll have one honest building inspector.* [He lies back on the bed now, looking up at the ceiling.] *This was a crazy day, a crazy day . . .*

He slowly walks toward wife, puts arm around her and sighs as they walk off

His eyes close and he dozes off.

FADE OUT.

THE END

The Big Deal

TELEVISION CRAFT

The Big Deal turned out an effective piece of television, but it is more suited to the stage. Actually, it would not have made as good a stage play as it did a television drama; but even so, its sheer weight and power are too much to be handled to television's fullest advantage. *The Big Deal* did not exploit the particular techniques of television. Of course, the mobility of the television camera, rudimentary as it is, allowed me to move this weighty chunk of theater along at a much faster clip than it would have come out on the stage. I was not confined to a one-scene set, nor did I have to write unnecessary lines of dialogue to justify characters being on that set when they would not naturally be there. I was able to concentrate the action of my story on the people directly involved. I was even able to catch more literal reality than I could have caught in a stage play. Nevertheless, *The Big Deal* is still too theatrical for my money. The main character is more obsessed than he is real, and the dialogue still falls far too frequently into the stagy pungent language that people in real life do not use.

Where *The Big Deal* went astray was in its basic approach. It is too obvious a drama for television. The story is too powerful. Obviousness is, unfortunately, one of the properties of the stage play. The stage play is directed to a large group of people—many of whom must be shouted to so that the words can be heard. On the stage, the writer does not capture the relationships between his characters; rather he projects them. We have caught Joe Manx, his wife, and his daughter on an exceptional day in their lives, a day dominated by a desperate pursuit of four thousand dollars culminating in the highest peak of crisis in Joe Manx's life. In terms of craft, this means that every scene—almost every line—is dominated by the heightened urgency of the story. It is my tentative belief that television does not do its best with dramas centered around a peak of tremendous crisis. Television is better suited to everyday crises through which the same depth of insight can be achieved, but without the excessive theatricality.

I do not want to get into what makes for good television material and what doesn't. This is something I would prefer to discuss using *Marty* and *The Mother*. Nor do I want to get into any comparisons between the hour television drama and the stage play or the movie. There is, indeed, a current tendency among the academicians of the theater to compare the three mediums. I have heard the television drama described—by myself as well as others—as an "extended one-act play" or "a small play" or a "three-quarter movie." At this moment, I believe the hour drama is none of these at all. Television writing is a form of drama peculiar to itself, more peculiar than any of us now writing for the medium really know. There is a special technique to writing television, a special craft, and its uniqueness is best shown by the dismal failure of successful Broadway playwrights and scenario writers to merely transfer to television.

The technique of a new writing form is not something that springs full-blown from anyone's head. The television writer has had to adjust laboriously to the distinct limitations of the medium, and it is within these adjustments that a new style and a particular sort of material is prescribed. Television has endless limitations that force upon the writer a distinct approach to his work.

In television, for example, you cannot handle comfortably more than four people on the screen at the same time. This means you cannot write mob scenes or capture expansive crowd moods like the nervous freneticism of a packed New Year's Eve party. If you have a story about a lynching or a political convention, forget it. The efforts of enterprising directors to capture the effect of five thousand people by using ten actors are pathetic. They are pathetic, for that matter, on the stage too; but on the stage there is a convention of impressionism. The audience will accept ten people standing as a crowd to indicate a much larger group. The audience will not accept this on television unless you are doing a highly impressionistic or expressionistic drama. For that matter, impressionistic and lyrical dramas suffer a bad fate on television. The use of blank sets with no scenery had a moment of novelty, but has faded out. Television has a camera, and the audience expects the camera to show it something real.

It costs about five hundred dollars to raise one camera to any appreciable height off the studio floor, which makes any real use of high-angle photography impractical. Besides, most studios in New York have relatively low ceilings. The major networks are now building large, high-ceilinged studios in Hollywood, but it is doubtful whether any of the hour drama programs will switch to Hollywood for a long time. The best actors, writers, and directors are in New York, and the only definite advantage Hollywood has is the steady sunshine required for any planned photography. The hour drama cannot be done well on film, at least not under present budget conditions. It takes at least three weeks to shoot a good hour feature film, and this is much too expensive. Film is fine for half-hour situation shows in which the lighting and the sets are ready and standing week in and week out. In shooting a different hour drama every week, you will have to reset all your lighting for each scene; and the fastest directors consider themselves lucky if they can get from five to ten pages of script shot in a day. Besides, the live show has a sense of continuity to it which helps the actor give an honest performance. In shooting a show on film, you shoot all the scenes that take place in one set at the same time—whether or not there is any continuity to them at all. The actor and the director work in bits and pieces, and the actor has little idea of how he felt the scene before or how he will feel the scene after. Certainly, the present crop of live hour shows are far superior to filmed dramas. Until the economics of television unwind themselves—permitting the bold expenditure required by a decent film—the live show will always be superior and the exodus to Hollywood will be delayed.

So you might as well resign yourself to the confinement of the ex-radio studios now being used for television purposes. Needless to say, you are limited in the number of your sets because the scene designer can fit just so many into the space he is allowed. You can probably get away with four fairly detailed sets and one or two insert sets. Insert sets are really nothing more than a few pieces of furniture with a blank flat behind them. For example, the hero leaves his house and goes to his office. His office, for all practical purposes, will consist of a desk with papers on it and a chair. The scene will be shot tight, hoping the audience will assume what the rest of the room looks like. If you write windows and glass doors into your scripts, you will be disturbed on blocking-out day to find out that there are no windows and the door is a wooden one. The reason for that is simple: if you have a window, you must be able to look out of it. This necessitates the construction of another set to represent the view. If windows are vital to your script, be careful not to have too many other sets—so that there will be space for a flat representing the view. Don't bother writing fires or floods, because the Fire Department and the Department of Buildings won't allow you. You will get some wisps of smoke and a small puddle of water. Avoid exteriors unless they are the main set of your script. Jungles come out on the screen like just so many potted plants, and a street scene is nakedly made of papier-mâché and plywood.

The mobility of television, while better than the stage, is still primitive. The actors have literally to run from one set to another to get into the next scene. This means you have to contrive endings to your scenes which allow for the actor to get about. Obviously, the actor cannot make any extensive costume or make-up changes while he races from one end of the studio to the other.

You cannot "cut" in television as you can in the movies. In the movies, a scene is shot from four or five different angles, and the editor cuts back and forth from each take as he sees fit. In television, you cut from one camera to another rather than by a splicing machine. Sharp cuts—as, for example, if you cut from one person to another during a telephone conversation—overlap and are usually embarrassing, as happened to me in *Holiday Song*. It is possible to make a sharp cut in television, but it requires the closest collaboration between the director, the head cameraman, the two cameramen on the floor, the floor manager, and the actors. Cuts should be reserved for vital dramatic movements and not for general pace. It is much wiser to dissolve from one scene to another; and if you have a telephone call in your script, it is better to split it in half rather than cut on each spoken line. This makes for a slower pace, but for a cleaner production.

The basic limitation in television is time. The hour drama is fifty-three minutes long. You can tell just so much in fifty-three minutes. A stage play, for purposes of comparison, plays about an hour and twenty minutes and a movie about an hour and a half. Transferred into terms of craft, this means you need only one subplot, never more than two. Television cannot take a thick, fully woven fabric of drama. It can only handle simple lines of movement and consequently smaller moments of crisis. The last act of *The Big Deal* shows a man closing in to the verge of a breakdown. Can you imagine this scene on a stage? It is a big scene; it should be played fully, with wideness and weight. David Opatashu gave a brilliant performance as the father, but in this scene he was physically restricted to rising and sitting and to occasional steps here and there. It is difficult to play a man fairly bursting from within himself with such physical restrictions. The crisis of *The Big Deal* was too big to be handled properly on television. The relationships between Joe Manx and his wife and his daughter needed to be seen more if the positive resolution of the play was to make honest sense. The point of the play was that this man had given the true values of life to his family—warmth, love, respect, dignity—which was a far more successful achievement than material wealth. I didn't have the time to show how he had given all these qualities. I had to be satisfied with some speeches in the third act to establish this, and only an indication here and there in the first two acts. We know almost nothing about his wife or what she got from her marriage. Where did the daughter learn the open generosity she evidences in the third act when she offers all her money without a second thought? Thanks to a careful portrayal of the part by Anne Jackson, we were able to see some of the love she held for her father; but it was not adequately written into the script. These are major flaws in the script, not just academic comments; and they are flaws not through any malfeasance of duty on my part, but because there just wasn't enough time in fifty-three minutes to build all the information required. The big dramatic story is not for television. There is much too much substance that goes into such a moment. Craftwise *The Big Deal* would have been better as a stage play.

Nor is the multiple-story proper for television. The multiple-story is the kind of thing only the movies can do well. This is the kind of script in which a number of independent stories wind around one focal incident. *The Bachelor Party* is a good example of this. Accurately written, *The Bachelor Party* should have told the individual stories of five men who go on a night about town, each of whom resolves something in his own life as a result of the party. This does not violate the basic rule which states that a script can be about only one leading character and that all other characters are used as they facilitate the main story. The leading character would still be Charlie, and the other four stories, independent as they would be, would still exist only as they shaped the main line. However, in the multiple-story, you build the body of your script by cutting from one story to the other as the basic line accumulates to its high point. This means there are no such things as first- and second-act curtains; one story or another is always moving along. In television, you have to have first- and second-act curtains for the reason that the commercials have to be introduced.

The very presence of commercials indicates the broadest and most all-inclusive limitation of television technique. Television is essentially an advertising and not an entertainment medium. The advertising agencies are interested only in selling their clients' products, and they do not want dramas that will disturb potential customers. This limits the choice of material markedly. You cannot write about adultery, abortion, the social values of our times, or almost anything that relates to adult reality. Compounding this fearful restriction is the ever-prevalent illusion that the audience only wants to see light drama, gay comedies about beautiful young people in love. If the girl and boy do not get married in the end, the script is referred to as "downbeat." Downbeat-type drama is almost as taboo as politically controversial stories.

These are the limitations that the first television writers were faced with. They can hardly be blamed for the incredible trash they wrote. The limitations are still with us, and much of the trash is;

but, in the desperate search to adjust, new areas of writing are being opened up, areas that are peculiar to their limitations. Television drama cannot expand in breadth, so it must expand in depth. In the last year or so, television writers have learned that they can write intimate dramas—"intimate" meaning minutely detailed studies of small moments of life. *Marty* is a good example of this stage of progress. Now, the word for television drama is depth, the digging under the surface of life for the more profound truths of human relationships. This is an area that no other dramatic medium has handled or can adequately handle. It is an area that sooner or later will run head-on into the taboos, not only of television, but of our entire way of life. Yet I cannot help but feel that this is where drama is going. These are strange and fretful times, and the huge inevitable currents of history are too broad now to provide individual people with any meaning to their lives. People are beginning to turn into themselves, looking for personal happiness. The offices of psychoanalysts are flooded with disturbed human beings; the psychiatric clinics of hospitals are too terribly understaffed to handle the demands of the public. Hardly a newspaper, at least in New York, does not carry a syndicated psychiatrist or similar columnist. The jargon of introspection has become everyday conversation. Our national best sellers are nonfiction books dealing with ways of achieving personal adjustments to life. The theater and all its sister mediums can only be a reflection of their times, and the drama of introspection is the drama that the people want to see. It may seem foolish to say, but television, the scorned stepchild of drama, may well be the basic theater of our century.

Marty

DIRECTED BY: DELBERT MANN
ASSOCIATE PRODUCER: GORDON DUFF
PRODUCED BY: FRED COE

Cast

MARTY	Rod Steiger
CLARA	Nancy Marchand
ANGIE	Joseph Mantell
MOTHER	Esther Minciotti
AUNT	Augusta Ciolli
VIRGINIA	Betsy Palmer
THOMAS	Lee Phillips
YOUNG MAN	Don Gordon
CRITIC	Nehemiah Persoff
BARTENDER	Howard Caine
TWENTY-YEAR-OLD	Andrew Gerado
ITALIAN WOMAN	Rosanna San Marco
SHORT GIRL	Rachel Maiori
GIRL	Mary Ann Reeves

ACT I

FADE IN: A butcher shop in the Italian district of New York City. Actually, we fade in on a close-up of a butcher's saw being carefully worked through a side of beef, and we dolly back to show the butcher at work, and then the whole shop. The butcher is a mild-mannered, stout, short, balding young man of thirty-six. His charm lies in an almost indestructible good-natured amiability.

The shop contains three women customers. One is a young mother with a baby carriage. She is chatting with a second woman of about forty at the door. The customer being waited on at the moment is a stout, elderly Italian woman who is standing on tiptoe, peering over the white display counter, checking the butcher as he saws away.

ITALIAN WOMAN: *Your kid brother got married last Sunday, eh, Marty?*

MARTY: [Absorbed in his work] *That's right, Missus Fusari. It was a very nice affair.*

ITALIAN WOMAN: *That's the big tall one, the fellow with the mustache.*

MARTY: [Sawing away] *No, that's my other brother Freddie. My other brother Freddie, he's been married four years already. He lives down on Quincy Street. The one who got married Sunday, that was my little brother Nickie.*

ITALIAN WOMAN: *I thought he was a big, tall, fat fellow. Didn't I meet him here one time? Big, tall, fat fellow, he tried to sell me life insurance?*

MARTY: [Sets the cut of meat on the scale, watches its weight register] *No, that's my sister Margaret's husband Frank. My sister Margaret, she's married to the insurance salesman. My sister Rose, she married a contractor. They moved to Detroit last year. And my other sister, Frances,*

135

she got married about two and a half years ago in Saint John's Church on Adams Boulevard. Oh, that was a big affair. Well, Missus Fusari, that'll be three dollars, ninety-four cents. How's that with you?

The Italian woman produces an old leather change purse from her pocketbook and painfully extracts three single dollar bills and ninety-four cents to the penny and lays the money piece by piece on the counter.

YOUNG MOTHER: [Calling from the door] *Hey, Marty, I'm inna hurry.*

MARTY: [Wrapping the meat, calls amiably back] *You're next right now, Missus Canduso.*

The old Italian lady has been regarding Marty with a baleful scowl.

ITALIAN WOMAN: *Well, Marty, when you gonna get married? You should be ashamed. All your brothers and sisters, they all younger than you, and they married, and they got children. I just saw your mother inna fruit shop, and she says to me: "Hey, you know a nice girl for my boy Marty?" Watsa matter with you? That's no way. Watsa matter with you? Now, you get married, you hear me what I say?*

MARTY: [Amiably] *I hear you, Missus Fusari.*

The old lady takes her parcel of meat, but apparently feels she still hasn't quite made her point.

ITALIAN WOMAN: *My son Frank, he was married when he was nineteen years old. Watsa matter with you?*

MARTY: *Missus Fusari, Missus Canduso over there, she's inna big hurry, and ...*

ITALIAN WOMAN: *You be ashamed of yourself.*

She takes her package of meat. turns, and shuffles to the door and exits. Marty gathers up the money on the counter, turns to the cash register behind him to ring up the sale.

YOUNG MOTHER: *Marty, I want a nice big fat pullet, about four pounds. I hear your kid brother got married last Sunday.*

MARTY: *Yeah, it was a very nice affair, Missus Canduso.*
YOUNG MOTHER: *Marty, you oughtta be ashamed. All your kid brothers and sisters, married and have children. When you gonna get married?*

> CLOSE-UP: Marty. He sends a glance of weary exasperation up to the ceiling. With a gesture of mild irritation, he pushes the plunger of the cash register. It makes a sharp ping.

> DISSOLVE TO: Close-up of television set. A baseball game is in progress. Camera pulls back to show we are in a typical neighborhood bar—red leatherette booths—a jukebox, some phone booths. About half the bar stools are occupied by neighborhood folk. Marty enters, pads amiably to one of the booths where a young man of about thirty-odd already sits. This is Angie. Marty slides into the booth across from Angie. Angie is a little wasp of a fellow. He has a newspaper spread out before him to the sports pages. Marty reaches over and pulls one of the pages over for himself to read. For a moment the two friends sit across from each other, reading the sports pages. Then Angie, without looking up, speaks.

ANGIE: *Well, what do you feel like doing tonight?*
MARTY: *I don't know, Angie. What do you feel like doing?*
ANGIE: *Well, we oughtta do something. It's Saturday night. I don't wanna go bowling like last Saturday. How about calling up that big girl we picked up inna movies about a month ago in the RKO Chester?*
MARTY: [Not very interested] *Which one was that?*
ANGIE: *That big girl that was sitting in front of us with the skinny friend.*
MARTY: *Oh, yeah.*
ANGIE: *We took them home alla way out in Brooklyn. Her name was Mary Feeney. What do you say? You think I oughtta give her a ring? I'll take the skinny one.*
MARTY: *It's five o'clock already, Angie. She's probably got a date by now.*
ANGIE: *Well, let's call her up. What can we lose?*

MARTY: *I didn't like her, Angie. I don't feel like calling her up.*

ANGIE: *Well, what do you feel like doing tonight?*

MARTY: *I don't know. What do you feel like doing?*

ANGIE: *Well, we're back to that, huh? I say to you: "What do you feel like doing tonight?" And you say to me: "I don't know, what do you feel like doing?" And then we wind up sitting around your house with a couple of cans of beer, watching Sid Caesar on television. Well, I tell you what I feel like doing. I feel like calling up this Mary Feeney. She likes you.*

Marty looks up quickly at this.

MARTY: *What makes you say that?*

ANGIE: *I could see she likes you.*

MARTY: *Yeah, sure.*

ANGIE: [Half rising in his seat] *I'll call her up.*

MARTY: *You call her up for yourself, Angie. I don't feel like calling her up.*

Angie sits down again. They both return to reading the paper for a moment. Then Angie looks up again.

ANGIE: *Boy, you're getting to be a real drag, you know that?*

MARTY: *Angie, I'm thirty-six years old. I been looking for a girl every Saturday night of my life. I'm a little, short, fat fellow, and girls don't go for me, that's all. I'm not like you. I mean, you joke around, and they laugh at you, and you get along fine. I just stand around like a bug. What's the sense of kidding myself? Everybody's always telling me to get married. Get married. Get married. Don't you think I wanna get married? I wanna get married. They drive me crazy. Now, I don't wanna wreck your Saturday night for you, Angie. You wanna go somewhere, you go ahead. I don't wanna go.*

ANGIE: *Boy, they drive me crazy too. My old lady, every word outta her mouth, when you gonna get married?*

MARTY: *My mother, boy, she drives me crazy.*

Angie leans back in his seat, scowls at the paper-napkin container. Marty returns to the sports page. For a moment a silence hangs between them. Then . . .

ANGIE: *So what do you feel like doing tonight?*
MARTY: [Without looking up] *I don't know. What do you feel like doing?*
They both just sit, Angie frowning at the napkin container, Marty at the sports page.

The camera slowly moves away from the booth, looks down the length of the bar, up the wall, past the clock—which reads ten to five—and over to the television screen, where the baseball game is still going on.

DISSOLVE SLOWLY TO: The television screen, now blank. The clock now reads a quarter to six.

Back in the booth, Marty now sits alone. In front of him are three empty beer bottles and a beer glass, half filled. He is sitting there, his face expressionless, but his eyes troubled. Then he pushes himself slowly out of the booth and shuffles to the phone booth; he goes inside, closing the booth door carefully after him. For a moment Marty just sits squatly. Then with some exertion—due to the cramped quarters—he contrives to get a small address book out of his rear pants pocket. He slowly flips through it, finds the page he wants, and studies it, scowling; then he takes a dime from the change he has just received, plunks it into the proper slot, waits for a dial tone . . . then carefully dials a number. . . . He waits. He is beginning to sweat a bit in the hot little booth, and his chest begins to rise and fall deeply.

MARTY: [With a vague pretense at good diction] *Hello, is this Mary Feeney? . . . Could I please speak to Miss Mary Feeney? . . . Just tell her an old friend . . .*
He waits again. With his free hand he wipes the gathering sweat from his brow.

. . . Oh, hello there, is this Mary Feeney? Hello there, this is Marty Pilletti. I wonder if you recall me . . . Well, I'm

kind of a stocky guy. The last time we met was inna mov-
ies, the RKO Chester. You was with another girl, and I was
with a friend of mine name Angie. This was about a month
ago . . .

> The girl apparently doesn't remember him. A sort of panic
> begins to seize Marty. His voice rises a little.

The RKO Chester on Payne Boulevard. You was sitting in
front of us, and we was annoying you, and you got mad,
and . . . I'm the fellow who works inna butcher shop . . .
come on, you know who I am! . . . That's right, we went to
Howard Johnson's and we had hamburgers. You hadda
milk shake . . . Yeah, that's right. I'm the stocky one, the
heavy-set fellow. . . . Well, I'm glad you recall me, because
I hadda swell time that night, and I was just wondering
how everything was with you. How's everything? . . .
That's swell . . . Yeah, well, I'll tell you why I called . . .
I was figuring on taking in a movie tonight, and I was won-
dering if you and your friend would care to see a movie
tonight with me and my friend . . . [His eyes are closed
now.] *Yeah, tonight. I know it's pretty late to call for a*
date, but I didn't know myself till . . . Yeah, I know, well
how about . . . Yeah, I know, well maybe next Saturday
night. You free next Saturday night? . . . Well, how about
the Saturday after that? . . . Yeah, I know . . . Yeah . . .
Yeah . . . Oh, I understand, I mean . . .

> He just sits now, his eyes closed, not really listening. After a
> moment he returns the receiver to its cradle and sits, his
> shoulders slack, his hands resting listlessly in the lap of his
> spotted white apron. . . . Then he opens his eyes, straightens
> himself, pushes the booth door open, and advances out into
> the bar. He perches on a stool across the bar from the bar-
> tender, who looks up from his magazine.

BARTENDER: *I hear your kid brother got married last week,*
Marty.
MARTY: [Looking down at his hands on the bar] *Yeah, it*
was a very nice affair.

BARTENDER: *Well, Marty, when you gonna get married?*
Marty tenders the bartender a quick scowl, gets off his perch,
and starts for the door—untying his apron as he goes.

MARTY: *If my mother calls up, Lou, tell her I'm on my way
home.*

DISSOLVE TO: Marty's mother and a young couple sitting
around the table in the dining room of Marty's home. The
young couple—we will soon find out—are Thomas, Marty's
cousin, and his wife, Virginia. They have apparently just been
telling the mother some sad news, and the three are sitting
around frowning.

The dining room is a crowded room filled with chairs and
lamps, pictures and little statues, perhaps even a small grotto
of little vigil lamps. To the right of the dining room is the
kitchen, old-fashioned, Italian, steaming, and overcrowded.
To the left of the dining room is the living room, furnished in
same fashion as the dining room. Just off the living room is
a small bedroom, which is Marty's. This bedroom and the living room have windows looking out on front. The dining room
has windows looking out to side alleyway. A stairway in the
dining room leads to the second floor.

The mother is a round, dark, effusive little woman.

MOTHER: [After a pause] *Well, Thomas, I knew sooner or
later this was gonna happen. I told Marty, I said: "Marty,
you watch. There's gonna be real trouble over there in
your cousin Thomas' house." Because your mother was
here, Thomas, you know?*

THOMAS: *When was this, Aunt Theresa?*

MOTHER: *This was one, two, three days ago. Wednesday.
Because I went to the fruit shop on Wednesday, and I
came home. And I come arounna back, and there's your
mother sitting onna steps onna porch. And I said: "Catherine, my sister, wadda you doing here?" And she look uppa
me, and she beganna cry.*

THOMAS: [To his wife] *Wednesday. That was the day you
threw the milk bottle.*

MOTHER: *That's right. Because I said to her: "Catherine, watsa matter?" And she said to me: "Theresa, my daughter-in-law, Virginia, she just threw the milk bottle at me."*

VIRGINIA: *Well, you see what happen, Aunt Theresa . . .*

MOTHER: *I know, I know . . .*

VIRGINIA: *She comes inna kitchen, and she begins poking her head over my shoulder here and poking her head over my shoulder there . . .*

MOTHER: *I know, I know . . .*

VIRGINIA: *And she begins complaining about this, and she begins complaining about that. And she got me so nervous, I spilled some milk I was making for the baby. You see, I was making some food for the baby, and . . .*

MOTHER: *So I said to her, "Catherine . . ."*

VIRGINIA: *So, she got me so nervous I spilled some milk. So she said: "You're spilling the milk." She says: "Milk costs twenny-four cents a bottle. Wadda you, a banker?" So I said: "Mama, leave me alone, please. You're making me nervous. Go on in the other room and turn on the television set." So then she began telling me how I waste money, and how I can't cook, and how I'm raising my baby all wrong, and she kept talking about these couple of drops of milk I spilt, and I got so mad, I said: "Mama, you wanna see me really spill some milk?" So I took the bottle and threw it against the door. I didn't throw it at her. That's just something she made up. I didn't throw it anywheres near her. Well, of course, alla milk went all over the floor. The whole twenny-four cents. Well, I was sorry right away, you know, but she ran outta the house.*
    Pause.

MOTHER: *Well, I don't know what you want me to do, Virginia. If you want me, I'll go talk to her tonight.*
    Thomas and Virginia suddenly frown and look down at their hands as if of one mind.

THOMAS: *Well, I'll tell you, Aunt Theresa . . .*

VIRGINIA: *Lemme tell it, Tommy.*

THOMAS: *Okay.*

VIRGINIA: [Leaning forward to the mother] *We want you to do a very big favor for us, Aunt Theresa.*

MOTHER: *Sure.*

VIRGINIA: *Aunt Theresa, you got this big house here. You got four bedrooms upstairs. I mean, you got this big house just for you and Marty. All your other kids are married and got their own homes. And I thought maybe Tommy's mother could come here and live with you and Marty.*

MOTHER: *Well . . .*

VIRGINIA: *She's miserable living with Tommy and me, and you're the only one that gets along with her. Because I called up Tommy's brother, Joe, and I said: "Joe, she's driving me crazy. Why don't you take her for a couple of years?" And he said: "Oh, no!" I know I sound like a terrible woman . . .*

MOTHER: *No, Virginia, I know how you feel. My husband, may God bless his memory, his mother, she lived with us for a long time, and I know how you feel.*

VIRGINIA: [Practically on the verge of tears] *I just can't stand it no more! Every minute of the day! Do this! Do that! I don't have ten minutes alone with my husband! We can't even have a fight! We don't have no privacy! Everybody's miserable in our house!*

THOMAS: *All right, Ginnie, don't get so excited.*

MOTHER: *She's right. She's right. Young husband and wife, they should have their own home. And my sister, Catherine, she's my sister, but I gotta admit, she's an old goat. And plenny-a times in my life I feel like throwing the milk bottle at her myself. And I tell you now, as far as I'm concerned, if Catherine wantsa come live here with me and Marty, it's all right with me.*

Virginia promptly bursts into tears.

THOMAS: [Not far from tears himself, lowers his face] *That's very nice-a you, Aunt Theresa.*

MOTHER: *We gotta ask Marty, of course, because this is*

his house too. But he's gonna come home any minute now.
VIRGINIA: [Having mastered her tears] *That's very nice-a you, Aunt Theresa.*
MOTHER: [Rising] *Now, you just sit here. I'm just gonna turn onna small fire under the food.*
> She exits into the kitchen.

VIRGINIA: [Calling after her] *We gotta go right away because I promised the baby sitter we'd be home by six, and it's after six now . . .*
> She kind of fades out. A moment of silence. Thomas takes out a cigarette and lights it.

THOMAS: [Calling to his aunt in the kitchen] *How's Marty been lately, Aunt Theresa?*
MOTHER: [Off in kitchen] *Oh, he's fine. You know a nice girl he can marry?*
> She comes back into the dining room, wiping her hands on a kitchen towel.

I'm worried about him, you know? He's thirty-six years old, gonna be thirty-seven in January.
THOMAS: *Oh, he'll get married, don't worry, Aunt Theresa.*
MOTHER: [Sitting down again] *Well, I don't know. You know a place where he can go where he can find a bride?*
THOMAS: *The Waverly Ballroom. That's a good place to meet girls, Aunt Theresa. That's a kind of big dance hall, Aunt Theresa. Every Saturday night, it's just loaded with girls. It's a nice place to go. You pay seventy-seven cents. It used to be seventy-seven cents. It must be about a buck and a half now. And you go in and you ask some girl to dance. That's how I met Virginia. Nice, respectable place to meet girls. You tell Marty, Aunt Theresa, you tell him: "Go to the Waverly Ballroom. It's loaded with tomatoes."*
MOTHER: [Committing the line to memory] *The Waverly Ballroom. It's loaded with tomatoes.*
THOMAS: *Right.*
VIRGINIA: *You tell him, go to the Waverly Ballroom.*

There is the sound of a door being unlatched off through the kitchen. The mother promptly rises.

MOTHER: *He's here.*

She hurries into the kitchen. At the porch entrance to the kitchen, Marty has just come in. He is closing the door behind him. He carries his butcher's apron in a bundle under his arm.

MARTY: *Hello, Ma.*

She comes up to him, lowers her voice to a whisper.

MOTHER: [Whispers] *Marty, Thomas and Virginia are* were *here. They had another big fight with your Aunt Catherine. So they ask me, would it be all right if Catherine come to live with us. So I said, all right with me, but we have to ask you. Marty, she's a lonely old lady. Nobody wants her. Everybody's throwing her outta their house. . . .*

MARTY: *Sure, Ma, it's okay with me.*

The mother's face breaks into a fond smile. She reaches up and pats his cheek with genuine affection.

MOTHER: *You gotta good heart.* [Turning and leading the way back to the dining room. Thomas has risen.] *He says okay, it's all right Catherine comes here.*

THOMAS: *Oh, Marty, thanks a lot. That really takes a load offa my mind.*

MARTY: *Oh, we got plenny-a room here.*

MOTHER: *Sure! Sure! It's gonna be nice! It's gonna be nice! I'll come over tonight to your house, and I talk to Catherine, and you see, everything is gonna work out all right.*

THOMAS: *I just wanna thank you people again because the situation was just becoming impossible.*

MOTHER: *Siddown, Thomas, siddown. All right, Marty, siddown. . . .*

She exits into the kitchen.

Marty has taken his seat at the head of the table and is waiting to be served. Thomas takes a seat around the corner of the table from him and leans across to him.

THOMAS: *You see, Marty, the kinda thing that's been hap-*

*pening in our house is Virginia was inna kitchen making
some food for the baby. Well, my mother comes in, and
she gets Virginia so nervous, she spills a couple-a drops . . .*

VIRGINIA: [Tugging at her husband] *Tommy, we gotta go.
I promise the baby sitter six o'clock.*

THOMAS: [Rising without interrupting his narrative] *So
she starts yelling at Virginia, waddaya spilling the milk
for. So Virginia gets mad . . .*

His wife is slowly pulling him to the kitchen door.

*She says, "You wanna really see me spill milk?" So Vir-
ginia takes the bottle and she throws it against the wall.
She's got a real Italian temper, my wife, you know that . .*

He has been tugged to the kitchen door by now.

VIRGINIA: *Marty, I don't have to tell you how much we
appreciate what your mother and you are doing for us.*

THOMAS: *All right, Marty, I'll see you some other time . .
I'll tell you all about it.*

MARTY: *I'll see you, Tommy.*

Thomas disappears into the kitchen after his wife.

VIRGINIA: [Off, calling] *Good-by, Marty!*

Close in on Marty, sitting at table.

MARTY: *Good-by, Virginia! See you soon!*

He folds his hands on the table before him and waits to be
served.

   The mother enters from the kitchen. She sets the meat plate
down in front of him and herself takes a chair around the
corner of the table from him. Marty without a word takes up
his knife and fork and attacks the mountain of food in front
of him. His mother sits quietly, her hands a little nervous on
the table before her, watching him eat. Then . . .

MOTHER: *So what are you gonna do tonight, Marty?*

MARTY: *I don't know, Ma. I'm all knocked out. I may just
hang arounna house.*

The mother nods a couple of times. There is a moment of
silence. Then . . .

MOTHER: *Why don't you go to the Waverly Ballroom?*

This gives Marty pause. He looks up.

MARTY: *What?*

MOTHER: *I say, why don't you go to the Waverly Ballroom? It's loaded with tomatoes.*

Marty regards his mother for a moment.

MARTY: *It's loaded with what?*

MOTHER: *Tomatoes.*

MARTY: [Snorts] *Ha! Who told you about the Waverly Ballroom?*

MOTHER: *Thomas, he told me it was a very nice place.*

MARTY: *Oh, Thomas. Ma, it's just a big dance hall, and that's all it is. I been there a hundred times. Loaded with tomatoes. Boy, you're funny, Ma.*

MOTHER: *Marty, I don't want you hang arounna house tonight. I want you to go take a shave and go out and dance.*

MARTY: *Ma, when are you gonna give up? You gotta bachelor on your hands. I ain't never gonna get married.*

MOTHER: *You gonna get married.*

MARTY: *Sooner or later, there comes a point in a man's life when he gotta face some facts, and one fact I gotta face is that whatever it is that women like, I ain't got it. I chased enough girls in my life. I went to enough dances. I got hurt enough. I don't wanna get hurt no more. I just called a girl this afternoon, and I got a real brush-off, boy. I figured I was past the point of being hurt, but that hurt. Some stupid woman who I didn't even wanna call up. She gave me the brush. That's the history of my life. I don't wanna go to the Waverly Ballroom because all that ever happened to me there was girls made me feel like I was a bug. I got feelings, you know. I had enough pain. No, thank you.*

MOTHER: *Marty . . .*

MARTY: *Ma, I'm gonna stay home and watch Sid Caesar.*

MOTHER: *You gonna die without a son.*

MARTY: *So I'll die without a son.*

MOTHER: *Put on your blue suit . . .*

MARTY: *Blue suit, gray suit, I'm still a fat little man. A fat little ugly man.*

MOTHER: *You not ugly.*

MARTY: [His voice rising] *I'm ugly . . . I'm ugly! . . . I'm UGLY!*

MOTHER: *Marty . . .*

MARTY: [Crying aloud, more in anguish than in anger] *Ma! Leave me alone! . . .*

> He stands abruptly, his face pained and drawn. He makes half-formed gestures to his mother, but he can't find words at the moment. He turns and marches a few paces away, turns to his mother again.

MARTY: *Ma, waddaya want from me?! Waddaya want from me?! I'm miserable enough as it is! Leave me alone! I'll go to the Waverly Ballroom! I'll put onna blue suit and I'll go! And you know what I'm gonna get for my trouble? Heartache! A big night of heartache!*

> He sullenly marches back to his seat, sits down, picks up his fork, plunges it into the lasagna, and stuffs a mouthful into his mouth; he chews vigorously for a moment. It is impossible to remain angry for long. After a while he is shaking his head and muttering.

MARTY: *Loaded with tomatoes . . . boy, that's rich . . .*

> He plunges his fork in again. Camera pulls slowly away from him and his mother, who is seated—watching him.

FADE OUT.

ACT II

FADE IN: Exterior, three-story building. Pan up to second floor . . . bright neon lights reading "Waverly Ballroom" . . . The large, dirty windows are open; and the sound of a fair-to-middling swing band whooping it up comes out.

DISSOLVE TO: Interior, Waverly Ballroom—large dance floor crowded with jitterbugging couples, eight-piece combination hitting a loud kick. Ballroom is vaguely dark, made so by papier-mâché over the chandeliers to create alleged romantic effect. The walls are lined with stags and waiting girls, singly and in small murmuring groups. Noise and mumble and drone.

DISSOLVE TO: Live shot—a row of stags along a wall. Camera is looking lengthwise down the row. Camera dollies slowly past each face, each staring out at the dance floor, watching in his own manner of hungry eagerness. Short, fat, tall, thin stags. Some pretend diffidence. Some exhibit patent hunger.

Near the end of the line, we find Marty and Angie, freshly shaved and groomed. They are leaning against the wall, smoking, watching their more fortunate brethren out on the floor.

ANGIE: *Not a bad crowd tonight, you know?*
MARTY: *There was one nice-looking one there in a black dress and beads, but she was a little tall for me.*
ANGIE: [Looking down past Marty along the wall right into the camera] *There's a nice-looking little short one for you right now.*
MARTY: [Following his gaze] *Where?*
ANGIE: *Down there. That little one there.*
The camera cuts about eight faces down, to where the girls are now standing. Two are against the wall. One is facing them, with her back to the dance floor. This last is the one Angie has in mind. She is a cute little kid, about twenty, and

149

she has a bright smile on—as if the other two girls are just amusing her to death.

MARTY: *Yeah, she looks all right from here.*

ANGIE: *Well, go on over and ask her. You don't hurry up, somebody else'll grab her.*

Marty scowls, shrugs.

MARTY: *Okay, let's go.*

They slouch along past the eight stags, a picture of nonchalant unconcern. The three girls, aware of their approach, stiffen, and their chatter comes to a halt. Angie advances to one of the girls along the wall.

ANGIE: *Waddaya say, you wanna dance?*

The girl looks surprised—as if this were an extraordinary invitation to receive in this place—looks confounded at her two friends, shrugs, detaches herself from the group, moves to the outer fringe of the pack of dancers, raises her hand languidly to dancing position, and awaits Angie with ineffable boredom. Marty, smiling shyly, addresses the short girl.

MARTY: *Excuse me, would you care for this dance?*

The short girl gives Marty a quick glance of appraisal, then looks quickly at her remaining friend.

SHORT GIRL: [Not unpleasantly] *Sorry. I just don't feel like dancing just yet.*

MARTY: *Sure.*

He turns and moves back past the eight stags, all of whom have covertly watched his attempt. He finds his old niche by the wall, leans there. A moment later he looks guardedly down to where the short girl and her friend are. A young, dapper boy is approaching the short girl. He asks her to dance. The short girl smiles, excuses herself to her friend, and follows the boy out onto the floor. Marty turns back to watching the dancers bleakly. A moment later he is aware that someone on his right is talking to him. . . . He turns his head. It is a young man of about twenty-eight.

MARTY: *You say something to me?*

YOUNG MAN: *Yeah. I was just asking you if you was here stag or with a girl.*

MARTY: *I'm stag.*

YOUNG MAN: *Well, I'll tell you. I got stuck onna blind date with a dog, and I just picked up a nice chick, and I was wondering how I'm gonna get ridda the dog. Somebody to take her home, you know what I mean? I be glad to pay you five bucks if you take the dog home for me.*

MARTY: [A little confused] *What?*

YOUNG MAN: *I'll take you over, and I'll introduce you as an old army buddy of mine, and then I'll cut out. Because I got this chick waiting for me out by the hatcheck, and I'll pay you five bucks.*

MARTY: [Stares at the young man] *Are you kidding?*

YOUNG MAN: *No, I'm not kidding.*

MARTY: *You can't just walk off onna girl like that.*

The young man grimaces impatiently and moves down the line of stags. . . . Marty watches him, still a little shocked at the proposition. About two stags down, the young man broaches his plan to another stag. This stag, frowning and pursing his lips, seems more receptive to the idea. . . . The young man takes out a wallet and gives the stag a five-dollar bill. The stag detaches himself from the wall and, a little ill at ease, follows the young man back past Marty and into the lounge. Marty pauses a moment and then, concerned, walks to the archway that separates the lounge from the ballroom and looks in.

The lounge is a narrow room with a bar and booths. In contrast to the ballroom, it is brightly lighted—causing Marty to squint.

In the second booth from the archway sits a girl, about twenty-eight. Despite the careful grooming that she has put into her cosmetics, she is blatantly plain. The young man and the stag are standing, talking to her. She is looking up at the young man, her hands nervously gripping her Coca-Cola glass.

We cannot hear what the young man is saying, but it is apparent that he is introducing his new-found army buddy and is going through some cock-and-bull story about being called away on an emergency. The stag is presented as her escort-to-be, who will see to it that she gets home safely. The girl apparently is not taken in at all by this, though she is trying hard not to seem affected.

She politely rejects the stag's company and will get home by herself, thanks for asking anyway. The young man makes a few mild protestations, and then he and the stag leave the booth and come back to the archway from where Marty has been watching the scene. As they pass Marty, we overhear a snatch of dialogue.

YOUNG MAN: . . . *In that case, as long as she's going home alone, give me the five bucks back. . . .*

STAG: . . . *Look, Mac, you paid me five bucks. I was willing. It's my five bucks. . . .*

They pass on. Marty returns his attention to the girl. She is still sitting as she was, gripping and ungripping the glass of Coca-Cola in front of her. Her eyes are closed. Then, with a little nervous shake of her head, she gets out of the booth and stands—momentarily at a loss for what to do next. The open fire doors leading out onto the large fire escape catch her eye. She crosses to the fire escape, nervous, frowning, and disappears outside.

Marty stares after her, then slowly shuffles to the open fire-escape doorway. It is a large fire escape, almost the size of a small balcony. The girl is standing by the railing, her back to the doorway, her head slunk down on her bosom. For a moment Marty is unaware that she is crying. Then he notices the shivering tremors running through her body and the quivering shoulders. He moves a step onto the fire escape. He tries to think of something to say.

MARTY: *Excuse me, Miss Would you care to dance?*

The girl slowly turns to him, her face streaked with tears, her lip trembling. Then, in one of those peculiar moments of simultaneous impulse, she lurches to Marty with a sob, and Marty takes her to him. For a moment they stand in an awkward embrace, Marty a little embarrassed, looking out through the doors to the lounge, wondering if anybody is seeing them. Reaching back with one hand, he closes the fire doors, and then, replacing the hand around her shoulder, he stands stiffly, allowing her to cry on his chest.

DISSOLVE TO: Exterior, apartment door. The mother is standing, in a black coat and a hat with a little feather, waiting for her ring to be answered. The door opens. Virginia stands framed in the doorway.

VIRGINIA: *Hello, Aunt Theresa, come in.*

The mother goes into the small foyer. Virginia closes the door.

MOTHER: [In a low voice, as she pulls her coat off] *Is Catherine here?*

VIRGINIA: [Helps her off with coat, nods—also in a low voice] *We didn't tell her nothing yet. We thought we'd leave it to you. We thought you'd put it like how you were lonely, and why don't she come to live with you. Because that way it looks like she's doing you a favor, insteada we're throwing her out, and it won't be so cruel on her. Thomas is downstairs with the neighbors . . . I'll go call him.*

MOTHER: *You go downstairs to the neighbors and stay there with Thomas.*

VIRGINIA: *Wouldn't it be better if we were here?*

MOTHER: *You go downstairs. I talk to Catherine alone. Otherwise, she's gonna start a fight with you.*

A shrill, imperious woman's voice from an off-stage room suddenly breaks into the muttered conference in the foyer.

AUNT: [Off] *Who's there?! Who's there?!*

The mother heads up the foyer to the living room, followed by Virginia, holding the mother's coat.

MOTHER: [Calls back] *It's me, Catherine! How you feel?*

At the end of the foyer, the two sisters meet. The aunt is a

spare, gaunt woman with a face carved out of granite. Tough,
embittered, deeply hurt type face.

AUNT: *Hey! What are you doing here?*

MOTHER: *I came to see you.* [The two sisters quickly embrace and release each other.] *How you feel?*

AUNT: *I gotta pain in my left side and my leg throbs like
a drum.*

MOTHER: *I been getting pains in my shoulder.*

AUNT: *I got pains in my shoulder, too. I have a pain in my
hip, and my right arm aches so much I can't sleep. It's a
curse to be old. How you feel?*

MOTHER: *I feel fine.*

AUNT: *That's nice.*

Now that the standard greetings are over, Aunt Catherine
abruptly turns and goes back to her chair. It is obviously her
chair. It is an old heavy oaken chair with thick armrests. The
rest of the apartment is furnished in what is known as "modern"—a piece from *House Beautiful* here, a piece from *Better
Homes and Gardens* there. Aunt Catherine sits, erect and for-
bidding, in her chair. The mother seats herself with a sigh in
a neighboring chair. Virginia, having hung the mother's coat,
now turns to the two older women. A pause.

VIRGINIA: *I'm going downstairs to the Cappacini's. I'll be
up inna little while.*

Aunt Catherine nods expressionlessly. Virginia looks at her
for a moment, then impulsively crosses to her mother-in-law.

VIRGINIA: *You feel all right?*

The old lady looks up warily, suspicious of this sudden
solicitude.

AUNT: *I'm all right.*

Virginia nods and goes off to the foyer. The two old sisters sit,
unmoving, waiting for the door to close behind Virginia.
Then the mother addresses herself to Aunt Catherine.

MOTHER: *We gotta post card from my son, Nickie, and his
bride this morning. They're in Florida inna big hotel.
Everything is very nice.*

AUNT: *That's nice.*

MOTHER: *Catherine, I want you come live with me in my house with Marty and me. In my house, you have your own room. You don't have to sleep onna couch inna living room like here.*

The aunt looks slowly and directly at the mother.

Catherine, your son is married. He got his own home. Leave him in peace. He wants to be alone with his wife. They don't want no old lady sitting inna balcony. Come and live with me. We will cook in the kitchen and talk like when we were girls. You are dear to me, and you are dear to Marty. We are pleased for you to come.

AUNT: *Did they come to see you?*

MOTHER: *Yes.*

AUNT: *Did my son Thomas come with her?*

MOTHER: *Your son Thomas was there.*

AUNT: *Did he also say he wishes to cast his mother from his house?*

MOTHER: *Catherine, don't make an opera outta this. The three-a you anna baby live in three skinny rooms. You are an old goat, and she has an Italian temper. She is a good girl, but you drive her crazy. Leave them alone. They have their own life.*

The old aunt turns her head slowly and looks her sister square in the face. Then she rises slowly from her chair.

AUNT: [Coldly] *Get outta here. This is my son's house. This is where I live. I am not to be cast out inna street like a newspaper.*

The mother likewise rises. The two old women face each other directly.

MOTHER: *Catherine, you are very dear to me. We have cried many times together. When my husband died, I would have gone insane if it were not for you. I ask you to come to my house because I can make you happy. Please come to my house.*

The two sisters regard each other. Then Aunt Catherine sits

again in her oaken chair, and the mother returns to her seat. The hardened muscles in the old aunt's face suddenly slacken, and she turns to her sister.

AUNT: *Theresa, what shall become of me?*

MOTHER: *Catherine . . .*

AUNT: *It's gonna happen to you. Mark it well. These terrible years. I'm afraida look inna mirror. I'm afraid I'm gonna see an old lady with white hair, like the old ladies inna park, little bundles inna black shawl, waiting for the coffin. I'm fifty-six years old. What am I to do with myself? I have strength in my hands. I wanna cook. I wanna clean. I wanna make dinner for my children. I wanna be of use to somebody. Am I an old dog to lie in fronta the fire till my eyes close? These are terrible years, Theresa! Terrible years!*

MOTHER: *Catherine, my sister . . .*

The old aunt stares, distraught, at the mother.

AUNT: *It's gonna happen to you! It's gonna happen to you! What will you do if Marty gets married?! What will you cook?! What happen to alla children tumbling in alla rooms?! Where is the noise?! It is a curse to be a widow! A curse! What will you do if Marty gets married?! What will you do?!*

She stares at the mother—her deep, gaunt eyes haggard and pained. The mother stares back for a moment, then her own eyes close. The aunt has hit home. The aunt sinks back onto her chair, sitting stiffly, her arms on the thick armrests. The mother sits hunched a little forward, her hands nervously folded in her lap.

AUNT: [Quietly] *I will put my clothes inna bag and I will come to you tomorrow.*

The camera slowly dollies back from the two somber sisters.

SLOW FADE-OUT.

CUT TO: Close-up, intimate, Marty and the girl dancing

cheek to cheek. Occasionally the heads of other couples slowly waft across the camera view, temporarily blocking out view of Marty and the girl. Camera stays with them as the slow dance carries them around the floor. Tender scene.

GIRL: . . . *The last time I was here the same sort of thing happened.*

MARTY: *Yeah?*

GIRL: *Well, not exactly the same thing. The last time I was up here was about four months ago. Do you see that girl in the gray dress sitting over there?*

MARTY: *Yeah.*

GIRL: *That's where I sat. I sat there for an hour and a half without moving a muscle. Now and then, some fellow would sort of walk up to me and then change his mind. I just sat there, my hands in my lap. Well, about ten o'clock, a bunch of kids came in swaggering. They weren't more than seventeen, eighteen years old. Well, they swaggered down along the wall, leering at all the girls. I thought they were kind of cute . . . and as they passed me, I smiled at them. One of the kids looked at me and said: "Forget it, ugly, you ain't gotta chance." I burst out crying. I'm a big crier, you know.*

MARTY: *So am I.*

GIRL: *And another time when I was in college . . .*

MARTY: *I cry alla time. Any little thing. I can recognize pain a mile away. My brothers, my brother-in-laws, they're always telling me what a goodhearted guy I am. Well, you don't get goodhearted by accident. You get kicked around long enough you get to be a real professor of pain. I know exactly how you feel. And I also want you to know I'm having a very good time with you now and really enjoying myself. So you see, you're not such a dog as you think you are.*

GIRL: *I'm having a very good time too.*

MARTY: *So there you are. So I guess I'm not such a dog as I think I am.*

GIRL: *You're a very nice guy, and I don't know why some girl hasn't grabbed you off long ago.*

MARTY: *I don't know either. I think I'm a very nice guy. I also think I'm a pretty smart guy in my own way.*

GIRL: *I think you are.*

MARTY: *I'll tell you some of my wisdom which I thunk up on those nights when I got stood up, and nights like that, and you walk home thinking: "Watsa matter with me? I can't be that ugly." Well, I figure, two people get married, and they gonna live together forty, fifty years. So it's just gotta be more than whether they're good-looking or not. My father was a real ugly man, but my mother adored him. She told me that she used to get so miserable sometimes, like everybody, you know? And she says my father always tried to understand. I used to see them sometimes when I was a kid, sitting in the living room, talking and talking, and I used to adore my old man because he was so kind. That's one of the most beautiful things I have in my life, the way my father and my mother were. And my father was a real ugly man. So it don't matter if you look like a gorilla. So you see, dogs like us, we ain't such dogs as we think we are.*

They dance silently for a moment, cheeks pressed against each other. Close-ups of each face.

GIRL: *I'm twenty-nine years old. How old are you?*

MARTY: *Thirty-six.*

They dance silently, closely. Occasionally the heads of other couples sway in front of the camera, blocking our view of Marty and the girl. Slow, sweet dissolve.

DISSOLVE TO: Interior, kitchen, Marty's home. Later that night. It is dark. Nobody is home. The rear porch door now opens, and the silhouettes of Marty and the girl appear—blocking up the doorway.

MARTY: *Wait a minute. Lemme find the light.*

He finds the light. The kitchen is suddenly brightly lit. The two of them stand squinting to adjust to the sudden glare.

MARTY: *I guess my mother ain't home yet. I figure my cousin Thomas and Virginia musta gone to the movies, so they won't get back till one o'clock, at least.*

The girl has advanced into the kitchen, a little ill at ease, and is looking around. Marty closes the porch door.

MARTY: *This is the kitchen.*

GIRL: *Yes, I know.*

Marty leads the way into the dining room.

MARTY: *Come on inna dining room.* [He turns on the light in there as he goes. The girl follows him in.] *Siddown, take off your coat. You want something to eat? We gotta whole halfa chicken left over from yesterday.*

GIRL: [Perching tentatively on the edge of a chair] *No, thank you . I don't think I should stay very long.*

MARTY: *Sure. Just take off your coat a minute.*

He helps her off with her coat and stands for a moment behind her, looking down at her. Conscious of his scrutiny, she sits uncomfortably, her breasts rising and falling unevenly. Marty takes her coat into the dark living room. The girl sits patiently, nervously. Marty comes back, sits down on another chair. Awkward silence.

MARTY: *So I was telling you, my kid brother Nickie got married last Sunday . . . That was a very nice affair. And they had this statue of some woman, and they had whisky spouting outta her mouth. I never saw anything so grand in my life.* [The silence falls between them again.] *And watta meal. I'm a butcher, so I know a good hunka steak when I see one. That was choice filet, right off the toppa the chuck. A buck-eighty a pound. Of course, if you wanna cheaper cut, get rib steak. That gotta lotta waste on it, but it comes to about a buck and a quarter a pound, if it's trimmed. Listen, Clara, make yourself comfortable. You're all tense.*

GIRL: *Oh, I'm fine.*

MARTY: *You want me to take you home, I'll take you home.*

GIRL: *Maybe that would be a good idea.*

> She stands. He stands, frowning, a little angry—turns sullenly and goes back into the living room for her coat. She stands unhappily. He comes back and wordlessly starts to help her into her coat. He stands behind her, his hands on her shoulders. He suddenly seizes her, begins kissing her on the neck. Camera comes up quickly to intensely intimate close-up, nothing but the heads. The dialogue drops to quick, hushed whispers.

GIRL: *No, Marty, please . . .*

MARTY: *I like you, I like you, I been telling you all night I like you . . .*

GIRL: *Marty . . .*

MARTY: *I just wanna kiss, that's all . . .*

> He tries to turn her face to him. She resists.

GIRL: *No . . .*

MARTY: *Please . . .*

GIRL: *No . . .*

MARTY: *Please . . .*

GIRL: *Marty . . .*

> He suddenly releases her, turns away violently.

MARTY: [Crying out] *All right! I'll take you home! All right!* [He marches a few angry paces away, deeply disturbed. Turns to her.] *All I wanted was a lousy kiss! What am I, a leper or something?!*

> He turns and goes off into the living room to hide the flush of hot tears threatening to fill his eyes. The girl stands, herself on the verge of tears.

GIRL: [Mutters, more to herself than to him] *I just didn't feel like it, that's all.*

> She moves slowly to the archway leading to the living room. Marty is sitting on the couch, hands in his lap, looking straight ahead. The room is dark except for the overcast of the dining-room light reaching in. The girl goes to the couch, perches on the edge beside him. He doesn't look at her.

MARTY: *Well, that's the history of my life. I'm a little, short, fat, ugly guy. Comes New Year's Eve, everybody starts arranging parties, I'm the guy they gotta dig up a date for. I'm old enough to know better. Let me get a packa cigarettes, and I'll take you home.*

He starts to rise, but doesn't . . . sinks back onto the couch, looking straight ahead. The girl looks at him, her face peculiarly soft and compassionate.

GIRL: *I'd like to see you again, very much. The reason I didn't let you kiss me was because I just didn't know how to handle the situation. You're the kindest man I ever met. The reason I tell you this is because I want to see you again very much. Maybe, I'm just so desperate to fall in love that I'm trying too hard. But I know that when you take me home, I'm going to just lie on my bed and think about you. I want very much to see you again.*

Marty stares down at his hands in his lap.

MARTY: [Without looking at her] *Waddaya doing tomorrow night?*

GIRL: *Nothing.*

MARTY: *I'll call you up tomorrow morning. Maybe we'll go see a movie.*

GIRL: *I'd like that very much.*

MARTY: *The reason I can't be definite about it now is my Aunt Catherine is probably coming over tomorrow, and I may have to help out.*

GIRL: *I'll wait for your call.*

MARTY: *We better get started to your house because the buses only run about one an hour now.*

GIRL: *All right.*

She stands.

MARTY: *I'll just get a packa cigarettes.*

He goes into his bedroom. We can see him through the doorway, opening his bureau drawer and extracting a pack of cigarettes. He comes out again and looks at the girl for the first

time. They start to walk to the dining room. In the archway,
Marty pauses, turns to the girl.

MARTY: *Waddaya doing New Year's Eve?*
GIRL: *Nothing.*
They quietly slip into each other's arms and kiss. Slowly their
faces part, and Marty's head sinks down upon her shoulder.
He is crying. His shoulders shake slightly. The girl presses her
cheek against the back of his head. They stand . . . there is
the sound of the rear porch door being unlatched. They both
start from their embrace. A moment later the mother's voice
is heard off in the kitchen.

MOTHER: *Hallo! Hallo, Marty?* [She comes into the dining room, stops at the sight of the girl.] *Hallo, Marty, when
you come home?*
MARTY: *We just got here about fifteen minutes ago, Ma.
Ma, I want you to meet Miss Clara Davis. She's a graduate of New York University. She teaches history in Benja-
min Franklin High School.*
This seems to impress the mother.

MOTHER: *Siddown, siddown. You want some chicken? We
got some chicken in the icebox.*
GIRL: *No, Mrs. Pilletti, we were just going home. Thank
you very much anyway.*
MOTHER: *Well, siddown a minute. I just come inna house.
I'll take off my coat. Siddown a minute.*
She pulls her coat off.

MARTY: *How'd you come home, Ma? Thomas give you a
ride?*
The mother nods.

MOTHER: *Oh, it's a sad business, a sad business.*
She sits down on a dining room chair, holding her coat in her
lap. She turns to the girl, who likewise sits.

MOTHER: *My sister Catherine, she don't get along with
her daughter-in-law, so she's gonna come live with us.*
MARTY: *Oh, she's coming, eh, Ma?*
MOTHER: *Oh, sure.* [To the girl] *It's a very sad thing. A*

woman, fifty-six years old, all her life, she had her own home. Now, she's just an old lady, sleeping on her daughter-in-law's couch. It's a curse to be a mother, I tell you. Your children grow up and then what is left for you to do? What is a mother's life but her children? It is a very cruel thing when your son has no place for you in his home.

GIRL: *Couldn't she find some sort of hobby to fill out her time?*

MOTHER: *Hobby! What can she do? She cooks and she cleans. You gotta have a house to clean. You gotta have children to cook for. These are the terrible years for a woman, the terrible years.*

GIRL: *You mustn't feel too harshly against her daughter-in-law. She also wants to have a house to clean and a family to cook for.*

The mother darts a quick, sharp look at the girl—then looks back to her hands, which are beginning to twist nervously.

MOTHER: *You don't think my sister Catherine should live in her daughter-in-law's house?*

GIRL: *Well, I don't know the people, of course, but, as a rule, I don't think a mother-in-law should live with a young couple.*

MOTHER: *Where do you think a mother-in-law should go?*

GIRL: *I don't think a mother should depend so much upon her children for her rewards in life.*

MOTHER: *That's what it says in the book in New York University. You wait till you are a mother. It don't work out that way.*

GIRL: *Well, it's silly for me to argue about it. I don't know the people involved.*

MARTY: *Ma, I'm gonna take her home now. It's getting late, and the buses only run about one an hour.*

MOTHER: [Standing] *Sure.*

The girl stands.

GIRL: *It was very nice meeting you, Mrs. Pilletti. I hope
I'll see you again.*
MOTHER: *Sure.*
    Marty and the girl move to the kitchen.
MARTY: *All right, Ma. I'll be back in about an hour.*
MOTHER: *Sure.*
GIRL: *Good night, Mrs. Pilletti.*
MOTHER: *Good night.*
    Marty and the girl exit into the kitchen. The mother stands,
    expressionless, by her chair watching them go. She remains
    standing rigidly even after the porch door can be heard being
    opened and shut. The camera moves up to a close-up of the
    mother. Her eyes are wide. She is staring straight ahead. There
    is fear in her eyes.

    FADE OUT.

ACT III

FADE IN: Film—close-up of church bells clanging away. Pan down church to see typical Sunday morning, people going up the steps of a church and entering. It is a beautiful June morning.

DISSOLVE TO: Interior, Marty's bedroom—sun fairly streaming through the curtains. Marty is standing in front of his bureau, slipping his arms into a clean white shirt. He is freshly shaved and groomed. Through the doorway of his bedroom we can see the mother in the dining room, in coat and hat, all set to go to Mass, taking the last breakfast plates away and carrying them into the kitchen. The camera moves across the living room into the dining room. The mother comes out of the kitchen with a paper napkin and begins crumbing the table.

There is a knock on the rear porch door. The mother leaves her crumbing and goes into the kitchen. Camera goes with her. She opens the rear door to admit Aunt Catherine, holding a worn old European carpetbag. The aunt starts to go deeper into the kitchen, but the mother stays her with her hand.

MOTHER: [In low, conspiratorial voice] *Hey, I come home from your house last night, Marty was here with a girl.*
AUNT: *Who?*
MOTHER: *Marty.*
AUNT: *Your son Marty?*
MOTHER: *Well, what Marty you think is gonna be here in this house with a girl?*
AUNT: *Were the lights on?*
MOTHER; *Oh, sure.* [Frowns suddenly at her sister] *The girl is a college graduate.*
AUNT: *They're the worst. College girls are one step from the streets. They smoke like men inna saloon.*

The aunt puts her carpetbag down and sits on one of the wooden kitchen chairs. The mother sits on another.

MOTHER: *That's the first time Marty ever brought a girl to this house. She seems like a nice girl. I think he has a feeling for this girl.*

At this moment a burst of spirited whistling emanates from Marty's bedroom.

CUT TO: Marty's bedroom—Marty standing in front of his mirror, buttoning his shirt or adjusting his tie, whistling a gay tune.

CUT BACK TO: The two sisters, both their faces turned in the direction of the whistling. The whistling abruptly stops. The two sisters look at each other. The aunt shrugs.

MOTHER: *He been whistling like that all morning.*

The aunt nods bleakly.

AUNT: *He is bewitched. You will see. Today, tomorrow, inna week, he's gonna say to you: "Hey, Ma, it's no good being a single man. I'm tired running around." Then he's gonna say: "Hey, ma, wadda we need this old house? Why don't we sell this old house, move into a nicer parta town? A nice little apartment?"*

MOTHER: *I don't sell this house, I tell you that. This is my husband's house, and I had six children in this house.*

AUNT: *You will see. A couple-a months, you gonna be an old lady, sleeping onna couch in your daughter-in-law's house.*

MOTHER: *Catherine, you are a blanket of gloom. Wherever you go, the rain follows. Some day, you gonna smile, and we gonna declare a holiday.*

Another burst of spirited whistling comes from Marty, off. It comes closer, and Marty now enters in splendid spirits, whistling away. He is slipping into his jacket.

MARTY: [Ebulliently] *Hello, Aunt Catherine! How are you? You going to Mass with us?*

AUNT: *I was at Mass two hours ago.*

MARTY: *Well, make yourself at home. The refrigerator is loaded with food. Go upstairs, take any room you want. It's beautiful outside, ain't it?*

AUNT: *There's a chill. Watch out, you catch a good cold and pneumonia.*

MOTHER: *My sister Catherine, she can't even admit it's a beautiful day.*

> Marty—now at the sink, getting himself a glass of water—is examining a piece of plaster that has fallen from the ceiling.

MARTY: [Examining the chunk of plaster in his palm] *Boy, this place is really coming to pieces.* [Turns to mother] *You know, Ma, I think, sometime we oughtta sell this place. The plumbing is rusty—everything. I'm gonna have to replaster that whole ceiling now. I think we oughtta get a little apartment somewheres in a nicer parta town ... You all set, Ma?*

MOTHER: *I'm all set.*

> She starts for the porch door. She slowly turns and looks at Marty, and then at Aunt Catherine—who returns her look. Mother and Marty exit.

> DISSOLVE TO: Church. The mother comes out of the doors and down a few steps to where Marty is standing, enjoying the clearness of the June morning.

MOTHER: *In a couple-a minutes nine o'clock Mass is gonna start—in a couple-a minutes ...* [To passers-by off] *hallo, hallo ...* [To Marty] *Well, that was a nice girl last night, Marty. That was a nice girl.*

MARTY: *Yeah.*

MOTHER: *She wasn't a very good-looking girl, but she looked like a nice girl. I said, she wasn't a very good-looking girl, not very pretty.*

MARTY: *I heard you, Ma.*

MOTHER: *She look a little old for you, about thirty-five, forty years old?*

MARTY: *She's twenny-nine, Ma.*

MOTHER: *She's more than twenny-nine years old, Marty. That's what she tells you. She looks thirty-five, forty. She didn't look Italian to me. I said, is she an Italian girl?*

MARTY: *I don't know. I don't think so.*

MOTHER: *She don't look like Italian to me. What kinda family she come from? There was something about her I don't like. It seems funny, the first time you meet her she comes to your empty house alone. These college girls, they all one step from the streets.*

Marty turns, frowning, to his mother.

MARTY: *What are you talkin' about? She's a nice girl.*

MOTHER: *I don't like her.*

MARTY: *You don't like her? You only met her for two minutes.*

MOTHER: *Don't bring her to the house no more.*

MARTY: *What didn't you like about her?*

MOTHER: *I don't know! She don't look like Italian to me, plenty nice Italian girls around.*

MARTY: *Well, let's not get into a fight about it, Ma. I just met the girl. I probably won't see her again.*

Marty leaves frame.

MOTHER: *Eh, I'm no better than my sister Catherine.*

DISSOLVE TO: Interior, the bar . . . about an hour later. The after-Mass crowd is there, about six men ranging from twenty to forty. A couple of women in the booths. One woman is holding a glass of beer in one hand and is gently rocking a baby carriage with the other.

Sitting in the booth of Act I are Angie and three other fellows, ages twenty, thirty-two, and forty. One of the fellows, aged thirty-two, is giving a critical résumé of a recent work of literature by Mickey Spillane.

CRITIC: *. . . So the whole book winds up, Mike Hammer, he's inna room there with this doll. So he says: "You rat, you are the murderer." So she begins to con him, you know? She tells him how she loves him. And then Bam!*

He shoots her in the stomach. So she's laying there, gasping for breath, and she says: "How could you do that?" And he says: "It was easy."

TWENTY-YEAR-OLD: *Boy, that Mickey Spillane. Boy, he can write.*

ANGIE: [Leaning out of the booth and looking down the length of the bar, says with some irritation] *What's keeping Marty?*

CRITIC: *What I like about Mickey Spillane is he knows how to handle women. In one book, he picks up a tomato who gets hit with a car, and she throws a pass at him. And then he meets two beautiful twins, and they throw passes at him. And then he meets some beautiful society leader, and she throws a pass at him, and . . .*

TWENTY-YEAR-OLD: *Boy, that Mickey Spillane, he sure can write . . .*

ANGIE: [Looking out, down the bar again] *I don't know watsa matter with Marty.*

FORTY-YEAR-OLD: *Boy, Angie, what would you do if Marty ever died? You'd die right with him. A couple-a old bachelors hanging to each other like barnacles. There's Marty now.*

Angie leans out of the booth.

ANGIE: [Calling out] *Hello, Marty, where you been?*

CUT TO: Front end of the bar. Marty has just come in. He waves back to Angie, acknowledges another hello from a man by the bar, goes over to the bar, and gets the bartender's attention.

MARTY: *Hello, Lou, gimme change of a half and put a dime in it for a telephone call.*

The bartender takes the half dollar, reaches into his apron pocket for the change.

BARTENDER: *I hear you was at the Waverly Ballroom last night.*

MARTY: *Yeah. Angie tell you?*

BARTENDER: [Picking out change from palm full of silver] *Yeah, I hear you really got stuck with a dog.*

Marty looks at him.

MARTY: *She wasn't so bad.*

BARTENDER: [Extending the change] *Angie says she was a real scrawny-looking thing. Well, you can't have good luck alla time.*

Marty takes the change slowly and frowns down at it. He moves down the bar and would make for the telephone booth, but Angie hails him from the booth.

ANGIE: *Who you gonna call, Marty?*

MARTY: *I was gonna call that girl from last night, take her to a movie tonight.*

ANGIE: *Are you kidding?*

MARTY: *She was a nice girl. I kinda liked her.*

ANGIE: [Indicating the spot in the booth vacated by the forty-year-old] *Siddown. You can call her later.*

Marty pauses, frowning, and then shuffles to the booth where Angie and the other two sit. The critic moves over for Marty. There is an exchange of hellos.

TWENTY-YEAR-OLD: *I gotta girl, she's always asking me to marry her. So I look at that face, and I say to myself: "Could I stand looking at that face for the resta my life?"*

CRITIC: *Hey, Marty, you ever read a book called* I, the Jury, *by Mickey Spillane?*

MARTY: *No.*

ANGIE: *Listen, Marty, I gotta good place for us to go tonight. The kid here, he says, he was downna bazaar at Our Lady of Angels last night and . . .*

MARTY: *I don't feel like going to the bazaar, Angie. I thought I'd take this girl to a movie.*

ANGIE: *Boy, you really musta made out good last night.*

MARTY: *We just talked.*

ANGIE: *Boy, she must be some talker. She musta been about fifty years old.*

CRITIC: *I always figger a guy oughtta marry a girl who's*

twenny years younger than he is, so that when he's forty,
his wife is a real nice-looking doll.

TWENTY-YEAR-OLD: *That means he'd have to marry the*
girl when she was one year old.

CRITIC: *I never thoughta that.*

MARTY: *I didn't think she was so bad-looking.*

ANGIE: *She musta kept you inna shadows all night.*

CRITIC: *Marty, you don't wanna hang around with dogs.*
It gives you a bad reputation.

ANGIE: *Marty, let's go downna bazaar.*

MARTY: *I told this dog I was gonna call her today.*

ANGIE: *Brush her.*

Marty looks questioningly at Angie.

MARTY: *You didn't like her at all?*

ANGIE: *A nothing. A real nothing.*

Marty looks down at the dime he has been nervously turning
between two fingers and then, frowning, he slips it into his
jacket pocket. He lowers his face and looks down, scowling at
his thoughts. Around him, the voices clip along.

CRITIC: *What's playing on Fordham Road? I think there's*
a good picture in the Loew's Paradise.

ANGIE: *Let's go down to Forty-second Street and walk*
around. We're sure to wind up with something.

Slowly Marty begins to look up again. He looks from face to
face as each speaks.

CRITIC: *I'll never forgive La Guardia for cutting burlesque*
outta New York City.

TWENTY-YEAR-OLD: *There's burlesque over in Union City.*
Let's go to Union City....

ANGIE: *Ah, they're always crowded on Sunday night.*

CRITIC: *So wadda you figure on doing tonight, Angie?*

ANGIE: *I don't know. Wadda you figure on doing?*

CRITIC: *I don't know.* [Turns to the twenty-year-old.]
Wadda you figure on doing?

The twenty-year-old shrugs.

Suddenly Marty brings his fist down on the booth table

with a crash. The others turn, startled, toward him. Marty rises in his seat.

MARTY: *"What are you doing tonight?" "I don't know, what are you doing?" Burlesque! Loew's Paradise! Miserable and lonely! Miserable and lonely and stupid! What am I, crazy or something?! I got something good! What am I hanging around with you guys for?!*

He has said this in tones so loud that it attracts the attention of everyone in the bar. A little embarrassed, Marty turns and moves quickly to the phone booth, pausing outside the door to find his dime again. Angie is out of his seat immediately and hurries after him.

ANGIE: [A little shocked at Marty's outburst] *Watsa matter with you?*

MARTY: [In a low, intense voice] *You don't like her. My mother don't like her. She's a dog, and I'm a fat, ugly little man. All I know is I had a good time last night. I'm gonna have a good time tonight. If we have enough good times together, I'm going down on my knees and beg that girl to marry me. If we make a party again this New Year's, I gotta date for the party. You don't like her, that's too bad.* [He moves into the booth, sits, turns again to Angie, smiles.] *When you gonna get married, Angie? You're thirty-four years old. All your kid brothers are married. You oughtta be ashamed of yourself.*

Still smiling at his private joke, he puts the dime into the slot and then—with a determined finger—he begins to dial.

FADE OUT.

THE END

Marty

Marty and *The Mother* are bundled together in one discussion because each represents in its own way the sort of material that does best on television. They both deal with the world of the mundane, the ordinary, and the untheatrical. The main characters are typical, rather than exceptional; the situations are easily identifiable by the audience; and the relationships are as common as people. The essence of these two shows lies in their literal reality. I tried to write the dialogue as if it had been wire-tapped. I tried to envision the scenes as if a camera had been focused upon the unsuspecting characters and had caught them in an untouched moment of life.

This sort of meticulous literalness is something that can be done in no other medium. On the stage, reality is a highly synthesized thing. The closest thing to reality I ever saw on the stage was in *Death of a Salesman*, but even this extraordinary play involved a suicide and an incident in which the son discovers his father in a hotel room with a woman other than his mother. These are excellent dramatic incidents, but they are not everyday occurrences in the life of the lower middle class. In writing the stage play, it is necessary to contrive exciting moments of theater. You may write about ordinary people, but the audience sees them in unordinary and untypical circumstances.

To a lesser degree, this is also true of the movies, especially American movies. *The Bicycle Thief*, an Italian masterpiece, got about as close to an ordinary day in an unemployed man's life as you can get in a movie; but even this picture required a special urgency of incident. Most movies, even the good ones, are based upon the extraordinary incident and the exceptional character.

In television, however, the same insights into a character or into a social milieu can be made with the most identifiable characters and the most commonplace situations. I set out in *Marty* to write a love story, the most ordinary love story in the world. I didn't want my hero to be handsome, and I didn't want the girl to be pretty. I wanted to write a love story the way it would literally have happened to the kind of people I know I was, in fact, determined to shatter the shallow and destructive illusions—prospered by cheap fiction and bad movies—that love is simply a matter of physical attraction, that virility is manifested by a throbbing phallus, and that regular orgasms are all that's needed to make a woman happy. These values are dominant in our way of life and need to be examined for what they are. Certainly I and everybody I know have at least once in our lives brushed off a girl we rather liked because our friends thought she was unattractive. In *Marty*, I ventured lightly into such values as the Oedipal relationship, the reversion to adolescence by many "normal" Americans, and the latent homosexuality of the middle class. I did not make a purposeful study of these values; I only mention them to show that as quiet as a television play may be, it need not yield anything in depth. An excellent story could be written about the latent homosexuality in the "normal" American male, and television would be the only medium I know of that could present the problem as it really exists.

On the stage, the incidents would have to be so definitized that the main character would not be a "normal" fellow. There are two plays on Broadway now [1954] dealing with homosexuality in one way or another. The first deals with a girl who married a homosexual. The second deals with an incident of alleged homosexuality in a boys' school. In both cases, the circumstances are exceptional and the main characters are not people that most of us know in our circle of friends. The homosexuality that television would explore would be one not of flagrant starkness, but of the hidden—sometimes terrifying—impulses deep within all of us. Most American men have decided homosexual impulses; the dramatic writer hardly needs Kinsey to prove that. We are for the most part an adolescent people; and adolescence is a semihomosexual stage in which the boys hang around together, feeling more comfortable among their own sex than with girls. Most of us grow older but never quite shake off our adolescent behavior patterns. Latent homosexuality is perfectly normal; but so much stigma is attached to it that it provokes fears and anxieties, guilts and depressions. It would be difficult to get most Americans to admit they have these impulses; indeed, most Americans hide from the thought of them.

The man who proudly proclaims how virile he is could very well be a man who is so unsure of his virility that he needs to re-establish it over and over again. The married man who chases other women might well be doing this to confirm his manliness in his own mind. He is probably being driven by a fear of homosexuality as it has manifested itself in his lack of desire for his wife, or even in more positive homosexual actions. This man would perhaps be revolted by the idea of making love to another man; he probably jokes about pansies and faggots as most of us do. He has a wife and three children. He likes to look at pictures of semi-dressed women. He is, in fact, a perfectly normal fellow except for the fact that he has to drive himself to make love to his wife. As bedtime approaches, he becomes more and more anxious, frightened of the demands his wife may make upon him, even more frightened that he will not be able to satisfy her demands. The fact that he does not have to satisfy her demands never enters his mind, for he is governed by a set of social values which tell him that virility is measured in orgasms. Rather than admit his inadequacy in the face of these impossible values, he blames his wife. ("My wife is a cold woman," "A man has to change his oil every now and then," "Man is not a monogamous person," etc.) In order to keep his sense of virility bolstered, he throws a pass at some other woman.

Certainly, this is not a study in abnormality. Thousands of married men throw thousands of passes at thousands of other women. It is as much a part of the American scene as honeysuckle. Nothing happens in this story except that a married man throws a pass at some girl. Yet deep within the framework of that gesture lies a wonderful area of drama and insight. Of course, the writer has to delineate his characters and select his sequence of scenes so that this very normal piece of behavior is clearly understood by the audience. But that's what makes writing.

If this story were done on the stage, you would find that the simple throwing of a pass barely makes your first-act curtain. You would have to invent much more incisive scenes and incidents. I cannot imagine a stage play on this subject which wouldn't require a scene showing the man ending up with a rank homosexual, so that the dramatic point is made. Or else you would have to write pages of pseudopsychoanalysis in order to get the point across. The theater audience is so far away from the actual action of the drama. They cannot see the silent reactions of the players. They must be told in a loud voice what is going on. The plot movement from one scene to another must be marked, rather than gently shaded as is required in television. In the end, you would have a play that would interest the audience a good deal, but not to the point where they would say, "My God, that's just like me."

Marty, of course, was not intended as a study of homosexuality or even as a study of the Oedipus complex. It was a comment on the social values of our times and, as such, its characters were not probed to the bottom. There is a distinct homosexual relationship between Marty and Angie, but to make anything of it would have been out of perspective. It likewise would have been in bad taste to develop Marty's relationship to his mother beyond what was shown. I was only interested in motivating the mother on a social level—that is, as a displaced ex-mother, rather than as a woman tied by deep emotional bonds to her son. For one thing, there is nothing abnormal about her attachment to her son. Marty does eventually break away from his mother. This was not a story about the silver cord.

In producing *Marty*, this is something to guard against vigilantly. Most of us are aware of the primitive Freudian explanations of our relationships to each other. The Oedipus complex is hardly an esoteric piece of psychoanalytic jargon; it is a commonly used and understood conversational phrase. Actors, and especially directors, rather imagine they are making astounding dramatic insights when they read such rudimentary psychology into the parts. *Marty* was not intended as a psychological study, and it should not be played that way. It is, of course, sound theater for the actors to know how they relate to the other actors of the script; but they must be disciplined from plunging beyond the level of the show. It is important that Marty and his mother be on terms of successful communication, and the actor should not play the profound resentments and antagonisms that are inherent in the Oedipus complex.

I must mention at this point that the actor who played Marty, Rod Steiger, is one of the most gifted young actors in the theater, and I owe him a genuine debt of gratitude for all that he contributed to this show.

The Mother, like *Marty*, is a good example of proper television material. It tells a small story about a familiar character and pursues this small story with relentless literalness to one small synthesized moment of crisis. But what makes *The Mother* particularly interesting to me is that it has begun to open up for me a whole new area of writing. The most fascinating character in the script is not the mother at all, but the daughter. Here is a study in subconscious guilts and resentments. I had to keep holding myself back from really exploring the daughter's story for fear the rest of my story would be thrown out of perspective.

The daughter is a girl who is still trying to buy her mother's love by sacrifice and by playing the role of the dutiful child. Children within a family fight fiercely for their mother's love, and this girl got the short end of the stick. She was obviously an unwanted child to whom the mother gave a grudging, dutiful attention. The girl grew up envious and resentful, fighting with her brother and sister, able only to negotiate with other people on the basis of sacrifice. She has become the sort of girl who is known as a generous, loyal friend and who is described by everyone as a person who would give you the shirt off her back. For she has learned only this way of gaining people's affection—by sacrificing, by constantly giving of herself. She cooks and cleans and sews for her husband; she does everything for her children, much too much, in fact. Throughout her life she will serve her mother slavishly, always hoping to be chosen as the favorite child. Under her thick surface of duty, she really resents—even hates—her mother. Her attempts to get her mother to give up her apartment represent subconscious desires to hurt her mother for denying her love.

If this strikes you as a quick piece of neopsychoanalysis, that is just what it is. Nevertheless, it is a pretty rational understanding of this girl, and it can be dramatized. As a kind of dramatic writing, it is unique. Playwrights have never plumbed the subconscious levels of their characters, except perhaps in the broadest and most primitive fashion. In television, you can dig into the most humble, ordinary relationships: the relationships of bourgeois children to their mother, of middle-class husband to wife, of white-collar father to his secretary—in short, the relationships of the people.

I do not like to theorize about drama. I suspect the academic writer, the fellow who can precisely articulate his theater. However, it is my current belief that the function of the writer is to give the audience some shred of meaning to the otherwise meaningless patterns of their lives. Our lives are filled with endless moments of stimulus and depression. We relate to each other in an incredibly complicated manner. Every fiber of relationship is worth a dramatic study. There is far more exciting drama in the reasons why a man gets married than in why he murders someone. The man who is unhappy in his job, the wife who thinks of a lover, the girl who wants to get into television, your father, mother, sister, brothers, cousins, friends—all these are better subjects for drama than Iago. What makes a man ambitious? Why does one girl always try to steal her kid sister's boy friends? Why does your uncle attend his annual class reunion faithfully every year? Why do you always find it depressing to visit your father? These are the substances of good television drama; and the deeper you probe into and examine the twisted, semiformed complexes of emotional entanglements, the more exciting your writing becomes.

Television is a strange medium, limited by a thousand technical problems, hemmed in by taboos and advertising policies, cheapened by the innumerable untalented and officious people you will always find in a billion-dollar industry. Nevertheless, for the writer there is still area for deep and unprobed work. I am just now becoming aware of this area, this marvelous world of the ordinary. This is an age of savage introspection, and television is the dramatic medium through which to expose our new insights into ourselves. The stage is too weighty, and the movies too intense, to deal with the mundane and all its obscured ramifications. More and more, the television writers are turning away from the slapdash activity of the violence show and turning to the needlelike perception of human relationships. Television need not be a demeaning sequence of panel shows and horror, of cooking classes and family situation comedies. You can write honest dramatic literature for television, rewarding to your sense of pride. Certainly, there were four or five hour shows last year that were far and away superior to anything on the current Broadway stage or anything issued by the movie industry. Perhaps they might even start paying the television writer a decent wage for his work.

The Mother

DIRECTED BY: DELBERT MANN
ASSOCIATE PRODUCER: GORDON DUFF
PRODUCED BY: FRED COE

Cast

OLD LADY	Cathleen Nesbitt
DAUGHTER	Maureen Stapleton
BOSS	David Opatoshu
SON-IN-LAW	George L. Smith
NEGRO WOMAN	Estelle Hemsley
SISTER	Perry Wilson
MRS. GEEGAN	Katherine Hynes
MRS. KLINE	Dora Weissman
BOOKKEEPER	Anna Berger
PUERTO RICAN GIRL	Violeta Diaz

ACT I

FADE IN: Film—a quick group of shots showing New York in a real thunderstorm—rain whipping through the streets—real miserable weather.

DISSOLVE TO: Close-up of an old woman, aged sixty-six, with a shock of gray-white hair, standing by a window in her apartment, looking out, apparently deeply disturbed by the rain slashing against the pane.

We pull back to see that the old woman is wearing an old kimono, under which there is evidence of an old white batiste nightgown. Her gray-white hair hangs loosely down over her shoulders. It is early morning, and she has apparently just gotten out of bed. This is the bedroom of her two-and-a-half-room apartment in a lower-middle-class neighborhood in the Bronx. The bed is still unmade and looks just slept in. The furniture is old and worn. On the chest of drawers there is a galaxy of photographs and portrait pictures, evidently of her various children and grandchildren. She stands looking out the window, troubled, disturbed.

Suddenly the alarm, perched on the little bed table, rings. Camera moves in for close-up of the alarm clock. It reads half past six. The old lady's hand comes down and shuts the alarm off.

CUT TO: Close-up of another alarm clock, ringing in another apartment. It also reads half past six; but it is obviously a different clock, on a much more modern bed table. This one buzzes instead of clangs. A young woman's hand reaches over and turns it off.

Camera pulls back to show that we are in the bedroom of a young couple. The young woman who has turned the clock off is a rather plain girl of thirty. She slowly sits up in bed, assembling herself for the day. On the other half of the bed, her husband turns and tries to go back to sleep.

SON-IN-LAW: [From under the blankets] *What time is it?*
DAUGHTER: [Still seated heavily on the edge of the bed]
It's half past six.
SON-IN-LAW: [From under the blankets] *What did you
set it so early for?*
DAUGHTER: *I wanna call my mother.* [She looks out at the
window, the rain driving fiercely against it.] *For heaven's
sake, listen to that rain! She's not going down today, I'll
tell you that, if I have to go over there and chain her in her
bed* . . . [She stands, crosses to the window, studies the
rain.] *Boy, look at it rain.*
SON-IN-LAW: [Still under the covers] *What?*
DAUGHTER: *I said, it's raining.*

> She makes her way, still heavy with sleep, out of the bedroom
> into the foyer of the apartment. She pads in her bare feet and
> pajamas down the foyer to the telephone table, sits on the
> little chair, trying to clear her head of sleep. A baby's cry is
> suddenly heard in an off room. The young woman absently
> goes "Sshh." The baby's cry stops. The young woman picks up
> the receiver of the phone and dials. She waits. Then . . .

DAUGHTER: *Ma? This is Annie. Did I wake you up?* . . . *I
figured you'd be up by now.* . . . *Ma, you're not going downtown today, and I don't wanna hear no arguments* . . . *Ma,
have you looked out the window? It's raining like* . . . *Ma,
I'm not gonna let you go downtown today, do you hear
me?* . . . *I don't care, Ma* . . . *Ma, I don't care* . . . *Ma, I'm
coming over. You stay there till* . . . *Ma, stay there till I
come over. I'm getting dressed right now. I'll drive over
in the car. It won't take me ten minutes* . . . *Ma, you're not
going out in this rain. It's not enough that you almost
fainted in the subway yesterday* . . . *Ma, I'm hanging up,
and I'm coming over right now. Stay there* . . . *all right,
I'm hanging up* . . .

> She hangs up, sits for a minute, then rises and shuffles quickly
> back up the foyer and back into her bedroom. She disappears
> into the bathroom, unbuttoning the blouse of her pajamas.

She leaves the bathroom door open, and a shaft of light suddenly shoots out into the dark bedroom.

SON-IN-LAW: [Awake now, his head visible over the covers] *Did you talk to her?*

DAUGHTER: [Off in bathroom] *Yeah, she was all practically ready to leave.*

SON-IN-LAW: *Look, Annie, I don't wanna tell you how to treat your own mother, but why don't you leave her alone? It's obviously very important to her to get a job for herself. She wants to support herself. She doesn't want to be a burden on her children. I respect her for that. An old lady, sixty-six years old, going out and looking for work. I think that shows a lot of guts.*

The daughter comes out of the bathroom. She has a blouse on now and a half-slip.

DAUGHTER: [Crossing to the closet] *George, please, you don't know what you're talking about, so do me a favor, and don't argue with me. I'm not in a good mood.* [She opens the closet, studies the crowded rack of clothes.] *I'm turning on the light, so get your eyes ready.* [She turns on the light. The room is suddenly bright. She blinks and pokes in the closet for a skirt, which she finally extracts.] *My mother worked like a dog all her life, and she's not gonna spend the rest of her life bent over a sewing machine.* [She slips into the skirt.] *She had one of her attacks in the subway yesterday. I was never so scared in my life when that cop called yesterday.* [She's standing in front of her mirror now, hastily arranging her hair.] *My mother worked like a dog to raise me and my brother and my sister. She worked in my old man's grocery store till twelve o'clock at night. We owe her a little peace of mind, my brother and my sister and me. She sacrificed plenty for us in her time.* [She's back at the closet, fishing for her topcoat.] *And I want her to move out of that apartment. I don't want her living alone. I want her to come live here with us, George, and I don't want any more arguments about that either. We can move Tommy in with the baby, and she can have Tommy's room. And that reminds me— the baby cried for a minute there. If she cries again, give her her milk because she went to sleep without her milk last night.* [She has her topcoat on now and is already at the door to the foyer.] *All right, I'll probably be back in time to make you breakfast. Have you got the keys to the car?* . . . [She nervously pats the pocket of her coat.] *No, I got them. All right, I'll see you. Good-by, George* . . .

She goes out into the foyer.

SON-IN-LAW: *Good-by, Annie* . . .

Off in some other room, the baby begins to cry again, a little more insistently. The husband raises his eyebrows and listens for a moment. When it becomes apparent that the baby isn't going to stop, he sighs and begins to get out of bed.

DISSOLVE TO: The old lady standing by the window again. She is fully dressed now, however, even to the black coat and hat. The coat is unbuttoned. For the first time, we may be aware of a black silk mourning band that the old lady has about the sleeve of her coat. Outside, the rain has abated considerably. It is drizzling lightly now. The old lady turns to her daughter, standing at the other end of the bedroom, brushing the rain from her coat. When the old lady speaks, it is with a mild, but distinct, Irish flavor.

OLD LADY: *It's letting up a bit.*

DAUGHTER: [Brushing off her coat] *It isn't letting up at all. It's gonna stop and start all day long.*

The old lady starts out of her bedroom, past her daughter, into her living room.

OLD LADY: *I'm going to make a bit of coffee for myself and some Rice Krispies. Would you like a cup?*

The daughter turns and starts into the living room ahead of her mother.

DAUGHTER: *I'll make it for you.*

OLD LADY: *You won't make it for me. I'll make it myself.*

She crowds past the daughter and goes to the kitchen. At the kitchen doorway, she turns and surveys her daughter.

OLD LADY: *Annie, you know, you can drive somebody crazy, do you know that?*

DAUGHTER: *I can drive somebody crazy?! You're the one who can drive somebody crazy.*

OLD LADY: *Will you stop hovering over me like I was a cripple in a wheel chair. I can make my own coffee, believe me. Why did you come over here? You've got a husband and two kids to take care of. Go make coffee for them, for heaven's sakes.*

She turns and goes into the kitchen, muttering away. She opens a cupboard and extracts a jar of instant coffee.

OLD LADY: *I've taken to making instant coffee, would you like a cup?*

The daughter is standing on the threshold of the kitchen now, leaning against the doorjamb.

DAUGHTER: *All right, make me a cup, Ma.*

The old lady takes two cups and saucers out and begins carefully to level out a teaspoonful of the instant coffee into each. The daughter moves into the kitchen, reaches up for something in the cupboard.

DAUGHTER: *Where do you keep your saccharin, Ma?*

The old lady wheels and slaps the daughter's outstretched arms down.

OLD LADY: *Annie, I'll get it myself!* [She points a finger into the living room.] *Go in there and sit down, will you?! I'll bring the cup in to you!*

The daughter leans back against the doorjamb, a little exasperated with the old lady's petulant independence. The old lady now takes an old teapot and sets it on the stove and lights a flame under it.

OLD LADY: *You can drive me to the subway if you want to do something for me.*

DAUGHTER: *Ma, you're not going downtown today.*

OLD LADY: *I want to get down there extra early today on*

the off-chance that they haven't given the job to someone
else. What did I do with that card from the New York
State Employment Service? . . .

> She shuffles out of the kitchen, the daughter moving out of
> the doorway to give her passage. The old lady goes to the table
> in the living room on which sits her battered black purse. She
> opens it and takes out a card.

OLD LADY: *I don't want to lose that.* [She puts the white
card back into her purse.] *I'm pretty sure I could have*
held onto this job, because the chap at the Employment
Service called up the boss, you see, over the phone, and
he explained to the man that I hadn't worked in quite a
number of years . . .

DAUGHTER: [Muttering] *Quite a number of years . . .*

OLD LADY: *. . . and that I'd need a day or so to get used to*
the machines again.

DAUGHTER: *Did the chap at the Employment Service ex-*
plain to the boss that it's forty years that you haven't
worked?

OLD LADY: [Crossing back to the kitchen] *. . . and the boss*
understood this, you see, so he would have been a little
lenient with me. But then, of course, I had to go and faint
in the subway, because I was in such a hurry to get down
there, you know, I didn't even stop to eat my lunch. I had
brought along some sandwiches, you see, cheese and to-
matoes. Oh, I hope he hasn't given the job to anyone
else . . .

> The old lady reaches into the cupboard again for a bowl of
> sugar, an opened box of Rice Krispies, and a bowl. The daugh-
> ter watches her as she turns to the refrigerator to get out a con-
> tainer of milk.

DAUGHTER: *Ma, when are you gonna give up?*

> The old lady frowns.

OLD LADY: *Annie, please . . .*

> She pours some Rice Krispies into the bowl.

DAUGHTER: *Ma, you been trying for three weeks now. If*

you get a job, you get fired before the day is over. You're too old, Ma, and they don't want to hire old people . . .

OLD LADY: *It's not the age . . .*

DAUGHTER: *They don't want to hire white-haired old ladies.*

OLD LADY: *It's not the age at all! I've seen plenty of old people with white hair and all, sitting at those machines. The shop where I almost had that job and he fired me the other day, there was a woman there, eighty years old if she was a day, an old crone of a woman, sitting there all bent over, her machine humming away. The chap at the Employment Service said there's a lot of elderly people working in the needle trades. The young people nowadays don't want to work for thirty-five, forty dollars a week, and there's a lot of old people working in the needle trades.*

DAUGHTER: *Well, whatever it is, Ma . . .*

OLD LADY: [Leaning to her daughter] *It's my fingers. I'm not sure of them any more. When you get old, y'know, you lose the sureness in your fingers. My eyes are all right, but my fingers tremble a lot. I get very excited, y'know, when I go in for a tryout, y'know. And I'll go in, y'know, and the boss'll say: "Sit down, let's see what you can do." And I get so excited. And my heart begins thumping so that I can hardly see to thread the needle. And they stand right over you, y'know, while you're working. They give you a packet of sleeves or a skirt or something to put a hem on. Or a seam or something, y'know. It's simple work, really. Single-needle machine. Nothing fancy. And it seems to me I do it all right, but they fire me all the time. They say: "You're too slow." And I'm working as fast as I can. I think, perhaps, I've lost the ability in my fingers. And that's what scares me the most. It's not the age. I've seen plenty of old women working in the shops.*

She has begun to pour some milk into her bowl of cereal; but she stops now and just stands, staring bleakly down at the worn oilcloth on her cupboard.

DAUGHTER: [Gently] *Ma, you worked all your life. Why don't you take it easy?*

OLD LADY: *I don't want to take it easy. Now that your father's dead and in the grave I don't know what to do with myself.*

DAUGHTER: *Why don't you go out, sit in the park, get a little sun like the other old women?*

OLD LADY: *I sit around here sometimes, going crazy. We had a lot of fights in our time, your father and I, but I must admit I miss him badly. You can't live with someone forty-one years and not miss him when he's dead. I'm glad that he died for his own sake—it may sound hard of me to say that—but I am glad. He was in nothing but pain the last few months, and he was a man who could never stand pain. But I do miss him.*

DAUGHTER: [Gently] *Ma, why don't you come live with George and me?*

OLD LADY: *No, no, Annie, you're a good daughter. . . .*

DAUGHTER: *We'll move Tommy into the baby's room, and you can have Tommy's room. It's the nicest room in the apartment. It gets all the sun . . .*

OLD LADY: *I have wonderful children. I thank God every night for that. I . . .*

DAUGHTER: *Ma, I don't like you living here alone . . .*

OLD LADY: *Annie, I been living in this house for eight years, and I know all the neighbors and the store people, and if I lived with you, I'd be a stranger.*

DAUGHTER: *There's plenty of old people in my neighborhood. You'll make friends.*

OLD LADY: *Annie, you're a good daughter, but I want to keep my own home. I want to pay my own rent. I don't want to be some old lady living with her children. If I can't take care of myself, I just as soon be in the grave with your father. I don't want to be a burden on my children . . .*

DAUGHTER: *Ma, for heaven's sakes . . .*

OLD LADY: *More than anything else, I don't want to be a*

burden on my children. I pray to God every night to let me keep my health and my strength so that I won't have to be a burden on my children . . . [The teapot suddenly hisses. The old lady looks up.] *Annie, the pot is boiling. Would you pour the water in the cups?*

The daughter moves to the stove. The old lady, much of her ginger seemingly sapped out of her, shuffles into the living room. She perches on the edge of one of the wooden chairs.

OLD LADY: *I been getting some pains in my shoulder the last week or so. I had the electric heating pad on practically the whole night. . . .* [She looks up toward the windows again.] *It's starting to rain a little harder again. Maybe, I won't go downtown today after all. Maybe, if it clears up a bit, I'll go out and sit in the park and get some sun.*

In the kitchen, the daughter pours the boiling water into each cup, stirs.

DAUGHTER: [To her mother, off in the living room] *Is this all you're eating for breakfast, Ma? Let me make you something else . . .*

DISSOLVE TO: A park bench. The old lady and two other old ladies are seated, all bundled up in their cheap cloth coats with the worn fur collars. The second old lady is also Irish. Her name is Mrs. Geegan. The third old lady is possibly Jewish, certainly a New Yorker by intonation. Her name is Mrs. Kline. The rain has stopped; it is a clear, bright, sunny March morning.

OLD LADY: *. . . Well, it's nice and clear now, isn't it? It was raining something fierce around seven o'clock this morning.*

MRS. GEEGAN: [Grimacing] *It's too ruddy cold for me. I'd go home except my daughter-in-law is cleaning the house, and I don't want to get in her way.*

MRS. KLINE: *My daughter-in-law should drop dead tomorrow.*

MRS. GEEGAN: *My daughter-in-law gets into an awful black temper when she's cleaning.*

MRS. KLINE: *My daughter-in-law should grow rich and own a hotel with a thousand rooms and be found dead in every one of them.*

MRS. GEEGAN: [To the old lady] *I think I'll go over and visit Missus Halley in a little while, would you like to go? She fell down the stairs and broke her hip, and they're suing the owners of the building. I saw her son yesterday, and he says she's awful weak. When you break a hip at that age, you're as good as in the coffin. I don't like to visit Missus Halley. She's always so gloomy about things. But it's a way of killing off an hour or so to lunch. A little later this afternoon, I thought I'd go to confession. It's so warm and solemn in the church. Do you go to Saint John's? I think it's ever so much prettier than Our Lady of Visitation. Why don't you come to Missus Halley's with me, Missus Fanning? Her son's a sweet man, and there's always a bit of fruit they offer you.*

OLD LADY: *I don't believe I know a Missus Halley.*

MRS. GEEGAN: *Missus Halley, the one that fell down the stairs last week and dislocated her hip. They're suing the owners of the building for forty thousand dollars.*

MRS. KLINE: *They'll settle for a hundred, believe me.*

MRS. GEEGAN: *Oh, it's chilly this morning. I'd go home, but my daughter-in-law is cleaning the house, and she doesn't like me to be about when she's cleaning. I'd like a bottle of beer, that's what I'd like. Oh, my mouth is fairly watering for it. I'm not allowed to have beer, you know. I'm a diabetic. You don't happen to have a quarter on you, Missus Fanning? We could buy a bottle and split it between us. I'd ask my son for it, but they always want to know what I want the money for.*

OLD LADY: [Looking sharply at Mrs. Geegan] *Do you have to ask your children for money?*

MRS. GEEGAN: *Oh, they're generous. They always give me*

*whenever I ask. But I'm not allowed to have beer, you
see, and they wouldn't give me the twenty-five cents for
that. What do I need money for anyway? Go to the movies? I haven't been to the movies in more than a year, I
think. I just like a dollar every now and then for an offering at mass. Do you go to seven o'clock novena, Missus
Fanning? It's a good way to spend an hour, I think.*

OLD LADY: *Is that what you do with your day, Missus
Geegan? Visit dying old ladies and go to confession?*

MRS. GEEGAN: *Well, I like to stay in the house a lot, watching television. There's ever so much fun on television in
the afternoons, with the kiddie shows and a lot of dancing and Kate Smith and shows like that. But my daughter-
in-law's cleaning up today, and she doesn't like me around
the house when she's cleaning, so I came out a bit early
to sit in the park.*

The old lady regards Mrs. Geegan for a long moment.

MRS. KLINE: *My daughter-in-law, she should invest all her
money in General Motors stock, and they should go bankrupt.*

A pause settles over the three old ladies. They just sit, hud-
dled, their cheeks pressed into the fur of their collars. After a
moment, the old lady shivers noticeably.

OLD LADY: *It's a bit chilly. I think I'll go home.* [She rises.]
Good-by, Missus Geegan . . . Good-by, Missus . . .

The other two old ladies nod their good-bys. The old lady
moves off screen. We hold for a moment on the remaining
two old ladies, sitting, shoulders hunched against the morning
chill, faces pressed under their collars, staring bleakly ahead.

DISSOLVE TO: Door of the old lady's apartment. It opens,
and the old lady comes in. She closes the door behind her,
goes up the small foyer to the living room. She unbuttons her
coat and walks aimlessly around the room, into the bedroom
and out again, across the living room and into the kitchen,
and then out of the kitchen. She is frowning as she walks and

rubs her hands continually as if she is quite cold. Suddenly
she goes to the telephone, picks it up, dials a number, waits.

OLD LADY: [Snappishly] *Is this Mister McCleod?! This is
Missus Fanning in Apartment 3F! The place is a refrigerator up here! It's freezing! I want some steam! I want it
right now! That's all there is to it! I want some steam right
now!*

She hangs up sharply, turns—scowling—and sits heavily down
on the edge of a soft chair, scowling, nervous, rocking a little
back and forth. Then abruptly she rises, crosses the living
room to the television set, clicks it on. She stands in front of
it, waiting for a picture to show. At last the picture comes on.
It is the WPIX station signal, accompanied by the steady
high-pitched drone that indicates there are no programs on
yet. She turns the set off almost angrily.

She is beginning to breathe heavily now. She turns nervously and looks at the large ornamental clock on the side-
board. It reads ten minutes after eleven. She goes to the small
dining table and sits down on one of the hard-back chairs. Her
black purse is still on the table, as it was during the scene with
her daughter. Her eyes rest on it for a moment; then she
reaches over, opens the purse, and takes out the white employment card. She looks at it briefly, expressionlessly. Then
she returns it to the purse and reclasps the purse. Again she
sits for a moment, rigid, expressionless. Then suddenly she
stands, grabs the purse, and starts out the living room, down
the foyer, to the front door of her apartment—buttoning her
coat as she goes. She opens the door, goes out.

Camera stays on door as it is closed. There is the noise of a
key being inserted into the lock. A moment later the bolts on
the lock shift into locked position. Hold.

FADE OUT.

ACT II

FADE IN: Film. Lunchtime in the needle-trade district of New York—a quick montage of shots of the streets, jammed with traffic, trucks, and working people hurrying to the dense little luncheonettes for their lunch.

DISSOLVE TO: Interior of the Tiny Tots Sportswear Co., Inc., 137 West Twenty-seventh Street, on the eighth floor. It is lunchtime. We dissolve in on some of the women operators at their lunch. They are seated at their machines, of which there are twenty—in two rows of ten, facing each other. Not all of the operators eat their lunch in: about half go downstairs to join the teeming noontime crowds in the oily little restaurants of the vicinity. The ten-or-so women whom we see —munching their sandwiches and sipping their containers of coffee and chattering shrilly to one another—all wear worn house dresses. A good proportion of the operators are Negro and Puerto Rican. Not a few of them are gray-haired, or at least unmistakably middle-aged.

The rest of the shop seems to consist of endless rows of pipe racks on which hang finished children's dresses, waiting to be shipped. In the middle of these racks is a pressing machine and sorting table at which two of the three men who work in the shop eat their lunch. At the far end of the loft—in a corner so dark that a light must always be on over it—is an old, battered roll-top desk at which sits the bookkeeper, an angular woman of thirty-five, differentiated from the hand workers in that she wears a clean dress.

Nearby is the boss, a man in his thirties. He is bent over a machine, working on it with a screw driver. The boss is really a pleasant man; he works under the illusion, however, that gruffness is a requisite quality of an executive.

Somehow, a tortured passageway has been worked out between the racks leading to the elevator doors; it is the only visible exit and entrance to the loft.

As we look at these doors, there is a growing whirring and clanging announcing the arrival of the elevator. The doors slide reluctantly open, and the old lady enters the shop. The elevator doors slide closed behind her. She stands surrounded by pipe racks, a little apprehensive. The arrival of the elevator has caused some of the people to look up briefly. The old lady goes to the presser, a Puerto Rican.

OLD LADY: *Excuse me, I'm looking for the boss.*

The presser indicates with his hand the spot where the boss is standing, working on the machine. The old lady picks her way through the cluttered pipe racks to the bookkeeper, who looks up at her approach. The boss also looks up briefly at her approach, but goes back to his work. The old lady opens her purse, takes out the white card, and proffers it to the bookkeeper. She mutters something.

BOOKKEEPER: *Excuse me, I can't hear what you said.*

OLD LADY: *I said, I was supposed to be here yesterday, but I was sick in the subway—I fainted, you see, and ...*

The boss now turns to the old lady.

BOSS: *What? ... What? ...*

OLD LADY: *I was sent down from the ...*

BOSS: *What?*

OLD LADY: [Louder] *I was sent down from the New York State Employment Service. I was supposed to be here yesterday.*

BOSS: *Yes, so what happened?*

OLD LADY: *I was sick. I fainted in the subway.*

BOSS: *What?*

OLD LADY: [Louder] *I was sick. The subway was so hot there, you see—there was a big crush at a Hundred and forty-ninth Street ...*

BOSS: *You was supposed to be here yesterday.*

OLD LADY: *I had a little trouble. They had my daughter down there and everything. By the time I got down here,*

*it was half past five, and the fellow on the elevator—not
the one that was here this morning—another fellow entirely. An old man it was. He said there was nobody up
here. So I was going to come down early this morning, but
I figured you probably had the job filled anyway. That's
why I didn't come down till now.*

BOSS: *What kind of work do you do?*

OLD LADY: *Well, I used to do all sections except joining
and zippers, but I think the fellow at the Employment
Service explained to you that it's been a number of years
since I actually worked in a shop.*

BOSS: *What do you mean, a number of years?*

OLD LADY: [Mumbling] *Well, I did a lot of sewing for the
Red Cross during the war, y'know, but I haven't actually
worked in a shop since 1916.*

BOSS: [Who didn't quite hear her mumbled words] *What?*

OLD LADY: [Louder] *Nineteen sixteen. October.*

BOSS: *Nineteen sixteen.*

OLD LADY: *I'm sure if I could work a little bit, I would be
fine. I used to be a very fast worker.*

BOSS: *Can you thread a machine?*

The old lady nods.

He starts off through the maze of pipe racks to the two rows
of machines. The old lady follows after him, clutching her
purse and the white card, her hat still sitting on her head, her
coat still buttoned. As they go up the rows of sewing machines,
the other operators look up to catch covert glimpses of the
new applicant. The boss indicates one of the open machines.

BOSS: *All right. Siddown. Show me how you thread a machine.*

The old lady sets her purse down nervously and takes the seat
behind the machine. The other operators have all paused in
their eating to watch the test. The old lady reaches to her side,
where there are several spools of thread.

OLD LADY: *What kind of thread, white or black? . . .*

BOSS: *White! White!*

She fumblingly fetches a spool of white thread and, despite the fact she is obviously trembling, she contrives to thread the machine—a process which takes about half a minute. The boss stands towering over her.

BOSS: *Can you make a sleeve?*

The old lady nods, desperately trying to get the thread through the eye of the needle and over the proper holes.

BOSS: *It's a simple business. One seam.*

He reaches into the bin belonging to the machine next to the one the old lady is working on and extracts a neatly tied bundle of sleeve material. He drops it on the table beside the old lady.

BOSS: *All right, make a sleeve. Let's see how you make a sleeve.*

He breaks the string and gives her a piece of sleeve material. She takes it, but is so nervous it falls to the floor. She hurriedly bends to pick it up, inserts the sleeve into the machine, and hunches into her work—her face screwed tight with intense concentration. She has still not unbuttoned her coat, and beads of sweat begin to appear on her brow. With painstaking laboriousness, she slowly moves the sleeve material into the machine. The boss stands, impatient and scowling.

BOSS: *Mama, what are you weaving there, a carpet? It's a lousy sleeve, for Pete's sake.*

OLD LADY: *I'm a little unsure. My fingers are a little unsure . . .*

BOSS: *You gotta be fast, Mama. This is week work. It's not piecework. I'm paying you by the hour. I got twenny dozen cottons here, gotta be out by six o'clock. The truckman isn't gonna wait, you know . . . Mama, Mama, watch what you're doing there . . .* [He leans quickly forward and reguides the material.] *A straight seam, for heaven's sake! You're making it crooked! . . . Watch it! Watch it! Watch what you're doing there, Mama . . . All right, sew. Don't let me make you nervous. Sew . . . Mama, wadda you sewing there, an appendicitis operation? It's a lousy*

*sleeve. How long you gonna take? I want operators here,
not surgeons . . .*

Through all this, the terrified old lady tremblingly pushes the
material through the machine. Finally she's finished. She
looks up at the boss, her eyes wide with apprehension, ready
to pick up her purse and dash out to the street. The boss picks
up the sleeve, studies it, then drops it on the table, mutters.

BOSS: *All right, we'll try you out for a while . . .*

He turns abruptly and goes back through the pipe racks to the
desk. The old lady sits, trembling, a little slumped, her
coat still buttoned to the collar. A middle-aged Negro woman,
sitting at the next machine over her lunch, leans over to the
old lady.

NEGRO WOMAN: [Gently] *Mama, what are you sitting there
in your hat and coat for? Hang them up, honey. You go
through that door over there.*

She points to a door leading into a built-in room. The old lady
looks up slowly at this genuine sympathy.

NEGRO WOMAN: *Don't let him get you nervous, Mama. He
likes to yell a lot, but he's okay.*

The tension within the old lady suddenly bursts out in the
form of a soft, staccato series of sighs. She quickly masters
herself.

OLD LADY: [Smiling at the Negro woman] *I'm a little unsure of myself. My fingers are a little unsure.*

CUT TO: The boss, standing by the desk. He leans down to
mutter to the bookkeeper.

BOSS: [Muttering] *How could I say no, will you tell me?
How could I say no? . . .*

BOOKKEEPER: *Nobody says you should say no.*

BOSS: *She was so nervous, did you see how nervous she
was? I bet you she's seventy years old. How could I say
no?* [The telephone suddenly rings.] *Answer . . .*

The bookkeeper picks up the receiver.

BOOKKEEPER: [On the phone] *Tiny Tots Sportswear . . .*

BOSS: [In a low voice] *Who is it?*

BOOKKEEPER: [On phone] *He's somewhere on the floor, Mister Raymond. I'll see if I can find him . . .*

She covers the mouthpiece.

BOSS: [Frowning] *Which Raymond is it, the younger one or the older one?*

BOOKKEEPER: *The younger one.*

BOSS: *You can't find me.*

The bookkeeper starts to relay this message, but the boss changes his mind. He takes the receiver.

BOSS: *Hello, Jerry? This is Sam . . . Jerry, for heaven's sake, the twenty dozen just came at half past nine this morning . . . Jerry, I told you six o'clock; it'll be ready six o'clock . . .* [Suddenly lowers his voice, turns away from the book-keeper, embarrassed at the pleading he's going to have to go through now] *Jerry, how about that fifty dozen faille sport suits . . . Have a heart, Jerry, I need the work. I haven't got enough work to keep my girls. Two of them left yesterday . . . Jerry, please, what kind of living can I make on these cheap cottons? Give me a fancier garment . . . It's such small lots, Jerry. At least give me big lots . . .* [Lowering his voice even more] *Jerry, I hate to appeal to you on this level, but I'm your brother-in-law, you know. . . . Things are pretty rough with me right now, Jerry. Have a heart. Send me over the fifty dozen failles you got in yesterday. I'll make a rush job for you . . . please, Jerry, why do you have to make me crawl? All right, I'll have this one for you five o'clock . . . I'll call up the freight man now. How about the failles? . . . Okay, Jerry, thank you, you're a good fellow. . . . All right, five o'clock. I'll call the freight man right now . . . Okay . . .*

He hangs up, stands a moment, sick at his own loss of dignity. He turns to the bookkeeper, head bowed.

BOSS: *My own brother-in-law . . .*

He shuffles away, looks up. The old lady, who had gone into

the dressing room to hang up her coat and hat, comes out of
the dressing room now. The boss wheels on her.

BOSS: *Watsa matter with you? I left you a bundle of
sleeves there! You're not even in the shop five minutes,
and you walk around like you own the place!* [He wheels
to the other operators.] *All right! Come on! Come on!
What are you sitting there?! Rush job! Rush job! Let's go!
Five o'clock the freight man's coming! Let's go! Let's go!*

CUT TO: The bedroom of the daughter's and son-in-law's
apartment. The bed has been made, the room cleaned up.
The blinds have been drawn open, and the room is nice and
bright. The son-in-law sits on one of the straight-back chairs,
slumped a little, surly, scowling. The daughter sits erectly on
the bed, her back to her husband, likewise scowling. Apparently, angry words have passed between them. The doorbell
buzzes off. Neither of them move for a moment. Then the
daughter rises. At her move, the son-in-law begins to gather
himself together.

SON-IN-LAW: *I'll get it.*

The daughter moves—in sullen, quick silence—past him and
out into the foyer. The son-in-law, who has started to rise, sits
down again.

In the hallway, the daughter pads down to the front door
of the apartment. She is wearing a house dress now and house
slippers. She opens the door. Waiting at the door is an attractive young woman in her early thirties, in coat and hat.

DAUGHTER: *Hello, Marie, what are you doing here?*

SISTER: *Nothing. I just came by for a couple of minutes,
that's all. I just brought the kids back to school, I thought
I'd drop in for a minute, that's all. How's George?*

She comes into the apartment. The daughter closes the door
after her. The sister starts down the hallway.

DAUGHTER: *You came in right in the middle of an argument.*

The son-in-law is now standing in the bedroom doorway

SON-IN-LAW: [To the sister] *Your sister drives me crazy.*

SISTER: *Watsa matter now?*

DAUGHTER: [Following her sister up the foyer] *Nothing's the matter. How's Jack? The kids?*

> The two women go into the bedroom, the son-in-law stepping back to let them in.

SISTER: *They're fine. Jack's got a little cold, nothing important. I just took the kids back to school, and I thought I'd drop in, see if you feel like going up to Fordham Road, do a little shopping for a couple of hours.* [To the son-in-law] *What are you doing home?*

SON-IN-LAW: *It's my vacation. We were gonna leave the kids with my sister, drive downna Virginia, North Carolina, get some warm climate. But your crazy sister don't wanna go. She don't wanna leave your mother . . .* [Turning to his wife] *Your mother can take care of herself better than we can. She's a tough old woman. . . . How many vacations you think I get a year? I don't wanna sit in New York for two weeks, watching it rain.*

SISTER: *Go ahead, Annie. Me and Frank will see that Mom's all right.*

DAUGHTER: *Sure, you and Frank. Look, Marie, I was over to see Mom this morning . . .*

SON-IN-LAW: *Half past six she got up this morning, go over to see your mother . . .*

DAUGHTER: *After what happened yesterday, I decided to put my foot down. Because Mom got no business at her age riding up and down in the subways. You know how packed they are. Anyway, I called Mom on the phone, and she gave me the usual arguments. You know Mom. So anyway, I went over to see her, and she was very depressed. We talked for about an hour, and she told me she's been feeling very depressed lately. It's no good Mom living there alone, and you know it, Marie. Anyway, I think I finally convinced her to move out of there and come and live over here.*

SON-IN-LAW: *You didn't convince me.*

DAUGHTER: *George, please . . .*

SON-IN-LAW: *Look, Annie, I like your mother. We get along fine. We go over visit her once, twice a week, fine. What I like about her is that she doesn't hang all over you like my mother does.*

DAUGHTER: *This is the only thing I ever asked you in our whole marriage . . .*

SON-IN-LAW: *This is just begging for trouble. You know that in the bottom of your heart . . .*

DAUGHTER: *I don't wanna argue any more about it . . .*

SISTER: *Look, Annie, I think George is right. I think . . .*

> The daughter suddenly wheels on her sister, a long-repressed fury trembling out of her.

DAUGHTER: [Literally screaming] *You keep outta this! You hear me?! You never cared about Mom in your whole life! How many times you been over there this week? How many times?! I go over every day! Every day! And I go over in the evenings too sometimes!*

> The sister turns away, not a little shaken by this fierce onslaught. The daughter sits down on the bed again, her back to both her husband and sister, herself confused by the ferocity of her outburst. The son-in-law looks down, embarrassed, at the floor. A moment of sick silence fills the room. Then without turning, but in a much lower voice, the daughter goes on.

DAUGHTER: *George, I been a good wife to you. Did I ever ask you for mink coats or anything? Anything you want has always been good with me. This is the only thing I ever ask of you. I want my mother to live here with me where I can take care of her.*

> The son-in-law looks up briefly at his wife's unrelenting back and then back to the floor again.

SON-IN-LAW: *All right, Annie. I won't argue any more with you about it.*

SISTER: *I guess I better go because I want to get back in*

*the house before three o'clock when the kids come home
from school.*

Nobody says anything, so she starts for the door. The son-in-law, from his sitting position, looks up briefly at her as she passes, but she avoids his eyes. He stands, follows her out into the foyer. They proceed silently down the foyer to the doorway. Here they pause a minute. The scene is conducted in low, intense whispers.

SON-IN-LAW: *She don't mean nothing, Marie. You know
that.*

SISTER: *I know, I know . . .*

SON-IN-LAW: *She's a wonderful person. She'd get up at
three o'clock in the morning for you. There's nothing she
wouldn't do for her family.*

SISTER: *I know, George. I know Annie better than you
know her. When she's sweet, she can be the sweetest person in the world. She's my kid sister but many's the time I
came to her to do a little crying. But she's gonna kill my
mother with all her sacrifices. She's trying to take away
my mother's independence. My mother's been on her own
all her life. That's the only way she knows how to live. I
went over to see my mother yesterday. She was depressed.
It broke my heart because I told Jack; I said: "I think my
mother's beginning to give up." My mother used to be so
sure of herself all the time, and yesterday she was talking
there about how maybe she thinks she is getting a little
old to work. It depressed me for the rest of the day . . .*

SON-IN-LAW: *Marie, you know that I really like your
mother. If I thought it would work out at all, I would
have no objection to her coming to live here. But the walls
in this place are made out of paper. You can hear everything that goes on in the next room, and . . .*

SISTER: *It's a big mistake if she comes here. She'll just dry
up into bones inside a year.*

SON-IN-LAW: *Tell that to Annie. Would you do that for me,
please?*

SISTER: *You can't tell Annie nothing. Annie was born at a wrong time. The doctor told my mother she was gonna die if she had Annie, and my mother has been scared of Annie ever since. And if Annie thinks she's gonna get my mother to love her with all these sacrifices, she's crazy. My mother's favorite was always our big brother Frank, and Annie's been jealous of him as long as I know. I remember one time when we were in Saint John's school on Daly Avenue —I think Annie was about ten years old, and . . . oh, well, look, I better go. I'm not mad at Annie. She's been like this as long as I know her.* [She opens the door.] *She's doing the worst thing for my mother, absolutely the worst thing. I'll see you, George.*

SON-IN-LAW: *I'll see you.*

The sister goes out, closing the door after her. The son-in-law stands a moment. Then, frowning, he moves back up the foyer to the bedroom. His wife is still seated as we last saw her, her back to the door, her hands in her lap—slumped a little, but with an air of rigid stubbornness about her. The son-in-law regards her for a moment. Then he moves around the bed and sits down beside his wife. He puts his arm around her and pulls her to him. She rests her head on his chest. They sit silently for a moment.

DISSOLVE TO: Interior, the shop. The full complement of working operators are there, all hunched over their machines, and the place is a picture of industry. The women chatter shrilly with each other as they work. A radio plays in the background. Occasionally, one of the operators lifts her head and bellows out: "Work! Work! Jessica! Gimme some work!" . . . The Bookkeeper, Jessica, scurries back and forth from her desk to the sorting table—where she picks up small cartons of materials, bringing them to the operators—and back to her desk.

DISSOLVE TO: The old lady and her immediate neighbor, the Negro woman, both bent over their machines, sewing away. The motors hum. The two women move their materials under

the plunging needles. The old lady hunches, intense and painfully concentrated, over her work. They sew in silent industry
for a moment. Then . . .

OLD LADY: [Without daring to look up from her work] *I'm
getting the feel back, you know?*

NEGRO WOMAN: [Likewise without looking up] *Sure,
you're gonna be all right, Mama.*

OLD LADY: *I used to be considered a very fast operator. I
used to work on the lower East side in those sweatshops,
y'know. Six dollars a week. But I quit in October 1916,
because I got married and, in those days, y'know, it was
a terrible disgrace for a married woman to work. So I quit.
Not that we had the money. My husband was a house
painter when we got married, which is seasonal work at
best, and he had to borrow the money to go to Atlantic
City for three days. That was our honeymoon.*

They lapse into silence. A woman's shrill voice from farther
down the row of machines calls out: "Work! Hey, Jessica!
Bring me some work!" The two women sew silently. Then . . .

OLD LADY: *I got a feeling he's going to keep me on here.
The boss, I mean. He seems like a nice enough man.*

NEGRO WOMAN: *He's nervous, but he's all right.*

OLD LADY: *I've been looking for almost four weeks now,
y'know. My husband died a little more than a month ago.*

NEGRO WOMAN: *My husband died eighteen years ago.*

OLD LADY: *He was a very sick man all his life—lead poison-
ing, you know, from the paints. He had to quit the trade
after a while, went into the retail grocery business. He
was sixty-seven when he died, and I wonder he lived this
long. In his last years, the circulation of the blood in his
legs was so bad he could hardly walk to the corner.*

NEGRO WOMAN: *My big trouble is arthritis. I get terrible
pains in my arms and in my shoulder sometimes.*

OLD LADY: *Oh, I been getting a lot of pains in my back, in
between my shoulder blades.*

NEGRO WOMAN: *That's gall bladder.*

OLD LADY: *Is that what it is?*

NEGRO WOMAN: *I had that. When you get to our age, Missus Fanning, you gotta expect the bones to rebel.*

OLD LADY: *Well, now, you're not such an old woman.*

NEGRO WOMAN: *How old do you think I am?*

OLD LADY: *I don't know. Maybe forty, fifty.*

NEGRO WOMAN: *I'm sixty-eight years old.*

> For the first time, the old lady looks up. She pauses in her work.

OLD LADY: *I wouldn't believe you were sixty-eight.*

NEGRO WOMAN: *I'm sixty-eight. I got more white hair than you have. But I dye it. You oughtta dye your hair too. Just go in the five-and-ten, pick up some kind of hair dye. Because most people don't like to hire old people with white hair. My children don't want me to work no more, but I'm gonna work until I die. How old do you think that old Greek woman over there is?*

OLD LADY: *How old?*

NEGRO WOMAN: *She's sixty-nine. She got a son who's a big doctor. She won't quit working either. I like working here. I come in here in the morning, punch the clock. I'm friends with all these women. You see that little Jewish lady down there? That's the funniest little woman I ever met. You get her to tell you some of her jokes during lunch sometime. She gets me laughing sometimes I can hardly stop. What do I wanna sit around my dirty old room for when I got that little Jewish woman there to tell me jokes all day? That's what I tell my children.*

> The old lady turns back to her sewing.

OLD LADY: *Oh, I'd like to hear a couple of jokes.*

> At this moment there is a small burst of high-pitched laughter from farther down the rows of machines. Camera cuts to long shot of the rows of operators, singling out a group of three Puerto Rican girls in their twenties. One of them has apparently just said something that made the other two laugh. A fourth Puerto Rican girl, across the table and up from them,

calls to them in Spanish: "What happened? What was so funny?" The Puerto Rican girl who made the others laugh answers in a quick patter of high-pitched Spanish. A sudden gust of laughter sweeps all the Puerto Rican girls at the machines. Another woman calls out: "What she say?" One of the Puerto Rican girls answers in broken English.

PUERTO RICAN GIRL: *She say, t'ree week ago, she make a mistake, sewed the belts onna dress backward. Nobody found out. Yesterday, she went in to buy her little girl a dress inna store. They tried to sell her one-a theese dresses . . .*

A wave of laughter rolls up and down the two rows of operators.

She say, the label onna dress say: "Made in California."
They absolutely roar at this.

CLOSE-UP: The old lady joining in the general laughter. She finishes the sleeve she has been working on. It is apparently the last of the bunch. She gathers together in front of her the two dozen other sleeves she has just finished and begins to tie them up with a black ribbon. She lifts her head up and—with magnificent professionalism—calls out.

OLD LADY: *Work! Work! . . .*
Camera closes down on the bundle of sleeves she has tied together with the black ribbon.

DISSOLVE TO: The same bundle of sleeves. We pull back and see it is now being held by the boss. He is frowning down at them. At his elbow is standing one of the Puerto Rican girls. She is muttering in broken English.

PUERTO RICAN GIRL: *So what I do? The whole bunch, same way . . .*

BOSS: [Scowling] *All right, all right. Cut them open, resew the whole bunch . . .*

PUERTO RICAN GIRL: *Cut! I didn't do! I can't cut, sew, five o'clock the truckman . . . I gotta sew them on the blouse. Take two hours . . .*

BOSS: *All right, all right, cut them open, sew them up again . . .*

The girl takes the bundle of sleeves and shuffles away. The boss turns, suddenly deeply weary. He goes to the desk.

BOSS: [To the bookkeeper] *The old lady come in today, she sewed all the sleeves for the left hand. She didn't make any rights. All lefts . . .*

BOOKKEEPER: *So what are you gonna do? It's half past four.*

BOSS: *Call up Raymond for me.*

The bookkeeper picks up the phone receiver, dials. The boss looks up and through the pipe racks at the old lady, sitting hunched and intense over her machine, working with concentrated meticulousness. The boss's attention is called back to the phone by the bookkeeper. He takes the phone from her.

BOSS: [In a low voice] *Jerry? This is Sam. Listen, I can't give you the whole twenty dozen at five o'clock. . . . All right, wait a minute, lemme . . . All right, wait a minute. I got fifteen dozen on the racks now . . . Jerry, please. I just got a new operator in today. She sewed five dozen sleeves all left-handed. We're gonna have to cut the seams open, and resew them . . . Look, Jerry, I'm sorry, what do you want from me? I can get it for you by six . . . Jerry, I'll pay the extra freight fee myself . . . Jerry . . . Listen, Jerry, how about those fifty dozen faille sport suits? This doesn't change your mind, does it? . . . Jerry, it's an accident. It could happen to anyone . . .* [A fury begins to take hold of the boss.] *Look, Jerry, you promised me the fifty dozen fai . . . Look, Jerry, you know what you can do with those fifty dozen failles? You think I'm gonna crawl on my knees to you?!* [He's shouting now. Every head in the shop begins to look up.] *You're a miserable human being, you hear that? I'd rather go bankrupt than ask you for another order! And don't come over my house no more! You hear?! I ain't gonna crawl to you! You hear me?! I ain't gonna crawl to you! . . .*

He slams the receiver down, stands, his chest heaving, his face flushed. He looks down at the bookkeeper, his fury still high.

BOSS: *Fire her! Fire her! Fire her!*

He stands, the years of accumulated humiliation and resentment flooding out of him.

FADE OUT.

ACT III

FADE IN: Interior of a subway car heading north to the Bronx during the rush hour—absolutely jam-packed. The camera manages to work its way through the dense crowd to settle on the old lady, seated in her black coat and hat, her hands folded in her lap, her old purse dangling from her wrist. She is staring bleakly straight ahead of herself, as if in another world. The train hurtles on.

DISSOLVE TO: Interior of the old lady's apartment—dark—empty. Night has fallen outside. The sound of a key being inserted into the lock. The bolts unlatch, and the door is pushed open. The old lady enters. She closes the door after herself, bolts it. She stands a moment in the dark foyer, then shuffles up the foyer to the living room. She unbuttons her coat, sits down by the table, places her purse on the table. For a moment she sits. Then she rises, goes into the kitchen, turns on the light.

It takes her a moment to remember what she came into the kitchen for. Then, collecting herself, she opens the refrigerator door, extracts a carton of milk, sets it on the cupboard shelf. She opens the cupboard door, reaches in, extracts the box of Rice Krispies and a bowl. She sets the bowl down, begins to open the box of cereal. It falls out of her hands to the floor, a number of the pebbles of cereal rolling out to the floor. She starts to bend to pick the box up, then suddenly straightens and stands breathing heavily, nervously wetting her lips. She moves out of the kitchen quickly now, goes to the table, sits down again, picks up the phone, and dials. There is an edge of desperation in her movements. She waits. Then . . .

OLD LADY: *Frank? Who's this, Lillian? Lillian, dear, this is your mother-in-law, and I . . . oh, I'm sorry, what? . . . Oh, I'm sorry . . . Who's this, the baby sitter? . . . This is Missus*

211

*Fanning, dear—Mister Fanning's mother, is he in? . . . Is
Missus Fanning in? . . . Well, do you expect them in? I
mean, it's half past six. Did they eat their dinner already?
. . . Oh, I see. Well, when do you . . . Oh, I see . . . No, dear,
this is Mister Fanning's mother. Just tell him I called. It's
not important.*

> She hangs up, leaving her hand still on the phone. Then she
> lifts the receiver again and dials another number. She places
> a smile on her face and waits. Then . . .

OLD LADY: *Oh, Marie, dear, how are you . . . this is mother
. . . Oh, I'm glad to hear your voice . . . Oh, I'm fine . . . fine.
How's Jack and the kids? . . . Well, I hope it's nothing serious . . . Oh, that's good . . .* [She is mustering up all the
good humor she has in her.] *Oh my, what a day I had. Oh,
wait'll I tell you. Listen, I haven't taken you away from
your dinner or anything . . . Oh, I went down to look for
a job again . . . Yes, that's right, Annie was here this morning . . . how did you know? . . . Oh, is that right? Well, it
cleared up, you know, and I didn't want to just sit around,
so I went down to this job, and I got fired again . . . The
stupidest thing. I sewed all left sleeves . . . Well, you know
you have to sew sleeves for the right as well as the left
unless your customers are one-armed people . . .* [She is
beginning to laugh nervously.] *Yes, it's comical, isn't it?
. . . Yes, all left-handed . . .*

> She bursts into a short, almost hysterical laugh. Her lip begins
> to twitch, and she catches her laughter in its middle and
> breathes deeply to regain control of herself.

*Well, how's Jack and the kids? . . . Well, that's fine. What
are you doing with yourself tonight? . . .*

> A deep weariness seems to have taken hold of her. She rests
> her head in the palm of her free hand. Her eyes are closed.

*Oh, do you have a baby sitter? . . . Well, have a nice time,
give my regards to your mother-in-law . . . No, no, I'm
fine . . . No, I was just asking . . . No, no, listen, dear, I'm
absolutely fine. I just come in the house, and I'm going to*

*make myself some Rice Krispies, and I've got some rolls
somewhere, and I think I've got a piece of fish in the refrigerator, and I'm going to make myself dinner and take
a hot tub, and then I think I'll watch some television.
What's tonight, Thursday? ... Well, Groucho Marx is on
tonight ... No, no, I just called to ask how everything was.
How's Jack and the kids? ... That's fine, have a nice time
... Good-by, dear ...*

> She hangs up, sits erectly in the chair now. Her face wears an
> expression of the most profound weariness. She rises now and
> shuffles with no purpose into the center of the dark room, her
> coat flapping loosely around her. Then she goes to the tele-
> vision set, turns it on. In a moment a jumble of lines appear,
> and the sound comes up. The lines clear up into Faye and
> Skitch Henderson engaging each other in very clever chitchat.
> The old lady goes back to a television-viewing chair, sits down
> stiffly—her hands resting on the armrests—and expression-
> lessly watches the show. Camera comes in for a close-up of the
> old lady, staring wide-eyed right through the television set,
> not hearing a word of the chitchat. She is breathing with some
> difficulty. Suddenly she rises and almost lurches back to the
> table. She takes the phone, dials with obvious trembling,
> waits ...

OLD LADY: *Annie? Annie, I wonder if I could spend the
night at your house? I don't want to be alone ... I'd appreciate that very much ... All right, I'll wait here ...*

> DISSOLVE TO: Interior of the old lady's bedroom. The son-
> in-law, in his hat and jacket, is snapping the clasps of an old
> valise together. Having closed the valise, he picks it off the bed
> and goes into the living room. The old lady is there. She is
> seated in one of the straight-back chairs by the table, still in
> her coat and hat, and she is talking to the daughter—who can
> be seen through the kitchen doorway, reaching up into the
> pantry for some of her mother's personal groceries.

OLD LADY: *... Well, the truth is, I'm getting old, and there's* *no point saying it isn't true.* [To her son-in-law as he sets the valise down beside her] *Thank you, dear. I always have so much trouble with the clasp. . . . Did you hear the stupid thing I did today? I sewed all left-handed sleeves. That's the mark of a wandering mind, a sure sign of age. I'm sorry, George, to put you to all this inconvenience . . .*

SON-IN-LAW: *Don't be silly, Ma. Always glad to have you.*

OLD LADY: *Annie, dear, what are you looking for?*

DAUGHTER: [In the kitchen] *Your saccharin.*

OLD LADY: *It's on the lower shelf, dear. . . . This isn't going to be permanent, George. I'll just stay with you a little while till I get a room somewheres with some other old woman . . .*

DAUGHTER: [In the kitchen doorway] *Ma, you're gonna stay with us, so, for heaven's sakes, let's not have no more arguments.*

OLD LADY: *What'll we do with all my furniture? Annie, don't you want the china closet?*

DAUGHTER: *No, Ma, we haven't got any room for it . . .*

OLD LADY: *It's such a good-looking piece. What we have to do is to get Jack and Marie and Frank and Lillian and all of us together, and we'll divide among the three of you whatever you want. I've got that fine set of silver—well, it's not the best, of course, silver plate, y'know—it's older than you are, Annie.* [To her son-in-law] *It was a gift of the girls in my shop when I got married. It's an inexpensive set, but I've shined it every year, and it sparkles.* [To her daughter in the kitchen] *Yes, that's what we'll have to do. We'll have to get all of us together one night and I'll apportion out whatever I've got. And whatever you don't want, well, we'll call a furniture dealer . . .* [To her son-in-law] *. . . although what would he pay me for these old things here? . . .* [To her daughter] *Annie, take the china closet . . . It's such a fine piece . . .*

DAUGHTER: *Ma, where would we put it?*

OLD LADY: *Well, take that soft chair there. You always liked that chair ...*

DAUGHTER: *Ma ...*

OLD LADY: *There's nothing wrong with it. It's not torn or anything. The upholstery's fine. Your father swore by that chair. He said it was the only chair he could sit in.*

DAUGHTER: *Ma, let's not worry about it now. We'll get together sometime next week with Marie and Lillian ...*

OLD LADY: *I want you to have the chair ...*

DAUGHTER: *Ma, we got all modern furniture in our house ...*

OLD LADY: *It's not an old chair. We just bought it about six years ago. No, seven ...*

DAUGHTER: *Ma, what do we need the ...*

OLD LADY: *Annie, I don't want to sell it to a dealer! It's my home. I don't want it to go piece by piece into a second-hand shop.*

DAUGHTER: *Ma ...*

SON-IN-LAW: *Annie! We'll take the chair!*

DAUGHTER: *All right, Ma, the chair is ours.*

OLD LADY: *I know that Lillian likes those lace linens I've got in the cedar chest. And the carpets. Now these are good carpets, Annie. There's no sense just throwing them out. They're good broadloom. The first good money your father was making we bought them. When we almost bought that house in Passaic, New Jersey. You ought to remember that, Annie. You were about seven then. But we bought the grocery store instead. Oh, how we scraped in that store. In the heart of the depression. We used to sell bread for six cents a loaf. I remember my husband said: "Let's buy a grocery store. At least we'll always have food in the house." It seems to me my whole life has been hand-to-mouth. Did we ever not worry about the rent? I remember as a girl in Cork, eating boiled potatoes every day. I don't know what it all means, I really don't ...* [She stares rather abstractedly at her son-in-law.] *I'm sixty-six*

years old, and I don't know what the purpose of it all was.
SON-IN-LAW: *Missus Fanning . . .*
OLD LADY: *An endless, endless struggle. And for what? For what?* [She is beginning to cry now.] *Is this what it all comes to? An old woman parceling out the old furniture in her house . . . ?*

> She bows her head and stands, thirty years of repressed tears torturously working their way through her body in racking shudders.

DAUGHTER: *Ma . . .*

> The old lady stands, her shoulders slumped, her head bowed, crying with a violent agony.

OLD LADY: [The words stumbling out between her sobs] *Oh, I don't care . . . I don't care . . .*

> Hold on the old lady, standing, crying.

> DISSOLVE TO: Film. Rain whipping through the streets of New York at night—same film we opened the show with—a frightening thunderstorm.

> DISSOLVE TO: The old lady's valise, now open, lying on a narrow single bed. We pull back to see the old lady—in a dress, but with her coat off—rummaging in the valise for something. The room she is in is obviously a little boy's room. There are a child's paintings and drawings and cutouts Scotch-taped to the wall, and toys and things on the floor. It is dark outside, and the rain whacks against the window panes. The old lady finally extracts from out of the valise a long woolen nightgown and, holding it in both arms, she shuffles to the one chair in the room and sits down. She sets the nightgown in her lap and bends to remove her shoes. This is something of an effort and costs her a few moments of quick breathing. She sits, expressionless, catching her breath, the white nightgown on her lap, her hands folded on it. Even after she regains her breath, she sits this way, now staring fixedly at the floor at her feet. Hold.

> DISSOLVE TO: The window of the child's bedroom. It is day-

light now, and the rain has stopped. The cold morning sun shines thinly through the white chintz curtains. The camera pulls slowly back and finally comes to rest on the old lady sitting just as we saw her last, unmoving, wrapped in thought, the white nightgown on her lap, her hands folded. From some room off, the thin voice of a baby suddenly rises and abruptly falls. The old lady looks slowly up.

Then she bends and puts her shoes on. She rises, sets the nightgown on the chair from which she has just risen, moves with a slight edge of purpose down the room to the closet, opens the door, reaches in, and takes out her coat. She puts it on, stands a moment, looking about the room for something. She finds her hat and purse sitting on the chest of drawers. She picks them up. Then she turns to the door of the room and carefully opens it. She looks out onto the hallway. Across from her, the door to her daughter's and son-in-law's bedroom stands slightly ajar. She crosses to the door, looks in. Her daughter and son-in-law make two large bundles under their blankets. For a moment she stands and surveys them. Then the daughter turns in her bed so that she faces her mother. Her eyes are open; she has not been asleep. At the sight of her mother in the doorway, she leans upon one elbow.

OLD LADY: [In an intense whisper] *Annie, it just wasn't comfortable, you know? I just can't sleep anywheres but in my own bed, and that's the truth. I'm sorry, Annie, honest. You're a fine daughter, and it warms me to know that I'm welcome here. But what'll I do with myself, Annie, what'll I do?* . . .

The daughter regards her mother for a moment.

DAUGHTER: *Where are you going, Ma, with your coat on?*

OLD LADY: *I'm going out and look for a job. And, Annie, please don't tell me that everything's against me. I know it. Well, I'll see you, dear. I didn't mean to wake you up.* . . .

She turns and disappears from the doorway. The daughter starts quickly from the bed.

DAUGHTER: *Ma . . .*

>   She moves quickly across the room to the door of the hallway.
>   She is in her pajamas. She looks down the hallway, which is
>   fairly dark. Her mother is already at the front door, at the
>   other end.

DAUGHTER: *Ma . . .*

OLD LADY: *I'm leaving the valise with all my things. I'll
pick them up tonight. And please don't start an argument
with me, Annie, because I won't listen to you. I'm a woman
of respect. I can take care of myself. I always have. And
don't tell me it's raining because it stopped about an hour
ago. And don't say you'll drive me home because I can get
the bus two blocks away. Work is the meaning of my life.
It's all I know what to do. I can't change my ways at this
late time.*

>   For a long moment the mother and daughter regard each
>   other. Then the daughter pads quietly down to the old lady.

DAUGHTER: [Quietly] *When I'm your age, Ma, I hope I'm
like you.*

>   For a moment the two women stand in the dark hallway.
>   Then they quickly embrace and release each other. The old
>   lady unbolts the door and disappears outside, closing the door
>   after her. The daughter bolts it shut with a click. She turns
>   and goes back up the dark foyer to her own bedroom. She goes
>   in, shuffles to the bed, gets back under the covers. For a mo-
>   ment she just lies there. Then she nudges her sleeping hus-
>   band, who grunts.

DAUGHTER: *George, let's drop the kids at your sister's for
a week or ten days and drive down to Virginia. You don't
want to spend your one vacation a year sitting in New
York, watching it rain.*

>   The son-in-law, who hasn't heard a word, grunts once or twice
>   more. The daughter pulls the blankets up over her shoulders,
>   turns on her side, and closes her eyes.

>   FADE OUT.

THE END

The Bachelor Party

DIRECTED BY: DELBERT MANN
ASSOCIATE PRODUCER: GORDON DUFF
PRODUCED BY: FRED COE

Cast

HELEN	Kathleen Maguire
CHARLIE	Eddie Albert
KENNETH	Bob Emmett
BOOKKEEPER	James Westerfield
BACHELOR	Joseph Mantell
GROOM	Douglas Gordon
JULIE	Anna Minot
BARTENDER	Ely Segall
BAR HAG	Elaine Eldridge
YOUNG FELLOW	Walter Kelly
GIRL	Bettye Ackerman
FIANCÉE	Olive Dunbar

ACT I

FADE IN: Interior, the one room of a one-and-a-half-room apartment in a low-income housing project in Jersey City, New Jersey. It is early morning, but the shades are drawn and the room is dark. The camera moves slowly across the room, over the large double bed on which Charlie and Helen Samson, a young couple in their late twenties, are sleeping. They are sleeping more or less on their sides, facing away from each other. One of Helen's pajama-clad legs projects from under the light covers. We close in slowly on Charlie's sleeping face.

The alarm clock at a distant end of the room suddenly bursts into a relentless buzz. Charlie's eyes open. There is a muffled movement at his side, and Helen gets up on one elbow. Then she sits up, rises, and pads barefooted—a rather pretty girl in rumpled pajamas—to the alarm clock and turns it off. Charlie's head turns on the pillow so that he can watch her. She pads back to the bed now and stands at the foot, looking down at her husband. She produces a smile that is more nearly a grimace, then turns and shuffles into the bathroom, where she turns on the wall switch. A shaft of light now pours into the bedroom.

Charlie sits up in bed. His shoes and socks are on the floor by his feet. He reaches down and starts to put them on. Suddenly, from the recesses of the bathroom, Helen's rather vague soprano bursts into song: "Ramona, I see you by the garden wall." Here it stops as abruptly as it began. Charlie's head slowly turns to look to the bathroom, then back again to the business of putting on his shoes. His face is expressionless, but there is no mistaking the sodden distaste he has for the world today.

He pushes his feet into his shoes and just sits there, head hanging, shoulders slumped. Behind him, the sudden noise of rushing tap water, then off. Then his wife comes back into the bedroom. She is carrying a bath towel with which she is drying her face. Finished, she drops the towel on the bed and begins to dress. She is in a position now where most of her is obscured from the camera either by the footboard of the bed or by Charlie's unmoving slumped figure. A moment later she pads around the corner of the bed to Charlie's front. She is still barefooted and wears her pajama top, but she has exchanged the trousers for a slip. Charlie hasn't moved a muscle since the Herculean effort required to put his shoes and socks on.

HELEN: *You think it's too early to call my mother?*

Charlie shrugs without looking up. Helen goes out of the bedroom. We stay on Charlie, slumped, unmoving, looking down at his hands dangling loosely between his knees. We hear a phone being dialed in the foyer, off—a pause—then Helen's voice.

HELEN: [Off] *Hello, Ma? Did I wake you up? This is Helen . . . Well, I'll be going to work in about twenty minutes, and I wanted to get ahold of you before I left. I called you last night. Where were you and Pop anyway? I kept calling you every half hour up till one o'clock . . . Oh, yeah? Did you have a nice time? . . .*

We slowly close in on Charlie's face, eyes closed.

Well, listen, Ma, I got something to tell you. I'm pregnant . . . Yeah, pregnant . . . Of course I'm sure . . . Yeah, Doctor Sloan . . . Yeah, he said I was pregnant. Third month. He says I can expect the baby next February . . . Well, Grandma, act a little excited, will you? . . . You bet I'm excited . . .

CLOSE-UP: Charlie. The bowed head rises slowly. The eyes open. He stares abstractedly ahead for a moment. Then he sighs a profound sigh. Then his eyes close again, and the head slowly sinks back to its previous abjection.

DISSOLVE TO: Interior, the kitchen of same apartment. Helen is sitting at the small table, carefully sipping a cup of coffee. She is reading yesterday's newspaper. At the same time she hums snatches of "Ramona." Charlie enters the kitchen. He is wearing his trousers now, but hasn't put on his shirt yet. He sits down at the other end of the table and begins to sip a cup of coffee that has already been poured for him. They sit silently a moment, Helen reading and sipping, Charlie study-ing the coffee in his cup.

CHARLIE: *A guy in my office is getting married Sunday.*

HELEN: [Without looking up] *Yeah, which one?*

CHARLIE: *Arnold. I told you about him. The guy who's got the sick mother.*

HELEN: *Oh, yeah.*

CHARLIE: *The rest of the guys are giving him a bachelor dinner tonight.*

HELEN: [Looking up now for the first time] *Do you want to go, Charlie?*

CHARLIE: *No, I don't want to go.*

HELEN: *Your cousin Julie is supposed to come over to-night, but I can call them up, tell them we won't be here.*

CHARLIE: *These bachelor dinners get kind of wild some-times. Everybody gets loaded. The whole philosophy is that it's the poor groom's last night before he goes into the electric chair. So it gets kind of wild.*

HELEN: *That's a good philosophy to start a marriage with.*

CHARLIE: *Well, you know, a bunch of guys get together, they like to tear up the town a little.*

Helen looks back to her newspaper, frowning a little. Then she looks up at Charlie again.

HELEN: *Maybe, you ought to go, Charlie.*

CHARLIE: *No, they asked me. I told them I didn't want to go.*

HELEN: *It might do you good to have a night out. I know you're upset about the baby ...*

CHARLIE: *I'm not upset ...*

HELEN: *Come on, Charlie, I know how you feel. Listen, you don't have to pretend you're excited about having a baby. We weren't figuring on a kid right now, and it's a shock. Listen, I wasn't exactly overjoyed when I began to suspect I was pregnant. I said: "Oh, boy, that's all I need, a baby." I had some bad days before I told you. I thought of all kinds of things. I'm ashamed to tell you what I thought of. I was real scared of having a baby. Then I said to myself: "If I'm having a baby, I'm having a baby, that's all there is to it." And I began to like the idea. We're going to have a family, Charlie. We're going to have a family. I like the idea.*

CHARLIE: *Well, there must be something wrong with me, Helen. Because all I can think about is that it's going to cost a lot of money, and we're going to be really tied down.*

HELEN: *Sure, I know. A baby takes up all your time.*

CHARLIE: *We were going to buy a car this year. We were going to go for a trip to Canada. We never even had a real honeymoon. Three days in a New York hotel. What kind of honeymoon is that? I'm old-fashioned. I want to see Niagara Falls.*

HELEN: *We'll get there.*

CHARLIE: *How are we going to get there? The car's out the window now, you know that. The guy in the grocery told me it costs about seven hundred bucks to have a baby.*

HELEN: *So we'll go to Niagara Falls in ten years. It isn't going to stop falling.*

CHARLIE: *All right. Helen, you're right. I know you're right. Give me a couple of days to get used to the whole idea. I'll be all right.*

HELEN: *I know you will, Charlie.*

CHARLIE: *Right now, it just seems that I got a ball and a chain hanging from every arm.*

HELEN: *I know, Charlie. That's why I think you ought to go to this bachelor party tonight. Get a little high. Laugh it up with your friends.*

CHARLIE: [Bursting out] *I don't want to go to this bachelor party!*

He looks down at his coffee, embarrassed at the outburs

I'm sorry I yelled.

HELEN: *Don't worry about it.*

CHARLIE: *I'm sorry I yelled like that, Heckie.*

HELEN: *What are you sorry about? Don't I yell at you all the time?*

We stay on Helen. She reads her newspaper, but there is a faint frown on her face.

CUT SHARPLY TO: Film. The Jersey City entrance to the Hudson and Manhattan tubes—eight-thirty in the morning— crowds of people pouring down into the subway.

CUT TO: Film. The Hudson and Manhattan subway hurtling along through its dark tunnel.

DISSOLVE TO: Interior of a crowded subway car. The camera pokes along between the bodies of the straphangers, comes to a halt on Charlie and another young married fellow, who are silently sitting, each with his hands folded in his lap. The friend, whose name is Kenneth Holman, is neatly dressed in collar, tie, and seersucker suit. Charlie has conceded more to the August heat. His jacket is folded across his lap, his collar is open, his tie loosely knotted. In short, two young white-collar workers on their way to work.

Hanging on to a strap directly in front of them is a full-blown young woman. Sitting to Kenneth's right is a pretty girl in her early twenties, reading a newspaper.

The two young husbands ride silently along for a moment, swaying in accordance with the train's movement. Kenneth ventures a quick look up at the girl swaying in front of him, then quickly looks down to his hands. After a moment he turns his head a little toward Charlie and speaks.

KENNETH: *Charlie, you ever think about other women?*

Charlie considers the question for a moment.

CHARLIE: *What do you mean, do I ever think about other women?*

KENNETH: *I mean, you're walking along in the street and*

some nice-looking girl walks by—I mean, do you ever think: "Hey, that's a nice-looking girl"?

Charlie considers again.

CHARLIE: *Why, do you?*

KENNETH: *Well, just because we're married don't mean we can't appreciate a good-looking girl when we see one.*

Charlie looks up at the girl swaying in front of them and down again. They ride along silently for a moment.

KENNETH: *You going to Arnold's bachelor dinner?*

CHARLIE: *I don't think so, Kennie.*

KENNETH: *Yeah, I was going to go, but I think I better not, because my kid, the young one, the girl, she's been acting up again lately. The doctor says she's got an allergy, they don't know what.*

CHARLIE: *These bachelor parties get a little out of hand sometimes. Eddie Watkins is making all the arrangements. If I know Eddie, he's probably lined up a whole bunch of chorus girls.*

KENNETH: *Yeah, do you think so?*

CHARLIE: *You know Eddie.*

KENNETH: *Boy, he really lives it up, don't he? Did you see that blonde who picked him up for lunch last week? Boy, sometimes I wish I was a bachelor.*

This last sentence came out a little unpremeditatedly, and both young husbands are embarrassed.

Well, you know what I mean. I been married six years, and I never seem to get out of the house any more, you know what I mean? So about once a week I go to the movies with my wife. We never even see the whole movie because my wife starts worrying about the kids. My youngest kid, the girl, she's allergic to something, we been trying to find out what it is. Anyway, it seems I never see anybody any more. Do you know how long it is since I seen Willie Duff? I haven't seen Willie in about six months. My wife can't stand his wife. You ever meet her, Willie's wife?

CHARLIE: *No. I didn't know Willie too well.*

KENNETH: *Boy, wait'll you get kids, boy. You'll never get out of the house.*

CHARLIE: *My wife's pregnant now.*

KENNETH: *No kidding.*

CHARLIE: *Yeah.*

KENNETH: *Congratulations!*

The two young husbands look down again at their hands and ride along silently. Kenneth sneaks a quick look up at the girl swaying in front of him; then his eye is caught by the girl on his right who is reading a newspaper. He slowly looks over at her.

At this point, a young fellow of about twenty-six elbows his way down through the crowded aisle until he spots the girl to Kenneth's right, pauses, crowds in next to the young woman swaying in front of Kenneth, grabs the strap, and—chewing gum determinedly—stares brazenly down at the girl reading the paper. The girl reading the paper, after a moment, becomes conscious of the young fellow ogling her, looks up quickly. The young fellow smiles pleasantly. The girl looks right back at her paper. Kenneth nudges Charlie.

CHARLIE: *What?*

KENNETH: *Dig this guy standing here. He's trying to pick up the girl here.*

Charlie leans a little forward and looks across at the young fellow and the girl. The former is chewing away, and the girl is reading with rigid nonchalance.

CHARLIE: *Yeah?*

KENNETH: *Was you with us about eight years ago when I picked up that chick in Paterson, New Jersey, in front of the bus stop?*

CHARLIE: *When was this?*

KENNETH: *Yeah, you were there. You were with that girl from Brooklyn. We just come from Palisades Amusement Park, and we were driving Frankie Klein's girl home, and the car broke down right in the middle of Route One.*

CHARLIE: [Beginning to smile] *Oh, yeah.*

KENNETH: [Beginning to laugh as he recalls the incident] *And Frankie opened up the hood, and the water cap blew right up in the air!*

CHARLIE: [Smiling] *And the cop come over . . .*

KENNETH: [Giggling so hard now he has to hide his face in one of his hands] *That's right, the cop. He thought Frankie shot off a gun. He was going to pull us all in . . .*

He sits in his seat, muffling his giggle under his hand, his shoulders shaking with hidden laughter.

Oh, man . . .

CHARLIE: *Oh, Frankie, he was funny.*

KENNETH: [Controlling himself, lets his hand fall back to his lap. An air of almost poignant memory settles on his face.] *Oh, that was a lot of fun, those days.*

He looks lazily over to the girl on his right. She is looking up over the top of her newspaper at the young fellow; they are staring steadfastly at each other. Kenneth turns back to Charlie.

KENNETH: *Hey, this guy's making out all right. She's giving him the eye now.*

CHARLIE: *No kidding.*

KENNETH: *I bet you he picks her up before we hit New York.*

Somehow this has a sobering effect on the two young husbands. Again they sit silently as the train buckets along.

CHARLIE: [Frowning down at his hands] *I don't know, Kennie. I've been feeling pretty miserable the last couple of weeks. It seems to me I got one really crummy life ahead of me. It just seems like I go to my job every day, and I come home, and we eat dinner, and then we go see Helen's mother and father or my mother and father. Or my cousin Julie and her husband. And now we got this kid coming. This is what the rest of my life is going to be like. I'm going to be a bookkeeper for seventy-two bucks a week the rest of my life. I don't know. Sometimes, I look at Helen. And she's a nice girl and all that. She's pretty. But I feel*

I'm missing something. I look at Helen, I say: "I must have felt something special to marry this girl." Something beautiful, you know what I mean? I mean, I love her, and all that, but . . . but what's love? You know what I mean?

He is quite nervous now at the turn his inarticulateness has taken. He breaks off abruptly. He sits frowning and disgruntled.

Listen, I hope I don't give you the idea I don't love my wife. I love Helen. Let's get that straight.

KENNETH: *Well, I hope I didn't give you the idea I don't love Alice. Alice and I get along fine.*

They sit silently again. The train hurtles along and then suddenly slows as it approaches New York. There is a rustle of movement among the passengers in the subway car. A few people start edging toward the doors. The girl at Kenneth's right folds her newspaper and rises almost directly in the young fellow's face. They regard each other steadily.

YOUNG FELLOW: [To the girl] *Excuse me, can you tell me how to get to Canal Street and Sixth Avenue?*

GIRL: *Just follow the signs. You'll see them all over.*

YOUNG FELLOW: *Are you getting out here?*

GIRL: *Yes.*

YOUNG FELLOW: *Well, I'll follow you then. That'll be easier. If you don't mind.*

GIRL: *No, not at all.*

They start to crowd down the aisle, in front of the two young husbands—who were following this interchange with deep interest. The heads of both young husbands turn slowly to watch their passage to the door. Then both young husbands look front again and just sit, both wearing expressions of the most poignant wistfulness. Fade out slowly.

CUT TO: Film. Interior of a moderately large office containing about seven girls and an odd number of young men at desks. The girls are typing away. We hear the click and clatter of a busy office staff.

CUT TO: Ground-glass door—gilt lettering: "Bookkeeping Department."

CUT TO: Interior of office, bookkeeping department—small office—typical—filing cabinets, etc.—four desks—window. Three of the desks are occupied. At the most downstage desk sits Kenneth, bent over his chores. At the most upstage desk sits Charlie. He has a sheaf of purchasing orders in front of him and a large ledger into which he transfers the totals from the purchasing orders. Occasionally he makes use of a small adding machine at his right elbow. At a desk stage-left of Charlie's desk sits a man in his late thirties, balding, a little stout. He too is bent over ledgers and statements. They are all in their shirt sleeves but wear ties. Throughout the ensuing scene, they never stop their bookkeeping, hardly even look up from their books. The fourth desk is empty.

For a moment the scene is one of industrious silence except for the occasional quick clatter of an adding machine.

BOOKKEEPER: [Without looking up from his work] *You guys going to Arnold's bachelor party tonight?*

KENNETH: [Without looking up] *No, I ain't going, are you?*

BOOKKEEPER: *No, I'm not going. I was going to go, but my wife's father came in from Akron, and he's only going to be here another couple of days. My wife bought tickets to the Radio City Music Hall. My father-in-law gave us a thousand bucks when I had my appendicitis last year, so the least I can do is go to the Radio City Music Hall with him.*

CHARLIE: *It looks like nobody's going to Arnold's party.*

BOOKKEEPER: *You ain't going?*

CHARLIE: *No, I ain't going.*

BOOKKEEPER: *Eddie's going to be mad.*

CHARLIE: *I told Eddie last week I couldn't make it. I mean, Eddie's a bachelor. It's okay for him to go rooting around town, picking up girls.*

BOOKKEEPER: *Yeah, you get married you give that kind of thing up.*

KENNETH: *Yeah, Charlie says Eddie had a whole bunch of chorus girls fixed up for us tonight.*

The bookkeeper's head comes up for the first time.

BOOKKEEPER: *No kidding.*

CHARLIE: *I didn't say that. I just said that if I knew Eddie, we'd probably wind up with some of his crazy girl friends.*

The bookkeeper looks back down again to his work.

KENNETH: *I don't know where he gets all these girls. He's a screwy-looking jerk.*

BOOKKEEPER: *Did you see that blonde that was up here looking for him last week?*

KENNETH: *Yeah. He told me she was a television actress. I think I saw her on* Martin Kane *once. Some lunatic was trying to strangle her with a necktie.*

BOOKKEEPER: *I'd like to strangle her with a necktie.*

KENNETH: *Now, Walter, an old married feller like you, you shouldn't talk that way.*

The bookkeeper looks up from his work, contemplates the wall in front of him.

BOOKKEEPER: *I get real jealous of Eddie sometimes. He's as free as a bird. Did you ever see that convertible he's got? You ought to see the old heap I got. He walks out of here on payday, he can spend the whole works on having himself a good time. I walk out of here, and I got three kids and a wife, all with their palms out. I lost two bucks playing poker at my house last week. It was an economic catastrophe. My wife didn't sleep all night.*

Frowning, he looks back to his work, then he looks up again.

Look, the jerk is twenty minutes late. If the boss walked in now, he'd fire him. What does Eddie care? So he scrambles around for another job. If that ever happened to me, I'd be afraid to go home.

He turns back again to his work. They work silently for a moment. Then the door opens, and a young man of twenty-eight enters. He is bespectacled, yet groomed in that Ripley clothes fashion that bespeaks the gay young blade about town. This is Eddie Watkins, but in this script he shall be known as the *Bachelor*. At the moment, he seems to have had very little sleep the night before. His eyes, behind the wire-rimmed glasses, are heavy-lidded. A cigarette dangles listlessly from his mouth. There is a perfunctory exchange of hellos and good mornings, establishing that this is Eddie. He shuffles wearily to his seat.

BACHELOR: [Muttering through reluctant lips] *The boss come in yet?*

KENNETH: *No.*

The Bachelor sits down at his desk, puffs his cigarette automatically for a moment; then he reaches over to a pile of telephone directories on the floor beside his desk, pulls up the Manhattan one, flips through the pages, finds the number he wants. He picks up his phone.

BACHELOR: *Mary, give me an outside line . . .*

He pauses, checks the number again in the telephone directory, then dials, waits.

Hello, is this Leathercraft on Madison Avenue? . . . This is Mr. Watkins. I was in about a week ago. I ordered a military set and a wallet. They were supposed to be ready today. . . . Yes, please, would you? . . .

He begins to search his jacket pockets while he waits, finds a piece of paper, pulls it out.

Yeah, a military set and a wallet . . . That's right. The following inscriptions should be on them: On the military set "To Arnold: Best Wishes on Your Marriage from Alex, Charlie, Eddie, Jerry, Kenneth, Mary, Olga, Phyllis, Walter, and The Boss." Now, on the wallet . . . Yeah, what? . . . Yeah, that's right—The Boss . . . Now, on the wallet, the following inscription: "To my best friend Arnold from his best man, Eddie." . . . No, "To my best friend Arnold" . . . That's right: "From his best man, Eddie." Now, can I come

*in at lunch and pick them up? . . . Okay, now have them
ready, because I only got a half an hour for lunch. . . .
Okay . . .*

Hangs up. Sits, listlessly puffs at the cigarette. He rubs his
eyes with two fingers to clear his head. In front of him, behind
him, and to his side his three colleagues bend to their work.
He picks the phone up again.

Mary, give me an outside line . . . [He waits, dials, waits
again.] *Miss Frances Kelly, please. I think it's room 417 . . .*

The three heads around him slowly look up from their respective work, naked interest manifest on their faces.

*Hello, Frances? This is Eddie . . . All right, wait a minute,
give me a chance to explain . . . I know I woke you up, but
if I didn't call you now, I would probably forget, and then
there'd really be a hassle. . . . Well, let me tell you what
happened. You know I'm supposed to be best man at this
fellow Arnold's wedding. So I called him up last night because I didn't know whether I was supposed to wear a
tuxedo or tails. Well, he didn't know, so he said: "Come on
over my girl's house with me tonight. They're making all
the arrangements for the wedding now." So I called you,
and left a message at the desk, saying I couldn't get over
till about ten o'clock . . . All right! That's what I'm going
to explain! . . .*

He holds the receiver against his chest and looks around at his
colleagues with the air of a man whose patience really is being
tried too much. He returns the receiver to his ear and listens
for a moment.

*All right. So I had to go over Arnold's girl's house with
Arnold last night. Well, there was about thirty people
there, and, man, you never saw such a crazy mess . . .*

Apparently the girl is off again. The Bachelor waits with
infinite patience again.

*All right, Frances, are you finished? All right. There was
about thirty people over there, and they're having a real
hassle. There was this little short bald-headed guy there.*

He's the bride's uncle. He's come all the way down from Boston with his whole family to go to the wedding. The only trouble is, he wasn't invited. Well, this crazy uncle, he grabs ahold of me, and he starts shaking me by the lapels. So I said: "What do you want from me? I ain't the groom! I'm just trying to find out whether I'm supposed to wear a tuxedo or tails." So I said to Arnold: "I'm cutting out of this madhouse." So they said: "Wait just a couple of minutes, because we're going to have a rehearsal." You'd think they were being married on television . . . [The Bachelor breaks into a smile.] *Funny, huh? . . . Look, Frances, I got to go to work now. I'm calling you from the office. How about letting me make this up to you? I'll take you out Saturday night . . . I can't make it tonight. The bachelor party's tonight . . . All right, Saturday night. It's a date . . . S'help me . . . I swear, right on time . . . Eight-thirty, okay? . . . Okay. We'll have a ball. Good-by. Go back to sleep.*

He hangs up. Sits listlessly in his chair again. The three heads around him drop again to their ledgers. With a sigh, the Bachelor picks up the phone again.

Mary, give me an outside line . . . What do you mean, personal calls?! These aren't personal calls! These are business calls! . . . Well, stop listening to other people's conversations. Give me a line! . . .

He gets the line. He dials, waits then, all sweetness.

Hello, who is this, Mrs. Stebbins? . . . This is Eddie, Mrs. Stebbins. I wonder if Edna is awake yet. Could I speak to her? . . . Thank you . . .

The three heads around him come up again, naked envy on every face.

Edna, baby, listen, sweetie, I can't make it Saturday night . . . I'm all loused up with this wedding I'm supposed to be the best man at . . . We have to rehearse the ceremony. You'd think they were getting married on television . . . Yes, sweetie. Why don't I call you Monday. Maybe, we'll

work out something before you go back to California . . .
All right, sweetie, good-by . . .

> He hangs up, sits a moment, then finally removes the cigarette from his mouth, crushes it in his ashtray, and turns to the three others.

Well, what do you say? I'm going to call up Louie's and make a reservation for a table for tonight. Who's coming, and who isn't? [To the bookkeeper] *Walter, you're coming, right?*

> The bookkeeper looks down at his ledger.

BOOKKEEPER: *Well, I'll tell you, Eddie . . . All right, I'm coming!* [To Kenneth] *Who wants to go to the Radio City Music Hall?*

KENNETH: *Yeah, Eddie, count me in. I'll call the wife, I'll tell her I'll be home a little late.*

BACHELOR: *How about you, Charlie?*

> Charlie is frowning down at the sheaf of purchasing orders in front of him.

CHARLIE: *I don't think so, Eddie.*

BACHELOR: [Nods, picks up the phone] *Mary, give me an outside line, and don't give me no trouble . . .*

KENNETH: *Ah, come on, Charlie. One night, we'll have a ball.*

BOOKKEEPER: *Sure, Charlie. A man has to bust loose every now and then.*

CHARLIE: [Angrily] *I said, I don't want to come!*

> Move in for intense close-up of Charlie, frowning, angry. Over this, the Bachelor's voice.

BACHELOR'S VOICE: *Hello, hello, Louie? This is Eddie Watkins. I'd like to reserve a table for four for tonight . . . For four . . .*

> CLOSE-UP. Charlie right up to the end

CHARLIE: *Hey, Eddie . . .*

BACHELOR'S VOICE: *What?*

CHARLIE: *Count me in*

He immediately bends back to his work, takes his pencil up again. Over this the Bachelor's voice.

BACHELOR'S VOICE: *Louie, make that five . . . Five guys . . . Yeah, a bachelor party . . .*

FADE OUT.

ACT II

Fade in: Exterior, small restaurant with small but bright neon sign reading "Louie's" . . .

Cut to: Interior the restaurant. Film. Crowded Villagey Italian restaurant—waiters—chatter—clatter.

Cut to: The table of the bachelor dinner. Charlie, Kenneth, Walter, Eddie, and a fifth young man of thirty-two. This is Arnold, whom we shall call the Groom. He is an amiable, rather ugly young man, reticent almost to the point of not speaking at all. At the moment he is smiling steadfastly and amiably, turning his head from one friend to the other as they talk, enjoying the rare privilege of being liked.

The dinner is over. During the ensuing scene, a bus boy continues to remove the used dishes. Several large bottles of beer and two fifths of Scotch are on the table. There is a welter of variously assorted glasses. Eddie, Walter, and Kenneth are smoking cigars, Charlie a cigarette. The Groom is not smoking. We have cut into the scene during a jumble of conversation. Walter is talking to Charlie, whose head is bent toward the older man. Kenneth is trying to tell the Groom a joke, but the Groom's attention is being distracted by the Bachelor, who is leaning across the table, trying to get Charlie's attention.

BACHELOR: *Hey, Charlie . . .*

BOOKKEEPER: [To Charlie] *. . . So we were stationed right outside Paris, about eight miles, a town called Chatou . . .*

BACHELOR: *. . . Hey, Charlie . . .*

BOOKKEEPER: [To Charlie] *. . . So the first night, a whole bunch of us swiped a jeep out of the motor court. We had a feller there who was a tech sergeant in the motor court. Oh, what a character he was! He used to get loaded every night on that vanilla extract.*

BACHELOR: *Hey, Charlie . . .*

237

CHARLIE: *What do you want, Eddie?*

BACHELOR: *Hey, Charlie, did I ever tell you about the time I was stationed at Buckley Field in Denver, and I picked up this girl in Lakeside Amusement Park?* . . .

BOOKKEEPER: *Hey, Eddie, listen to this story I'm telling Charlie. Hey, Arnold, I'm telling Charlie about the time me and that crazy tech sergeant from the motor court went to Paris. . . . Hey, Kenneth* . . .

KENNETH: *Hey, what happened to the Giants today?*

BOOKKEEPER: *Hey, Kenneth, listen to this story. I was stationed outside of Paris about eight miles* . . .

KENNETH: *Oh, that Paris! I was there for two days! Clubs! You had to beat the women off with clubs!*

BACHELOR: *Hey, Charlie* . . .

BOOKKEEPER: *Well, let me tell you what happened* . . .

BACHELOR: *Hey, you know what was a great town for dames, Hamburg!*

KENNETH: *Hamburg! Clubs! Clubs! You had to beat them off with clubs!*

BOOKKEEPER: *Kennie, pass me that Scotch, will you?*

BACHELOR: *Boy, the first night I was in Hamburg, two Fräuleins come walking right in the barracks. So I said to the lieutenant* . . .

> The bookkeeper, who is mildly lit, suddenly stands and bangs the table mightily with his fist.

BOOKKEEPER: [Bellowing out] *The best fighting outfit in the whole fighting army was the fighting Hundred and Fourth Infantry Division, General Terry Allen, Commanding!*

> This brings the jumbled conversation to a halt. The bookkeeper surveys the other four, looking for signs of disagreement, then sits heavily down.

KENNETH: *Hey, somebody give Arnold a drink.*

GROOM: *No, I* . . .

BOOKKEEPER: [Promptly pouring a thick tumblerful] *Somebody give Arnold a drink.*

GROOM: *I had about three or four . . .*

BACHELOR: [As the bookkeeper extends the tumbler to the Groom] *Arnold, you have to get loaded. That's your duty.*

BOOKKEEPER: [Thrusting the tumbler under the nose of the vaguely protesting Groom] *Arnold, I was stationed outside of Paris, about eight miles. So the first night about ten of us hop in a jeep, and we start off for Paris . . .*

KENNETH: *Say, who wants to go to the Polo Grounds tomorrow afternoon?*

BOOKKEEPER: *So the ten of us were piled in this jeep, and this crazy tech sergeant was driving . . .*

KENNETH: *Hey, Charlie, you want to go to the ball game tomorrow afternoon?*

> The Groom has been twisting his head from side to side, trying to follow both speakers, never relinquishing his polite smile of interest.

BACHELOR: *Arnold, drink up!*

> This startles the Groom into swallowing down the tumbler. The others halt in their stories to watch the process.

BOOKKEEPER: *One gulp, Arnold, one gulp . . .*

BACHELOR: *That's my boy . . .*

BOOKKEEPER: *Boy, you know, I put about eight ounces in that one . . .*

CHARLIE: *Don't drink it too fast, Arnold . . .*

KENNETH: *That's all right, Arnold, that's all right! . . .*

> The Groom finally sets the tumbler down empty and sits, the smile gone from his face, his chest heaving heavily.

BACHELOR: *You okay, Arnold?*

> The Groom brings his hand to his face and rubs his brow lightly.

CHARLIE: *Arnold, you want some water?*

> The Groom smiles wanly.

BACHELOR: *You okay, Arnold?*

GROOM: [Weakly] *Man, that crazy whisky!*

BACHELOR: [Beaming] *Sure, Arnold's all right.*

> Move in fast for big close-up of the Bachelor—crying out.

BACHELOR: *Man! We're having a ball!*

Hold on the broadly smiling close-up of the Bachelor.

> CUT TO: Interior, kitchen of Charlie's and Helen's apartment. Helen is standing in front of the laundry part of the sink, washing her things. She has on a house smock, and her sleeves are rolled up. Seated at the small table behind her is a second young wife, Julie, Charlie's cousin. She is smoking.

JULIE: *Yeah, so?*

HELEN: [Washing away] *Well, he's worried about the baby. He's worried I'm going to have to quit my job. Charlie's a big worrier. But he'll be all right. I know Charlie. He thinks everything out, and then one day, he wakes up, and he's all full of jokes again.*

JULIE: *My husband Mike, during the entire nine months, he acted like he was ashamed of me. I never forgive him for that. He used to walk a couple of steps in front of me in the street, as if he didn't know who that woman with the stomach was.*

HELEN: *Well, Mike was just a kid when you had your first baby, Julie. How old was he, twenty-two? He was a baby himself. But Charlie is a pretty intelligent guy. This just came as a big shock to him. And he's been generally feeling kind of low lately. But he'll be all right.*

JULIE: *Well, I wouldn't let my husband Mike go to a bachelor party.*

HELEN: *What can they do? Get a little drunk? Charlie doesn't drink anyway.*

JULIE: *Are you kidding?*

HELEN: *What do you think they're going to do, find some girls in the street? If some girl came over to Charlie, he would sit there, frowning and thinking it all out for about an hour, and then he'd get up and he'd say: "Well, miss, I really don't think so."*

> She turns from her washing to Julie, smiling now out of deep fondness for her husband.

He's so sweet, you know? I guess this is the way you get when you're having a baby. Everything and everybody seems rosy to you. I look at Charlie sometimes, and he looks handsome to me. I woke up in the middle of the night last night, and I look down at him. He looks so sweet. So I pushed him a little. So he says: "What?" His eyes are still closed. He's still sleeping. I said: "Charlie, you love me?" So he wakes up now. So he says: "Something the matter, honey?" So I said: "How much do you love me, Charlie?" So he says—his eyes are half closed, he can hardly keep awake—he says: "What do you mean, how much? What do you want me to do, write you out a profit-and-loss statement?" He's a bookkeeper, you know. I thought that was so funny. Don't you think that's funny?

JULIE: *Yeah.*

HELEN: *It sounds stupid now, but in the middle of the night like that—he was half asleep—it sounded so funny. I just lay in bed giggling for about an hour.*

Turns back to her wash, stares down at the suds, somehow deeply moved.

I'm crazy about him.

JULIE: *Well, you only been married three years. Wait'll you been married eleven years like me and Mike.*

HELEN: *Nobody knows how nice he really is. My brother died in Korea, he used to stay up with me every night till three, four o'clock in the morning. I used to cry all night, and he used to sit on the bed and talk with me. He only had one year of college, but he's really very smart. I used to look at him talking there, and I used to think: "What would I do without this sweet guy here? I'd go crazy."*

JULIE: *My husband comes home from work, he pulls out his paper, that's the last word I hear out of him all night.*

HELEN: *As hard as I try, I just can't picture Charlie getting drunk and picking up some tramp in the street. I think I'd kill myself if I ever thought he was with another girl.*

The phone rings in the foyer off the kitchen. Helen turns, still

a little bemused. It rings again. This returns her to reality. She
takes her hands out of the suds, holding them up like a
surgeon.

HELEN: *Julie, give me that towel there, will you?*

Julie hands her a kitchen towel, and Helen crosses into the
foyer, drying her hands as she goes. The foyer is unlit, but
there is ample light pouring in from the kitchen. The telephone is on a little telephone table. It rings again. Helen sits
down beside the table, picks up the phone.

HELEN: *Hello . . .* [Smiles gently] *Hello, Charlie, where
are you calling from? . . . You sound like you're having a
nice time . . . Oh, you're having a ball, huh? . . . Well, what
time do you think you'll be coming home? . . .*

 Cut to: Charlie in a telephone booth. He obviously is having a ball. He is smiling broadly.

CHARLIE: *Well, that's what I'm calling you about, honey.
I think a couple of the guys are taking off now. I think
Kennie's going. His kid's sick. But I was wondering if you
wanted me home for any particular reason.*

 Cut Back to: Helen sitting in her foyer.

HELEN: *Just a minute, Charlie . . .*

 She rises, goes to kitchen door, still holding the phone. She
 leans into kitchen to Julie.

HELEN: *Excuse me, Julie. It's Charlie . . .*

 A little embarrassed, she closes the kitchen door. The foyer is
 quite dark now. She goes back to the telephone table, sits
 down, wipes a lock of hair back.

HELEN: *Charlie? . . . Charlie, come on home now. I miss
you . . No, I feel all right. I just miss you. Julie's here, and
we were talking about you, and I just miss you . . . Ah,
come on . . .* [Frowns a little] *Well, no, if you're having
such a good time, stay out and enjoy yourself . . . No,
Charlie, I don't want you to come home if you're having a
good time . . . I'm not lonely. Julie's here. We're talking.
I'm washing my things . . . I know, Charlie, that's what I*

told you this morning. You finally got one night off for yourself. I don't want you to feel guilty about it . . . Charlie, do you love me? . . . You sound angry, that's why I ask . . . No, come home any time you want . . . [She wets her lips nervously.] *Charlie . . .* [She lets her head sink down onto the palm of her free hand.] *Charlie, there's no girls at this party, is there? . . . I'm not checking up on you, Charlie. I just miss you, that's all . . . All right, Charlie, please, I don't want to argue with you. Julie's in the kitchen . . . All right, Charlie, have a good time, stay out as long as you want . . . All right, Charlie, good-by . . .*

She slowly hangs up the receiver, sits slumped and abject, all the buoyancy she had at the beginning of the scene evaporated.

Cut to: Charlie in the phone booth. The broad grin has disappeared from his face. As seen through the closed glass doors of the booth, he is a very sullen and despondent young man. He stands now, pushes the doors open, and marches—frowning—out of the booth.

Cut Sharply to: The restaurant table. The bookkeeper, the Bachelor, and Kenneth. They are on their feet. The Groom is mildly tight and smiling vacantly. We come into the scene as the Bachelor is shouting.

BACHELOR: *Where are you guys going?! You're breaking up the party! This is just the shank of the evening! The shank!*

BOOKKEEPER: *I told my wife I'd meet her at the Radio City Music Hall!*

BACHELOR: *The Radio City Music Hall! How bourgeois can you get?! You men terrify me! You absolutely terrify me! Can't you get one night off from your wives?! What are you rushing home for?! What's so special in your home?! You got a floor show every night? Who are you guys married to, Linda Darnell? Sit down! We're just starting! Hey, waiter! . . .*

KENNETH: *Eddie, we gotta go. My kid's sick.*

BOOKKEEPER: *Yeah, we gotta go, Eddie . . .* [To Arnold], who musters a smile for him] *Arnold, since I ain't going to see you again before the marriage, congratulations and best wishes in the coming future to both you and the bride.*

KENNETH: *Yeah, Arnold, many happy returns.*

GROOM: *Thanks a lot, fellows, for coming. And thanks for the presents. I never expected anything like that.*

He is genuinely, if soggily, touched. Tears well in his eyes. He contrives to stand, if a little shakily.

I mean it, I really mean it. This night has been one of the nicest things that ever happened to me . . .

BACHELOR: [Smiling] *Boy, Arnold is really loaded . . .*

GROOM: *I mean it. This was the first party that was ever given to me in my whole life! I never even had a birthday party! I appreciate this.*

BACHELOR: *All right, Arnold, all right . . .*

Helps Arnold back into his seat.

GROOM: *I want to thank you fellows . . .*

KENNETH: *That's all right, Arnold . . .*

GROOM: *I really mean it. I want to . . .*

BACHELOR: *All right, Arnold! Stop thanking them. They just ate dinner with you. They didn't elect you President!*

Charlie comes into view.

KENNETH: *We're going, Charlie. You going?*

CHARLIE: *No, I don't think so, Kennie.*

BACHELOR: *Well, we got one man here who still has hair in his blood.* [Muttering] *Radio City Music Hall. A bunch of tourists I got for friends.* [To Kenneth and the book-keeper] *Well, so long, you dragons. Arnold, me, and Charlie, we're going to have a ball. Right, Charlie?*

CLOSE-UP: Charlie.

CHARLIE: *Right!*

DISSOLVE TO: A bar—fairly crowded. As we dissolve in, a strong though tremulous and not always on-key baritone voice is singing a high-school alma mater. Pull back to show that the Groom is singing. He is sitting soddenly at the bar, with Charlie and the Bachelor at his left—both of whom sit restless and scowling, muttering to each other here and there through the song.

GROOM: *De-Witt-C L I N T O N*
Boom!
Clinton!
Oh, Cli-i-inton
Ever to theeeee!
Fai-rest of high schools
Give her three times three
Oh, fellows ...
Rah! Rah! Rah!
Long may we cherish thee

BACHELOR: *How did he ever get on this alma mater kick?*
CHARLIE: *Hey, Eddie, this joint is dead. Let's get out of here.*

GROOM: *Faithful we'll be*
Clinton, oh, Clinton
For you and me ...
Da ... da ... da ...
da ... da ...

BACHELOR: *Want to go down Greenwich Village?*
CHARLIE: *Anything doing down there?*
BACHELOR: *A lot of spots down there.*

GROOM: *Crash through that line of blue,*
And send the backs around the end ...
Fight hard for every yard ...
Clinton's honor to defend ...
Rah! Rah! Rah!

BACHELOR: *There he goes with those fullbacks again.*
CHARLIE: [Angry] *Well, let's go!*

Dissolve to: Film. Interior, small Village night club—tiny dance floor, crowded.

Cut to: A small table hedged in by elbows on all sides. Charlie, the Bachelor, and the Groom. The Bachelor is craning his neck, peering around—looking for someone he knows. The Groom sort of hangs over him, talking with a desperate urgency.

GROOM: *So what do you think of my girl, Eddie—you saw her last night. Tell me the truth. I mean, be honest with me. I had the feeling you didn't like her.*

BACHELOR: *Wait a minute. I think I see someone I used to know.*

He rises abruptly and exits.

GROOM: *Listen, Charlie, I'd like to ask you a little advice. I mean, you're a married man. This girl I'm supposed to marry, she's all right, but I'm not really attracted to her, you know what I mean? That's important, isn't it? I kissed her a couple of times, but I . . . I don't know why I'm getting married, Charlie.*

CHARLIE: *What did you say, Arnold?*

GROOM: *I said, I don't know why I'm getting married, Charlie. I did pretty good for thirty-two years without getting married. I get along fine at home. My mother's a good cook. I have a nice life. What do I want to break it all up?*

CHARLIE: *Well, Arnold, everybody feels that way just before they get married.*

GROOM: *Yeah? Did I ever show you a picture of my girl?*

CHARLIE: *No, you didn't, Arnold.*

GROOM: *Do you want to see a picture?*

CHARLIE: *Yeah, I would.*

The Groom clumsily hauls out his wallet and extracts a picture. He gives it to Charlie, who twists at an angle in order to get some light on it.

GROOM: *I want you to give me your honest impression,*

Charlie. Tell me what you think of her. She isn't much, is she?

CHARLIE: *She looks like a nice, pretty girl to me, Arnold.*

GROOM: *Well, I wouldn't say that. We were matched up, you know. I was brought over to her house by my mother and father. Then her mother and father and my mother and father and she and me, we sat around the table in the dining room, and we settled the whole deal. She's some kind of tenth cousin. We went out a couple of times. She's all right. She's quiet. I kissed her a couple of times. She just sat there and I kissed her. I mean, she didn't respond. What do you think, Charlie? I want to have a girl. I'm human. I've got the same desires everybody else got. So my mother and father, we fixed it up with her mother and father. She's about four years older than me.*

CHARLIE: *Well, that don't make any difference, Arnold.*

GROOM: *We're going to live with her mother and father. Do you think that's a good idea, Charlie? I like her, but she ain't much. What do you think I ought to do?*

CHARLIE: *What do you mean, Arnold?*

GROOM: *I mean, you think I ought to marry her?*

CHARLIE: *Well, Arnold, even if I knew the girl, I wouldn't answer that question. I may not like her, but she may be great for you.*

GROOM: *Because I'm thinking of calling the whole thing off.*

CHARLIE: *It's kind of late for that, ain't it, Arnold?*

GROOM: *I'm scared stiff, Charlie.*

CHARLIE: *What are you scared about?*

GROOM: *What am I going to do with her, Charlie. She's one of these quiet ones. I'm not much of a talker myself. Somebody's got to do the talking. What are me and this girl going to do, just sit there, nobody talking?*

CHARLIE: *I thought you said you went out with her a couple of times.*

GROOM: *Yeah. That's what happened. We sat around, no-body talked. I don't understand marriage, Charlie. What are you supposed to do with your wife? I mean, most of the time.*

CHARLIE: [Thinking] *Most of the time, Arnold, you don't even see each other. You're away working. You come home, and you eat. Then one of you washes the dishes. Then, if you're not tired, you can go to the movies or visit somebody. Or you watch Tee Vee.*

GROOM: *I do that now with my mother.*

This gives Charlie pause.

CHARLIE: *I don't know just what there is to marriage, Arnold. I suppose it's to have kids. It doesn't seem like much, does it? My wife's pregnant. In her third month.*

GROOM: *That's wonderful, Charlie.*

Charlie turns slowly to the Groom, then looks down at the table.

CHARLIE: *Arnold, I've been planning something in my mind a long time. I didn't even tell my wife this. I want to go back to college and get my degree in Business and Ac-counting. That was the stupidest thing I ever did, leaving college. What am I now? A bookkeeper. If I had a degree in Accounting, I'd have a future. I could become a CPA, have my own office. How am I going to go back to college if my wife's pregnant? She's going to have to quit her job. Somebody's going to have to support the family. I don't think it's so wonderful about this kid.* [Pause]

GROOM: *So what do you think I ought to do? You think I ought to marry this girl?*

CHARLIE: [A little angry] *Arnold, I can't answer that.*

The Bachelor sidles back into his seat.

BACHELOR: *There was a girl there I knew. She was with another guy, or I would have brought her over. So where you want to go now, Charlie?*

CHARLIE: [Angry with the Bachelor, Arnold, his wife, him-self, the world] *Let's go somewheres, for Pete's sake! Let's get drunk or something! You're supposed to be the big lover, Eddie! Where's all the women?! What have we been doing?! Running from one dumpy night club to another?! Roaming around the city like a couple of sailors! Where's all these beautiful blondes and these fancy tomatoes who live in hotels?! Let's do something, for Pete's sakes!*

BACHELOR: [Likewise shouting] *All right! What are you getting mad at? You want to find some women?!*

CHARLIE: *Yeah, I want to find some women!*

BACHELOR: *All right, well, let's go find some women!*

Close in on Charlie, angry, confused, almost trembling.

FADE OUT.

ACT III

FADE IN: A large wall clock reading twenty-five minutes to three. The camera slowly pans down the wall. We are in an Eighth Avenue bar. It is almost entirely empty except for the bartender, Charlie, the Groom, and the Bachelor, who are leaning wearily against the bar over their drinks; and a worn, battered old veteran of the streets, a woman in her late forties, bespectacled, who is perched on a bar stool at the far end of the bar, gloomily reading a newspaper. The camera moves down and in on Charlie, the Groom, and the Bachelor.

BACHELOR: . . . *I mean, you can't compare the two. This kid Mantle, how long has he been up, two years? What did he hit, .310, .315? Musial led the National League in hitting six times. He's having one of the worst years of his career this year, and he's still hitting .320. Musial is an all-time great! This kid Mantle, for my dough, he still has to make the varsity . . .*

CHARLIE: [Mumbling] *Yeah, I guess so.*

The Groom, who by now is sodden, leans heavily toward the Bachelor.

GROOM: *So what do you think, Eddie? You think I ought to go through with this marriage?*

BACHELOR: *If it was me, boy, I'd be in China by now.* [Leaning across the Groom to Charlie] *All right, let's take them position by position. Who have the Yankees got on first? Thirty guys named Joe. Who's this last guy they pulled up from Kansas City, Trianhos or something? Well, I mean, is there any argument? Hodges is the best first baseman in both leagues . . . Pick up any paper. He's hitting about .320 or something. He's got about thirty-five home runs. He's driven in over one hundred runs already . . .*

250

GROOM: [With sodden persistence] *So, Eddie, what do you think? You think I ought to marry her, go to China, or what?*

BACHELOR: *Arnold, if it bothers you so much, call her up and tell her to forget the whole deal.* [To Charlie] *All right, who's on second? Billy Martin or Gilliam, and this isn't even counting Jackie Robinson, head and shoulders the best second baseman in both leagues, if they let him play there . . .*

GROOM: *So Eddie . . .*

BACHELOR: *Arnold! Get rid of her! You're driving me crazy!*

> The Groom lowers his heavily steadfast eyes, frowns, and suddenly ponders the top of the bar. The Bachelor turns back to Charlie.

BACHELOR: *What's Billy Martin hitting? .250? What's Gilliam hitting? .283 . . . This Gilliam is a flashy fielder. Supposed to be even better than Robinson . . .*

> The Groom heavily turns from the bar and moves out of camera.

BACHELOR: *Don't forget Gilliam gets a lot of bases on balls, and, once he's on the bases, man, it unnerves the pitcher . . .*

BARTENDER: [From a little down the bar] *Yeah, but what's Brooklyn going to do for pitching?*

> The Bachelor turns to the bartender.

BACHELOR: *What's wrong with Erskine?*

BARTENDER: *What have you got to compare with Raschi, Lopat, Ford, Reynolds? . . .*

BACHELOR: *Reynolds hasn't pitched a full game since last year.*

BARTENDER: *The best relief pitcher in both leagues.*

BACHELOR: *What's the matter with Billy Loes?*

BARTENDER: *How do you come to compare Billy Loes with Reynolds?*

BACHELOR: *What are you, a Yankee fan?*

BARTENDER: *Yeah.*

BACHELOR: *Well, drop dead.* [Turns angrily back to Charlie] *He's a Yankee fan.*

There is a sudden bellow off.

GROOM'S VOICE: *Hey!*

Charlie and the Bachelor slowly turn to look in the Groom's direction. The camera slowly looks with them, panning across the floor of the bar to the telephone booth opposite. . . . The Groom is standing unsteadily in front of it.

GROOM: *I did it!*

BACHELOR: *You did what?*

The Groom staggers a few paces into the center of the empty bar.

GROOM: *I called her up! I told her I wouldn't marry her because I'm having a ball!*

Then, suddenly and effortlessly, he sinks down onto the floor —out cold. For a moment the Bachelor and Charlie regard the prostrate form. Then they move to him.

CHARLIE: *You know, I think he just called his girl and broke his engagement.*

He kneels down beside the Groom. The Bachelor likewise squats beside the body of his friend, and the two young men contrive to lift the Groom and get him onto a bar stool during the following lines.

BACHELOR: *Is that what he was yelling about?*

CHARLIE: *That's what he said.*

BACHELOR: *No kidding. You think he did it because I was needling him there before? You think he took me seriously? I was just kidding.*

CHARLIE: *Eddie, we better get him home.*

BACHELOR: *Ah, let's not break it up yet.*

CHARLIE: *It's three o'clock already, for Pete's sakes.*

BACHELOR: *Look at him, he's out cold. Let him sleep it off a little.*

CHARLIE: [Shaking the Groom] *Arnold, come on, wake up.*

BACHELOR: *What do you want to go home for?*

CHARLIE: *It's going to take us an hour to get Arnold home.*

He lives up in the Bronx somewheres. By the time I get back to Jersey City, it'll be daybreak. What are you going to do, stay up all night long? Don't you want to go home sometimes?

BACHELOR: *What am I going to do home? Everybody's sleeping.*

CHARLIE: *Well, go to sleep, too.*

BACHELOR: *Ah, don't go home, Charlie. I feel like doing something.*

CHARLIE: *What? Argue about the Yankees and the Dodgers? This is just what we used to do before I got married. The whole bunch of us would wander around the streets, making cracks at girls, and then we'd wind up in a bar, drinking beer and yelling at each other. Who's got a lower earned-run average, Van Lingle Mungo or Tarzan Parmalee? Then we'd hang around the corner, because we hate to go home. We were looking, looking, always looking for something. That's what we've been doing all night tonight. Going from one place to another, looking. What are we looking for? Go home, Eddie, go to bed. I'll take Arnold home, explain to everybody he was drunk, he didn't mean anything. [Grips the Groom around his shoulders.] Come on, Arnold, kid. We're going home now.*

The Groom, who is awake though his eyes are closed, manages to get off the stool and—with Charlie's firm arm holding him—starts for the exit. The Bachelor remains at the bar, covertly watching the two figures making their way down the length of the bar to the door. They exit. The door is shut behind them.

For a moment the Bachelor regards the closed door. Then he looks back to his schooner of beer without taking it up. He is profoundly weary. His shoulders slump, his face sags. He runs his hand down his face and shakes his head as if to clear it. He turns and looks down the other end of the bar, where the Bar Hag sits engrossed in her newspaper. He watches her for a moment.

BACHELOR: [Spiritlessly] *Hiya, honey, what are you, a Yankee fan or a Dodger fan?*

The Bar Hag slowly turns to regard him over the rims of her glasses.

BAR HAG: *Hiya, honey.*

Bleakly, the Bachelor shuffles slowly down the long length of the bar to where the battered old woman sits.

DISSOLVE TO: Interior, subway car as it hurtles along up to the Bronx. It is half past three in the morning, and the car is absolutely empty except for Charlie and the Groom. The Groom is sprawled across the straw seat, one leg buckled beneath him, the other on the floor, sleeping heavily. Charlie sits expressionless, obviously involved in deep introspection.

We hear suddenly the clicking of a woman's high heels approaching. We hear them before Charlie does. At last he looks up. The camera looks up with him. Slowly ambling down the length of the empty car is a tall, not unpleasant-looking young woman. She sees Charlie and the sprawled Groom. She ambles along slowly past the two young men, her heels clicking, and takes the corner seat of the straw bench, directly under a sign that says: "No Smoking."

She opens her purse, extracts a pack of cigarettes, takes one, lights it up, puffs deeply, returns the pack, reclasps her purse. Then slowly she turns her head to regard Charlie.

Charlie and she exchange a stare for a moment. Then Charlie looks down again to his hands in his lap, frowning. Then he smiles ever so little, and he looks up at the girl and shakes his head no, almost imperceptibly. The girl raises her nostrils with an air of ineffable disdain, rises, and starts for the next car, her heels clicking gradually off into silence.

The car buckets along into the night. The Groom sleeps, sprawled. Charlie returns to his introspection.

FADE OUT.

DISSOLVE TO: Interior, narrow hallway on third floor of Bronx apartment house. A small overhead bulb provides a thin, sketchy light. We see enough of the corridor to see two apartment doors, lettered "3D" and "3C."

Charlie and the Groom enter. . . . The Groom is awake now, but miserable. Charlie helps him down the corridor to apartment "3D." They pause outside the door. The scene is played in low mutters and whispers.

GROOM: *Well, thanks a lot, Charlie.*

CHARLIE: *You okay?*

GROOM: *Yeah, I'm okay. I'm a little groggy, but I'm awake anyway. You don't want to come in, do you?*

CHARLIE: *No, I don't think so.*

GROOM: *I think my mother and father are up. I hear voices. My girl must have called them because they wouldn't be up at this hour.*

CHARLIE: *Well, you go on in and tell them you're drunk, and you're sorry, and you call your girl the first thing in the morning . . . because she must really be upset about this.*

GROOM: [Who has been listening at his door] *I think she's here.*

CHARLIE: *Who?*

GROOM: *My girl. I think I hear her voice in there.*

CHARLIE: *Well, be nice to her, Arnold. Remember you woke her up in the middle of the night and probably scared her to death.*

GROOM: *Charlie, what should I say to her?*

Charlie frowns, shuffles a few paces to the railing of the landing, leans against it. The Groom moves to him.

CHARLIE: *Say to her what you said to me. Tell her you're scared. Tell her you don't think you can be a good husband. Tell her you're afraid you're not going to have anything to say to each other. Tell her everything you're scared about. Everybody's scared, Arnold. Everybody's got things in them they're ashamed of. That's what a wife's for. To make you feel you don't have to be ashamed of yourself. Then she tells you what makes her feel misera-*

ble. . . . Then, that's your job. It's your job to make her feel
she's not as bad as everybody makes her think she is.
That's what marriage is, Arnold. It's a job. You work at it.
You work at it twenty-four hours a day. It's your job to
make that person feel happy. You have to sit and think:
"How am I going to make that person feel happy?" And,
boy, sometimes you feel tired, and you just want to be left
alone, and you wish somebody would start thinking about
how to make you happy. . . . Then you just got to stop
thinking that, because it's your job to make that other person happy. And, if your girl is halfway decent, she's going
to make it her job to make you happy. Then you get to feel,
I can depend on this person. And that's love, man. That's
the greatest thing in the world. There's nothing like it. I
have moments sometimes with my wife, Arnold . . . We're
just lying sometimes in bed, you know, before you go to
sleep. We're just talking . . . You know how you can get to
feel sometimes . . . What's the sense of working? What's
it all mean? What do you get out of this crazy life, but people yelling at you all day and trying to save a couple of
bucks every week. And then my wife tries to talk to me.
She'll say: "Look, you got a wife who loves you. Your
mother, your father, your kid brother loves you. You got
friends . . . " Arnold, I don't know how to explain this to
you . . . but that's what my wife does for me. She's the one
that makes life worth living.

> Tears have welled in his eyes, and he hurriedly puts his hand
> to his face, shading his reddening eyes.

CHARLIE: [Having difficulty getting the words out] *Arnold, I got a kid coming, for heaven's sakes. That's our kid.
I mean, that's what life is, ain't it? What else you going to
do if you don't have a family and kids? That's why we're
living. That's what everybody is looking for.*

> He turns away from the Groom, crying quietly. The Groom
> stands, a little embarrassed at this display of his friend's emo-
> tion. After a moment he speaks.

GROOM: *Well, I'm going to go in, Charlie. Now you suggest that I just tell her everything on my mind.* [Charlie, still hiding his eyes, nods. The Groom smiles.] *Well, at least this girl and I, we'll have something to talk about for a change . . . because I have a lot of things on my mind.* [He smiles briefly again.] *Well, Charlie, thanks for taking care of me. Thanks for the presents you guys bought me.*

CHARLIE: *You better get in, Arnold.*

GROOM: *Yeah, well, I'll see you Monday. No, I'll be on my honeymoon. So I'll see you two weeks from Monday.*

CHARLIE: *All right, Arnold. Have a nice honeymoon.*

The Groom shuffles back to the door of his apartment, rings the bell lightly, takes a deep breath. A moment, and then the door opens. A girl of about thirty-five, bespectacled, rather plain but with a sensitive face, stands in the doorway. She has on a topcoat, and her face is drawn in anxiety. The Groom stands, his head down in shame.

GROOM: *Hello, Louise. I'm very sorry, honest.*

FIANCÉE: *Sure, Arnold, come on in.*

She looks anxiously over the Groom's shoulder in Charlie's direction. The Groom lumbers past her into the apartment. She follows him in. The door closes.

DISSOLVE TO: The door to Charlie's apartment. The apartment is dark. There is the light sound of a key being inserted into the lock, and then the bolt clicks. The door opens. Charlie enters. He closes the door softly behind him, locks the bolt. He moves down the short corridor and turns into the open doorway of the bedroom. Helen lies in bed just as we saw her at the beginning of Act I, sleeping quietly, one pajama-clad leg projecting from under the covers. Charlie moves a few silent paces into the room and stands, looking down at her. His face has no expression. . . . He takes his jacket off, drapes it around the back of a standing chair. He begins to undo the knot of his tie. Turning, he moves quietly into the bathroom, pulls the door almost shut. A moment later a sliver of light shoots through the still open part of the doorway. There is the sound of rushing water. Then, suddenly, a light tenor voice issues from the bathroom: "Ramona, I see you by the garden wall." It ends as abruptly as it started.

The singing causes Helen to turn slightly on the bed. She assumes a new position under the covers and buries her head in the pillows. Just the slightest trace of a smile slips across her face.

FADE OUT.

THE END

The Bachelor Party

THE DIRECTOR AND THE ACTORS

The Bachelor Party is laid out like a short story—a straight chronology of scenes as we follow the course of the party through the evening. The first act has a semblance of normal dramatic structure, but the second act abandons even this pretense, and the third act embarks on an entirely new story. It is, frankly, not the best-structured television script I have read. It played beautifully, however. The excellent reception it received was to a great extent due to the delicate direction of Delbert Mann and to the acting of the whole cast, especially Eddie Albert, who played the lead.

The television director, like the director in the other mediums, has a complex and frightening job. On the half-hour show—where there is usually only one director—he is casting and designing next week's show even as he is rehearsing this week's. At the same time he is reading and approving scripts for shows three, four, and five weeks ahead. On the hour show, the director rarely sees his script more than a week before rehearsals begin and usually less. He must cast his show within a few days and on a strictly limited budget. He must start the scene designer on the sets so that they can be constructed and painted in time for the show. He has to have some sort of idea of the layout of the sets even before the scene designer brings in his rough sketches of the floor plan. He has to know where he intends to set up his cameras on each scene so that he can dolly, pan, or cross-shoot without seeing part of the next set. He must detail a full list of props so that the property man can start procuring them. He has conferences with the producer to discuss the show in terms of the program policy. For example, the men from the advertising agency may have wanted the Italian character in the second act changed for fear of offending the millions of Italians in the country, or they may have wanted the ending adjusted so that the young couple decide not to get a divorce but get back together again for the

259

sake of the child. The director then proceeds into rehearsal, where for seven to ten days he tries to convey his dramatic interpretation of the script to each actor. He decides on the costumes and the make-up. He chooses the music. He fights with the continuity and legal departments of the network for lines of dialogue that border on the tabooed. Two days before the show he sits down with the technical supervisor of the show, the light man, and the audio man and painfully goes over each second of the script, detailing which camera will be where, the sort of lighting on each scene, and the placing of the audio booms so that the incredible mélange of machinery on the floor of the studio will not get mixed up. On the day before the show the director blocks out the show. He sits in the control room with the technical director on his right and the head audio man on his left. Behind him are the music man with his trio of player-recorders, the contrast man sitting behind his panel board, and the light man. Down on the floor beneath them, the actors are seeing the sets for the first time. The floor of the studio is laced with innumerable camera and microphone cables. The entire studio is crowded with technical personnel: cameramen, sound men, light men, stagehands, costumers, make-up men, and carpenters. The sets stand, makeshift and trembling—a third of a living room, the corner of an office, two isolated bus seats, a table and two wooden chairs— all turned at odd angles to each other with no sense of continuity except in the director's mind. Then, with laborious meticulousness, the director puts the actors through their scenes, checking each line, movement, and cue for camera position. On the day of the show the director runs a technical rehearsal; then the dress rehearsal, followed by feverish final refinements; and then the show. During the show, the director cues every change, cut, dissolve, music cue, exit, and entrance from his seat in the control room. It is, to say the least, a desperate and anxious hour for him.

The director is, furthermore, the father of the production. In the jangled, frenetic atmosphere of a theatrical production, someone has to give everyone else the feeling that everything is all right, that things are moving along well, and that—no matter how disturbed matters seem at the moment—it will all come out fine.

Despite this mountain of responsibility, the director's function is essentially an invisible one. He does not get up in front of the audience as the actors do, nor can he claim any vanity from the words of the script as does the writer. Directing is an interpretative job. Most directors who take their work seriously prefer, however, to think of themselves as creative artists. I do not know exactly what a creative artist is; it is, I suspect, a conception worked up by theater people to bolster their own sense of inadequacy in a bourgeois world. There is nothing any more creative in acting, directing, or writing than there is in any other kind of work. Nevertheless, theater people like to think of themselves as creators, and nowhere is this sort of thinking more unfortunate than in the case of directors. In order to identify their work to the audience, so many directors will force their own artistic compulsions on a script. They will dig into the words to find overheightened theatrical moments and effective camera shots. They will shoot scenes from underneath tables, through the crook of someone's elbow, or between the legs of a herd of cattle. They will involve the actors in the most intricate analyses of their roles even where such probing is out of perspective with the level of the script. They will find lyric poetry in the simplest moments. They will shroud the whole production in mood. They become more interested in excitement rather than truth, in theatricality rather than reality.

Needless to say, the relationship of the writer to the creative director is a delicate one. A director may have the highest regard for the writer's talent, but he will still resent any violation of his province of activity. He will react to the writer's criticisms at rehearsal either by defending himself or by nodding his head quickly in a posture of impatient interest and then promptly going about his own way. Some directors are flatly belligerent, and some, usually the least talented, will improvise on the script, adding new lines and cutting old ones. (Since most writers are either barred from or don't bother coming down to rehearsals, this has become almost an accepted part of the director's business.) I have never met the director, from Elia Kazan down, who could cut or rewrite my own scripts better than I could myself. I have also found that most directors take a somewhat different approach to my scripts than I do. We will vary on the tone, mood, and even the meaning of the play. Directors, after all, come to their work with their own highly personalized beliefs and emotions. A director whose mother abandoned him when he was four years old is going to have a definite attitude on how to treat the role of a mother in a given script. The homosexual director cannot have an accurate understanding of either the relationship between two men or that between a young man and a young woman. A director may be very impressed by the stark, bare-stage sort of drama of the 1930's, and he may impose this attitude on the most conventional comedy. The writer must protect his script against these violations.

When I say protect his script, I do not mean like a wounded mother tiger. If there is anything more trying than the arrogant director, it is the defensive playwright. A writer must come into rehearsal leaving any paternalistic feelings he may have for his script behind him. The show, after all, will come out under his name; and he should have only one purpose in mind, and that is to see that the show comes out on screen as best as it can be done. He must watch each scene as it matures between the actors, searching for moments of untruth or boredom. He must cut with ruthless incisiveness, regardless of how well-turned the phrase of dialogue may be. If the director says he cannot make sense out of a scene, the playwright must rewrite the scene. If the actors do not understand a given moment, he must rewrite the moment. The writer should have no concern for his words; he should only be interested in the final playing. Therefore, when a writer protects his script, he is protecting not his lines but an interpretation, tone, or approach that he considers best for the show. This will take him into the province of the director; but the director should also be approaching the show with the single purpose of making it the best possible one, and he should accept the writer's suggestions. The writer must always negotiate with the director, never with the actors. This is an inviolable tradition of theater and a sound one. There can only be one boss at rehearsals, and that is the director. It is therefore vital that the writer extend himself to get along with his director. The relationship is always difficult, frequently circumspect, and sometimes impossible. If the writer cannot get along with his director, then it is my sincere advice that he shouldn't write for that program again. It is impossible to produce a good show that offers any satisfaction to the writer unless he has a working relationship with his director. I, personally, depend a great deal upon my director. I do not write literature; I write drama, and drama depends entirely on how it is played, and the only man who can make a script play well is the director.

More often than not, the script has holes in it, and a good director can cover them up. Such was certainly the case in *The Bachelor Party*. I am not sure to this day where the basic approach was wrong; but obviously the line of the story is six inches off from beginning to end, and the third-act resolution is hardly an inevitable outgrowth of the preceding two acts. The most obvious structural defect lies in the second act, where there is almost no line of graduated movement. The act, which in its published version is much improved over the original draft, consists of a succession of scenes, each a repetition of the preceding one, gathering at best a gradual weight of deterioration. I wanted to show the emptiness of an evening about town, and emptiness is one of the most difficult of all qualities to dramatize. What Delbert Mann, the director, did was to balance each scene delicately so that the emptiness became heavier and heavier. The act still required some line relating to the other two acts, and we decided the line that the first act indicated was the leading character's desire to go to bed with a woman other than his wife. It is impossible to write such blatant adultery in a television script and even more impossible to write an honest motivation for it. It was up to the director and the actor to convey this basic thought to the audience. It was done with simple stage business and by a quality in the acting. In the first scene of the act, a girl crossed past Eddie Albert, and he gave her a restless attention throughout the scene. There was nothing conclusive in his looking at the girl, just the first visible stirrings of desire. This desire was irritated by his sense of guilt toward his wife in the telephone-call scene—so that when we pick him up again in the high-school scene, he is frankly restless, impatient to go to Greenwich Village. In the final scene of the act, his desire erupts into open acknowledgment, and he asks the Bachelor to find him a girl.

This is a sound, honest line of movement. The second-act curtain is the inevitable high point promised by the first act, and it makes the audience willing to sit through a commercial to see the rest of the play. It was not written or even clearly conceived in the script. It was the work of the director that made this act play as sharply as it did.

Delbert Mann's finest gift as a director lies in his ability to see the whole show in its proper shape. This is a rare quality in a director. Most directors are fine when they handle the moment at hand; in fact, they are much too concerned with individual beats and theatricalities. They lose the forest for the single trees. The result of this kind of directing is a show jagged and spotted with intensities that spoil the smooth, swift flow of a story. Delbert also has a keen understanding of normal bourgeois life. He is an amiable middle-class fellow himself, who looks rather like a young associate professor of sociology. He does not strike the poses usually associated with the creative director. He does not clasp his brow or plummet into ten minutes of abstracted silence as he ponders the hidden subtleties of a characterization. Nor does he try to impress the actors by giving them lessons. Most actors actually are not aware they are being directed by Delbert until the fourth or fifth day of rehearsal. He lets them alone—assuming they are professional people—unless, of course, they violate his basic line of reasoning or unless they want to discuss their parts. Delbert also has the secure ability to accept my meddling without defending his prestige. If he likes my ideas, he uses them; if he doesn't like them, he says so. Generally, I would say that Delbert is much more interested in what the audience thinks of the show than in what it thinks of him. He is a rare fellow, and I owe him more than I care to acknowledge.

The relationship of the writer to the actors is quite a different matter entirely. There are all sorts of actors, many of them highly intelligent or amusing, but as a class they have a poor sense of theater. There are very few actors whose opinion of a script I would trust. They have a thin sense of reality; they are eager to emotionalize any line of dialogue that comes their way. It is only natural for them to play their lines for everything they are worth, and so few of them stop to think of playing the scene as they would in real life. Most young actors today are what is known as "method" actors. The method is a school of acting that is so broad that it defies definition, but it generally involves a depth of understanding of the role that approaches psychoanalysis. It is based on the Moscow Art Theater, and it is certainly the finest approach to acting that I know of. Method actors are after the inner truth of their roles, that is to say, the deeper motivations of the character—so that the actual lines of dialogue represent far more than what they say. So it is a continual shock to me to see how shallow is the result of their intellectualizing and probing. They still read the simplest improvised lines of dialogue as if they were epic statements. They still whirl and turn on-stage with the magnified clarity of a ballet dancer instead of with the mundane casualness of real life. One of the basic rules of acting is to relate to the other people in the scene, but it hardly requires that they stare eye to eye at each other as they say: "Hello, what's new?" The truth of the matter is that many of the method actors are not as perceptive as the method requires them to be; and if they are, they frequently do not have their talent refined enough to play what their intelligence has uncovered. The actor is basically a refined mechanism that can produce the truthful emotion required of a role at a given time. A truthful emotion is a difficult thing to produce. It implies a naked exposure of the actor's own emotions, and most people, including actors, do not like to expose their emotions. A smile does not mean joy, nor a frown mean tragedy. A wealth of complicated inward emotion must be dredged up to produce a genuine feeling of joy or disaster. It requires great skill and long experience. The idea, indicated in the film *All about Eve*, that a girl can walk up on to a stage and with no previous experience play a role adequately, let alone with excitement, is ridiculous. Anyone who dreams of becoming a fine actor without years of intensive training and work is fooling himself. Acting is difficult, lonely work.

To pick any one actor out as the best in the business is inaccurate, because each actor can play things that other actors can't. Nobody doubts the superb ability of Marlon Brando, but he could not have played Charlie in *The Bachelor Party* as ingeniously as did Eddie Albert.

Eddie Albert has been playing movie juveniles for so long that people have forgotten what a superlative actor he is. Eddie has an advantage over most actors today because he was trained for many years in the precise comedy of the 1930 Broadway stage. His stage-craft is impeccable, his timing as sharp as Jack Benny's. But these are the surface techniques of acting. Under Eddie Albert's casual performance lie layer upon layer of meticulous thinking. In the part of Charlie, he was given only the sketchiest of roles. I conceived Charlie as one of those quiet fellows, thoughtful, pensive, introspective. It is much easier to play an articulate character than an intro-spective one, for in the latter case the actor has to achieve his effects by silent relationships. How does an actor let the audience know what he is really thinking unless he can speak words? The bad actor mugs, the competent actor conceives a certain amount of surface detail. I have only a vague idea of what the fine actor does even though I watched Eddie Albert carefully build his part, thought by thought, gesture by gesture. During rehearsals, Eddie spent hours closeted in corner conferences with Delbert Mann, plumbing into the role, experimenting, improvising. In the mornings he would come in with fresh ideas that he had dug up overnight. How, for example, does a fine actor convey with no breach of taste and with literal reality the hungry, restless, amorphous desire to sleep with another woman when he won't even admit this desire to himself? The bad actor strikes a facial expression of lust, delivers his line with a broad undercurrent of passion. The good actor digs into himself to remember what he was like under similar or the same circum-stances. He tries to recall the precise accuracy of what he looked like, what he was really feeling, how he talked to the others around him, what his attitude toward his wife was, the layers of guilt con-fused with need. Piece by piece he reconstructs the moment just as it would be if it were happening to him. Then he improvises the whole moment to himself until he has captured an over-all quality. Then he refines it, details it, identifies it for the audience. Eddie

Albert's reconstruction of his role in *The Bachelor Party* was a tribute to acting. I am constantly amazed by what a fine actor can do to a part.

Even the best actors, however, require ceaseless guidance. This is the director's job: it is patently not the writer's. If the writer has anything to say, he says it to the director. It is the director's responsibility to drag out of the actors the exact feelings he wants on every line. Each actor has to be approached differently, each will respond only to a specific image or stimulus. Kim Stanley, one of the most gifted actresses I have ever worked with, seems to work on a purely analytical level. She discusses her role with all the familiar jargon of psychoanalysis. She is, I think, the only actress who can take these academic terms and reduce them to surface effects that the audience will understand. Most psychoanalytical actors can discuss their roles, but cannot produce the delicate edges of reality they have just discussed. Nehemiah Persoff is another actor who is able to make dramatic sense out of an intellectual understanding. Cathleen Nesbitt, who played the leading role in *The Mother*, gave an incredible performance, to my mind the best character performance ever done on television, without ever discussing her role beyond the simplest level. Joe Mantell needs two words from the director, and he spurts back with the corrected refinement. Some actors like to talk their roles a lot, some of them just do whatever the director tells them. Each actor is a highly individual mechanism, and this ability to use actors for their best is one of the most difficult aspects of directing.

The writer should stay away from the actors except to let them know how much he is delighted by them. Actors, like everyone else in show business, need this constant reward. Don't flatter an actor unless he deserves it, but most professional actors, if they are responsive, will give you frequent cause for praise. Other than this, don't meddle with them. Actors will always come up to the writer, if he is around rehearsals, and try to talk their parts out with him. The writer must refer them to the director. The director has his own idea of how to approach each actor, and advice from the writer will just confuse the actor and diffuse the director's authority.

Actors are the only important people once rehearsals start. They are the ones who will be up on the screen, and the entire responsibility for the show is ultimately theirs. They must be made to feel completely comfortable in their roles. If the actor suggests changes in the dialogue because he feels better with these changes, his needs must be granted unless they damage the show—and this is not too frequent. There are really very few basic lines in a script that are vital to the story. Occasionally, there is an actor who rather prides himself on his directing and writing ability and who will try to take over the show. This is a dangerous situation. Actors have no business writing or directing a show they are in. There is sometimes little you can do except to scream or simply fire the actor. Fortunately, this is not too usual a situation. Actors for the most part are co-operative and eager people.

There is nothing in show business that I know of to match successful rehearsals. The writer who enjoys his director and has a good cast can have a wonderful time.